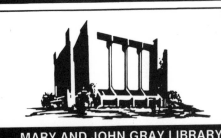

Learning to Keyboard

June Dostal

Business Technology Department Coordinator
Naperville Central High School
Naperville, Illinois

Consultants

Floyd Crank
Emeritus Professor
Northern Illinois University

Dr. Randy Joyner
East Carolina University

West Publishing Company
St. Paul   New York   Los Angeles   San Francisco

Book design: Gary Hespenheide
Copyediting: Barbara Ferenstein
Composition: American Composition & Graphics, Inc.
Art: Gloria Langer
Additional art: Randy Miyake
Cover design: Mary Schlesinger
Index: Anita Cullinan
Photo credits: **3** (top) Courtesy of International Business Machines; **3** (bottom) Courtesy of Tandy Corporation; **4** (top and bottom) Courtesy of Apple Computer, Inc.; **123** Photos by Bart Richmond; **126** Photos by Bart Richmond; **A-2** (top) Photo by Bart Richmond; **A-2** (Bottom) Courtesy of International Business Machines.

WEST'S COMMITMENT TO THE ENVIRONMENT
In 1906, West Publishing Company began recycling materials left over from the production of books. This began a tradition of efficient and responsible use of resources. Today, up to 95% of our legal books and 70% of our college and school texts are printed on recycled, acid-free stock. West also recycles nearly 22 million pounds of scrap paper annually—the equivalent of 181,717 trees. Since the 1960s, West has devised ways to capture and recycle waste inks, solvents, oils, and vapors created in the printing process. We also recycle plastics of all kinds, wood, glass, corrugated cardboard, and batteries, and have eliminated the use of Styrofoam book packaging. We at West are proud of the longevity and the scope of our commitment to the environment.

Contents

Section 5

More Word Processing Functions 174

Section 6

Producing Different Documents 206

Section 7

Review and Simulation   307

Section 8

Timed Writings   324

Appendices

Preface

Learning to Keyboard is one of the first texts written exclusively for middle school and junior high school students learning to keyboard on computers, not typewriters. Since many of the existing junior high keyboarding texts were originally written for high school students, or for students working at typewriters rather than computers, *Learning to Keyboard* will be especially valuable to you and your students if you are teaching keyboarding at the middle school/junior high level, on computers.

A major advantage to *Learning to Keyboard* for students and teachers working exclusively with computers is that there are no dual directions for typewriters and computers within the body of the text. *Learning to Keyboard* assumes that all students are working at a computer. Therefore, all the directions, diagrams, and drills are written for students using computers—there are no typewriter diagrams and directions to get in the way and confuse students. [Please note, however, that the text does include a typewriting appendix, which provides basic information for students using a typewriter. After studying this appendix students working at typewriters can do the drills in *Learning to Keyboard*.]

If you are teaching middle school and junior high students, you will find a second major advantage to *Learning to Keyboard* in the method used to present new keys. Only *two* new keys are introduced in each lesson, and every *third* lesson is a review lesson. Slowing down the pace and providing more "breather" lessons makes the course less stressful for the younger students and thereby improves their overall performance.

A third major advantage to *Learning to Keyboard* is that junior high students will find the exercises and the copy they key more interesting and enjoyable than the similar kinds of material in more traditional texts, which have been aimed at older, more mature students. Here are just a few of the *Learning to*

Keyboard features that will help keep the students' attention and improve their attitude and behavior in the keyboarding lab.

- **Conversational Writing Style**—Unlike most keyboarding texts, *Learning to Keyboard* is written in a friendly, informal style that talks directly to the students in their own language. This means the students can and will read and do more on their own without the need for as much teacher explanation.
- **High Interest Copy**—Students don't key dull, dry business letters and documents. Instead, they key jokes, poems, riddles, and stories. The copy they key involves such topics as backpacking, fashion, "Things That Drive Teachers Crazy," and handwriting analysis.
- **Language Arts Mysteries**—Most Keyboarding texts contain language arts exercises. *Learning to Keyboard* goes a step further, making these exercises interesting and fun. Students have to play detective to find errors. And there's added interest in that they are looking for errors in copy about such topics as bubble gum, "The Father of Frozen Food," sword swallowing, and pretzel makers.
- **Games**—Because most middle school and junior high students love to compete against the clock and against each other, *Learning to Keyboard* presents many of the accuracy and speed drills in the form of games. A few examples are "Key-A-Thon," "Link Up," "Categories," obstacle races, and word scrambles.
- **Composing Activities**—In the "Composing at the Computer" feature students do a great deal of composing. Because composing is not easy for middle school/junior high students, the composing activities begin with single-word responses, progress to short phrases, and then to sentences and paragraphs. Only after they've gone through this progression do they compose their own reports, stories, invitations, etc.

While *Learning to Keyboard* attempts to make the keyboarding course as interesting and enjoyable as possible for middle school and junior high students, it is not all fun and games. In addition to the basic goal of learning the keyboard and developing their keying skills, students learn a great deal about how to use their computer. Students learn word processing features such as search and replace, centering, hard hyphens, boldfacing, and indents. They learn to format a variety of documents, including flyers, book reports, outlines, personal notes, and tables, by first keying from arranged copy, then unarranged copy, and finally composing and formatting their own documents. Students participate in a culminating simulation in which they compose documents as part of a student-run business. Students also do countless proofreading and language arts exercises. Thus, *Learning to Keyboard* provides a complete keyboarding course, with an introduction to Word Processing, for the middle school/junior high student.

Research indicates that the majority of schools are offering keyboarding units in the 6- to 9-week range, with many teaching a full semester course, and a few teaching as much as an entire year of keyboarding. Because of this range of offerings, the *Learning to Keyboard* program has been developed to make it as flexible as possible. By using the textbook and varying combinations of the supplements, you can structure a course to fit your particular situation, whether you are teaching a 4-week unit or full year course. In the *Teacher Resource Book* you will find suggested course outlines for the most common course lengths of 9 weeks, 18 weeks, and 36 weeks.

The components of the Learning to Keyboard program, in addition to the student text, are as follows:

- **Teacher's Annotated Edition**—This text is the same book as the student text, but with the addition of annotations (teacher notes) in the margins and a Teacher Manual bound into the back of the student text. The extensive annotations, which provide step-by-step guidance on how to teach each lesson, will be especially helpful to beginning teachers and those not trained to teach keyboarding. Many of the answers to exercises in the student text are also provided in the annotations.

  The Teacher's Manual bound into the back of the annotated edition contains background information for teaching a keyboarding course, in-depth explanations of the various kinds of activities found in the text, and answers too lengthy to fit in the margins of the student pages. These answers include a complete key to all the document formatting applications.

- **Teacher Resource Book**—This book contains a variety of material to help you teach with and supplement the student text. In addition to the detailed course outlines previously mentioned, this book contains a technique evaluation chart, quizzes, grammar rules used in the text's "Language Arts Mysteries," progress charts, and lots of supplemental applications. You are free to photocopy and distribute all of the pages in this book to your students.

- **Timed Writing Software**—Available for both Apple and MS-DOS computers, this software provides 1-minute, 3-minute, and 5-minute timed writings. The computer scores speed and accuracy for each timing and allows students the option of printing their timings.

- **Keyboard Carnival**—This software consists of animated games for developing speed and accuracy. Students will enjoy playing games such as "Dunk Fuzzball," "Milk Bottle Knockdown," and "Ring the Bell" while improving their speed and accuracy at the same time.

- **Learning to Study**—A workbook consisting of 50 lessons to help middle school and junior high students improve their study skills while composing at the computer. Students learn time management skills, test-taking tips, memory aids, the importance of their study environment, and much more.

It is our belief that the *Learning to Keyboard* textbook program is a complete, flexible, original approach to teaching keyboarding skills and word processing to middle school and junior high school students. Please send any comments and suggestions for future editions to the School Division, Editorial Department of West Publishing Company, 30851 W. Agoura Road, Agoura Hills, California 91301.

The author and the publisher would like to thank the following teachers for their valuable comments and suggestions throughout the development of this textbook.

Elizabeth Beavers
Bradley Middle School
San Antonio, TX

Tom Bookler
Indian Trails Junior High School
Addison, IL

Mary Buchanan
Westlake Junior High School
Broomfield, CO

Lynn Comé
Sycamore Middle School
Pleasant View, TN

Beatrice Foster
James W. Robinson Junior High School
Fairfax, VA

Michelle Hulse
Castle Junior High School
Evansville, IN

Linda Lawrence
Jackson Middle School
Grand Prairie, TX

Marie Lenert
Thomas Boushall Middle School
Richmond, VA

Leroy Mack
Lakeview Middle School
Winter Garden, FL

Phyllis Melick
Kokomo High School
Kokomo, IN

Gail Stoner
Carmel Junior High School
Charlotte, NC

Abbreviations:
  period key after, 50
  postal, A13
Alignment scale, A1
Announcements:
  composing, 211–212
  formatting, 207–210, 308
Apostrophe, 100–103
Asterisk, 170–173, A10

Backspace key, 126
Bell, on typewriter, A7
Boldfacing, 136, 140
Business letters, 240–247, 321

Caps Lock key, 91–94
Centering tables:
  on computer, 201–207
  on typewriter, A8–A9
Centering text horizontally:
  on computer, 129–133
  on typewriter, A7
Centering text vertically:
  on computer, 184–187
  on typewriter, A8
Colon, 106–113
Comma, 78–81, A10
Computers. *See* Computer
  Operation; Computer Parts
  and Equipment (Skills &
  Exercises Index)
Copying text, 180–184
Correction fluid, A6
Correction tape, A6
Correcting errors:
  on computer, 11–12, 126
  on typewriter, A5–A7
Cover page:
  composing, 288–290, 323
  formatting, 283–288, 317,
    323
  keying in, 284
  model for, 285
CPU (central processing unit),
  5
Cursor movement keys, 123

Default settings:
  for margins, 124
  for tabs, 198–201

Delete key, 126
Diagonal key, 103–108
Disk drive, 5
Disks:
  care of, 5
  saving on, 12
Dollar sign, 163–166

Electronic typewriter. *See*
Typewriter(s)
Elite pitch, A4
Enumerations:
  composing, 218–220, 321
  formatting, 213–217, 309,
    321
Equals key, 117–120
Error messages, 9
Errors, correcting:
  on computer, 11–12, 126
  on typewriter, A5–A7
Exclamation mark, 170–173

Flyers:
  composing, 232–233
  formatting, 228–232,
    310–311, 319
Fractions, A11

Hand span, 18
Hard drive computers, 5
Hard hyphen, 131
Hard page break, 135
Hard space, 131
Home row keys, 14–22
Hyphen, 95–100, A10
  hard, 131

Impact selector, A1
Indented text, 139–143
Inserting page numbers, 275
Inserting text, 135–136
Invitations and
announcements:
  composing, 211–212
  formatting, 207–210, 308

Keyboard:
  defined, 2
  height of, 14
  proper distance from,

18–19, 22, 31–32, 42
  proper elbow position at,
    27–28, 53, 65, 77
  proper foot position at, 21,
    31
  proper posture at, 22, 35,
    38, 54
  proper wrist position at, 21,
    23–24, 31, 36, 59, 65, 73,
    75–76, 84
  typewriter, A11
Keyboarding, 2
  preparing for, on computer,
    2–13
  preparing for, on typewriter,
    A3
  on typewriter, A10–A11
Keys. *See* Keys (Skills &
Exercises Index)

Left Shift key, 56–59
Letters:
  personal business,
    240–247, 321
  personal, 312
Lift–off tape, A5
Line space regulator, A1
Line spacing, 125
Listening for bell, A7
Lists. *See* Enumerations

Margin scale, A1
Margins:
  on computer, 124–128,
    130–131
  on typewriter, A4–A5
Misspelled words, commonly,
  A15–A16
Misstrokes, 11
Monitor, 5
Moving text, 175–179
Multi–page reports, 316–317
  keying in, from script,
    273–283

Numbers:
  keying in. *See* Number Drill
    Exercises (Skills &
    Exercises Index) page,
    274–275

One–page reports:
  composing, 262–264,
    270–272, 323
  containing proofreaders'
    marks, 265–272
  formatting, 257–262,
    269–272, 314–315, 323
Outlines:
  composing, 253–256,
    265–272
  formatting, 248–252,
    270–272, 313–314, 322

Page breaks, 135
Page numbers, 274
  inserting, 275
Paper bail, A1
Paper guide, A1
Paper release lever, A1
Parentheses, 167–169
Percent sign, 163–166
Period key, 47–51
  after abbreviations, 50
  spacing after, 53, 61, 64, 69,
    72–73, 76, 80
Personal letters, 242–244, 312
Personal notes:
  composing, 238–240, 320
  formatting, 234–237,
    311–312
Phrases, 49
Pica pitch, A4
Pitch select key, A1
Platen, A1
Platen knob, A1
Plus sign, 117–120
Poems:
  composing, 225–227
  formatting, 220–224,
    226–227, 309, 320
Position at keyboard. *See*
Keyboard
Postal abbreviations, A13
Powering down, 9–10
Powering up, 7–9
Print carrier, A1
Printer, 5, 10–11

Question mark, 81–85
Quiet hand technique, 73

Accuracy Exercises

alphabetic sentences, 228, 232, 238, 245, 253, 263
decoding while keying, 225
hyphenated words, 189, 199, 203–204, 284
long words, 115, 118, 185
one–hand words, 101, 176–177, 181, 194–195, 218, 299
opposite–hand letters, 96, 111
travel game, 54–55
"weak finger" words, 271
word patterns, 211
words with same letter combinations, 152, 159, 165

Applications

business letters, 247, 321
cover pages, 286–287, 289, 317, 323
enumerations, 215–217, 219–220, 309, 321
flyers, 230, 233, 310–311, 319
invitations and announcements, 209–210, 212–213
multi–page reports, 316–317
one–page reports, 259–262, 314–315, 323
outlines, 250–252, 255–256, 313–314, 322
personal letters, 242–244, 312
personal notes, 236–237, 239–240, 311–312, 320
poems, 222–224, 226–227, 320
reference pages, 294–297, 317, 323
reports containing proofreader's marks, 267–270, 272
tables, 204–205, 301–303, 315, 321

Composing Exercises

alphabetical lists, 101
alphabetical sentences, 89, 93, 202
announcements, 212–213
answers to given phrases, 122

apostrophes, 111
business letters, 247
categories game, 111
coining phrases, 151–152
colons, 115
completing adages, 134
cover pages, 323
dialogue for cartoons, 155
enumerations, 219–220, 321
famous quotations, 184
filling in blanks with own words, 147
flyers, 233
homonyms, 171–172
horoscopes, 180
hyphenated words, 106
invitations, 212–213
job desired, 188
listing favorites, 129–130
listing objects in classroom (treasure hunt), 118
Murphy's Law, 165
one–page reports, 264, 323
opposite meanings, 92
outlines, 255–256
personal notes, 239–240, 320
poems, 226–227
quotation marks, 118
reference pages, 298–299, 323
reports containing proofreader's marks, 272
rhymes, 106
riddles, 193, 196, 198
sentences from other students' words, 168
sentences starting with given letters, 158, 162
tables, 305–306
"weak finger" drill, 102
words containing double letters, 97
words starting with given letters, 88, 114
words with same beginnings or endings, 96

Computer Operation

error correction, 11–12
error messages, 9

networks and, 5
powering down, 9–10
powering up, 7
saving and retrieving words, 12
start–up routine on, 12–13

Computer Parts and Equipment

care of, 5, 11
CPU (central processing unit), 5
disk drive, 5
disks, 5, 12
dual–floppy computers, 5, 7–9
keyboard, 4
monitor, 5
printer, 5, 10–11

Games

Beat the Clock, 51, 63
counting, 166, 169, 173
designs with capital–letter keys, 113
key–a–thon, 77, 81, 85
Keyboarding 500, 120
keyboarding tag, 59
Link–up, 90
Number Challenge, 149, 153, 156, 160, 163
obstacle course, 99–100, 108
passing notes, 116
travel, 54–55
unscrambling letters, 69, 74

Keying from Script

246, 249, 254, 258, 263, 266, 271, 289, 297, 300, 304

Keying with Proofreader's Marks

246, 249, 254, 258, 263–264, 266–270, 272, 289, 297–298, 300, 305

Keys Introduced

A	 17	B	 47
C	 4	D	 17
E	 25	F	 17
G	 26	H	 24
I	 33	J	 17
K	 17	L	 17
M	 66	N	 56
O	 44	P	 70
Q	 81	R	 33
S	 17	T	 37
U	 28	V	 60
W	 66	X	 70
Y	 60	Z	 78
0	 150	1	 145
2	 150	3	 153
4	 160	5	 157
6	 160	7	 153
8	 157	9	 145
"	113, A10	!	 170
$	 163	%	 163
'	 100	(	 167
)	 167	*	170, A10
+	 117	,	78, A10
–	95, A10	.	 47
/	 103	:	 106
;	 17	=	 117
?	 81		

Other Keys

Backspace, 126
Caps Lock, 91
cursor movement, 123
Delete, 126
fractions, A11
home row, 14–22
Left Shift, 56
Return/Enter, 16
Right Shift, 37
keys on typewriter, A10–A11
Tab, 87

Language Arts Mystery

apostrophes, 112, 156
capitalization, 89–90
choppy sentences, 166
colons, 172–173
commas before conjunctions, 152
commas in series, 148, 152
commas with appositives, 119
double negatives, 162–163
homonyms, 94
possessive case apostrophes, 156
punctuation, 107, 119, 148, 152, 172–173
quotation marks, 169
run–on sentences, 102–103, 159
sentence fragments, 116
verbs, 98

Number Drill Exercises

207, 211, 214, 218–219, 221, 228, 229, 232, 235, 238, 241, 246, 248, 254, 257–258, 263, 265–266, 271, 274, 284, 289, 292, 297, 300, 304

Proofreader's Marks Introduced

capitalize, 208, A14
close up, 212, A14
delete, 221, A14
insert, 219, A14

let it stand (stet), 239, A14
lower case, 229, 233, A14
paragraph, 235, A14
space, A14
spell out, A14
switch around (transpose), 214, A14

Proofreading Exercises

132, 136–137, 141, 177, 181–182, 186, 190, 200, 204

Shifting Technique

39–40, 42, 46–47, 58, 64–65, 67–68, 75, 80

Space Bar Technique

15, 43, 52, 65, 77

Speed Exercises

alternate–hand letter combinations, 273, 288
alternate–hand letters, 114, 117–118, 185, 189
alternate–hand phrases, 207, 240
alternate–hand sentences, 221, 234
alternate–hand word patterns, 296–297
alternate–hand words, 172, 176, 181, 194, 199, 248, 257, 265

common phrases, 148, 155, 162, 168–169
different key rows, 203
introduction to, 56–57, 66
key–a–thon, 77, 81, 85
punctuation marks, 291, 304
short words, 95–96, 101
speed paragraphs, 104–105, 109–110
speed pyramid, 87–89, 92

Timed Writings

short, 325–334
sustained, 335–342

Typewriter Parts and Operations

A1–A16

Word Processing Functions

boldfacing, 136, 140
centering tables, 201–207
centering text vertically, 184–187
centering text horizontally, 129–133
copying text, 180–184
correcting errors, 11–12, 126
default settings, 124, 198–201
hard hyphen, 131
hard page break, 135
hard space, 131
indenting text, 139–143

inserting page numbers, 275
inserting words, 135–136
line spacing, 125
margin settings, 124–128, 130–131
moving text, 175–179
page breaks, 135
page numbers, 274–275
searching and replacing text, 193–198
searching text, 188–192
strikeover (typeover), 135–136
tab settings, 198–201
underlining, 136, 140
wordwrap, 123–124

SECTION 1

Getting Ready to Keyboard; Learning the Basic Keys

LESSON 1

Getting Ready To Keyboard

What is Keyboarding?

You are about to learn an exciting new skill. You will use this skill throughout your school days and even after graduation when you enter the world of work. That skill is called **keyboarding**.

More and more, information is being entered into computers for processing. The method used to enter this information is called keyboarding.

There are different ways to enter information into a computer using a keyboard. You are going to learn the most efficient way. It is called the **touch method** of keyboarding. This means that the operator uses the fingers on both hands to strike the keys. The experienced operator does not need to look at the keyboard to find the location of those keys. By the time you finish this book, and with proper practice, you also should be able to read what you are keyboarding and enter that information without having to search for the location of the keys. What's more, you should be able to do that with a good amount of speed and accuracy.

Besides developing keyboarding skill, as you progress through the book, you will learn how to use your computer for word processing. This means you will learn how to do different things *electronically* with words, such as storing them, changing them, retrieving them, and printing them. You will learn how to produce different kinds of documents, and you will sharpen your ability to compose thoughts right at the computer screen. Composing this way is much faster than composing with pencil and paper.

As you can see, you are going to learn many exciting new skills that will serve you well in the future. Let's start by taking a look at the equipment you will be using.

PART B

Parts of the Computer

Find the diagram on the next two pages that is similar to the computer you are using. If you are unsure, ask your teacher. As you read about the five basic parts described below, see if you can locate them on the diagram and then on your own computer.

1. **Keyboard:** An arrangement of keys either attached or apart from the computer.

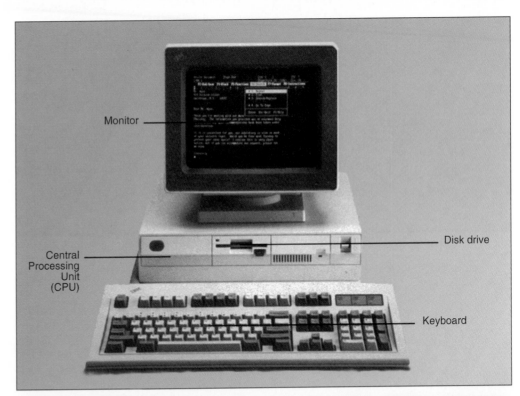

Monitor

Disk drive

Central
Processing
Unit
(CPU)

Keyboard

IBM PS/2 30-286

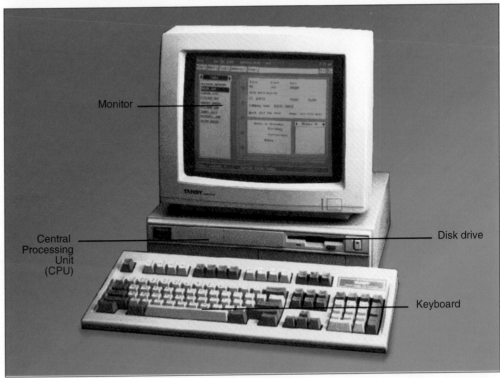

Monitor

Disk drive

Central
Processing
Unit
(CPU)

Keyboard

Tandy 2500XL

Apple IIe

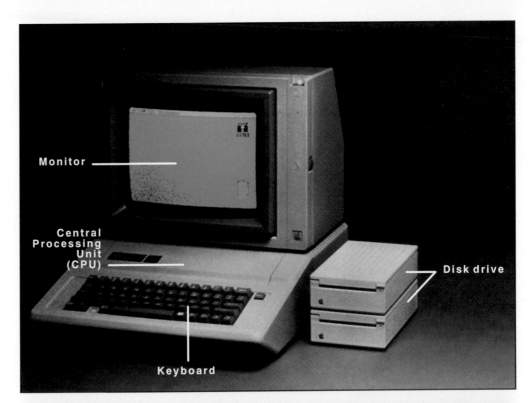

Monitor

Central
Processing
Unit
(CPU)

Disk drive

Keyboard

Macintosh Classic

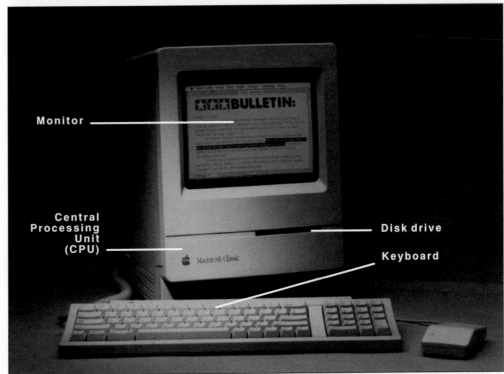

Monitor

★★★BULLETIN:

Central
Processing
Unit
(CPU)

Disk drive

Keyboard

2. **Monitor:** A picture tube similar to that found on a television used to display text. (Also known as Video Display Terminal or CRT, Cathode Ray Tube.)

3. **CPU (Central Processing Unit):** The "brains" of the computer.

4. **Printer:** A unit attached to the computer that produces on paper a permanent copy of the words on the screen.

5. **Disk Drive:** A unit into which a disk is inserted to be read by the CPU. Computers that have two visible disk drives are called **dual-floppy computers**. Most computers that have just one visible drive are called **hard drive computers**.

Networks

Some computers may be joined together to form a network. A network links all computers together to form a communications system. Connecting computers allows all users to share the same files, software programs, and printers. A device called a file server contains the master files and network programs on a fixed disk. Your teacher will tell you if you are on a network.

Care of Disks

Disks come in two sizes—3.5 and 5.25 inches. Both sizes are called by many names—diskettes, disks, floppies. The 3.5-inch disks are covered with a protective plastic cover. The 5.25-inch disks are not; they usually come in a protective sleeve or envelope.

Damage to a disk can result in loss of all or part of the information stored on that disk. To prevent loss of data, it is important that you handle disks carefully and observe the following guidelines for their care:

1. Do not bend or fold the disk.

2. Do not attach a paper clip to the disk.

3. Keep disks away from magnetic fields.

4. Keep disks away from direct sunlight.

5. Keep disks away from extreme heat or cold.

6. Do not touch the exposed areas on the disk.

7. Use a felt-tip pen when writing on a 5.25-inch disk.

8. Use the disk only on equipment for which it is designed to be used.

9. Place the disk in its protective sleeve when not in use.

10. Do not spill liquids on the disk.

a. Do not bend or fold the disk.

b. Do not attach a paper clip to a disk.

c. Keep disks away from magnetic fields.

d. Keep disks away from direct sunlight.

e. Keep disks away from extreme heat or cold.

f. Do not touch the exposed area on the disk.

g. Use a felt tip pen when writing on a 5.25" disk.

h. Use the disk only on equipment for which it is designed to be used.

i. Place the disk in its protective sleeve when not in use.

j. Do not spill liquids on the disk.

Powering Up

Turning on the power is called powering up or booting the computer. Procedures for starting some of the most common computers are listed below. Follow the steps for your computer. (Your teacher will explain other procedures you should follow at the beginning of each class period to get ready for keyboarding.)

 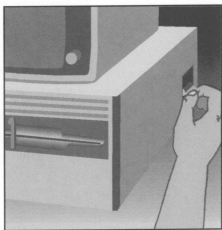 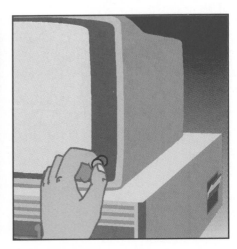

Apple Single and Dual Floppies (without hard drives)

1. Turn on the monitor.

2. Open the disk drive door.

3. With the disk label facing up, insert the oval-window edge of the disk into the slot of the disk drive. If there is more than one disk drive, use the drive your instructor recommends.

4. Close the disk drive door. If it doesn't close easily, remove the disk and insert it again. Do not force the door closed.

5. Turn on the CPU. Or, if the computer is already on, hold down the Control, Open Apple, and Reset keys at the same time. This procedure restarts the system.

6. A disk drive light will turn on and you will hear a whirring sound. If the light does not go out after about 20 seconds, turn the computer off, remove the disk, and reinsert it in the drive. Turn the computer on again.

7. Follow the start-up procedures required by your software.

MS or PC-DOS Dual Floppies (without hard drives)	1. Open the disk drive door. Insert the disk with the label facing up. Close the disk drive door.
	2. Turn on the computer. If the monitor is separate from the CPU, turn it on also. If the computer is already on, hold down the CTRL (control), ALT (alternate), and DEL (delete) keys at the same time. This procedure restarts the system.
	3. When the computer prompts you to enter the date, key in the date or bypass this by pressing the Enter key. Your teacher will tell you which option to follow.
	4. When the computer prompts you to enter the time, key in the time or bypass this by pressing the Enter key. Your teacher will tell you which option to follow.
	5. Follow the start-up procedures required by your software.
Apple Mac + (with floppy)	1. Put the disk in the top drive and turn on the machine.
	2. Double click on the application icon and find the correct start-up icon. Double click on that icon.
Apple Mac (with hard drive)	1. Do not put the disk in the external drive. Turn the power on.
	2. If the application is on the hard drive, find the correct icon and double click on it to start.
	3. If the application is on the floppy disk, open the icon that corresponds to the disk. Then open the application icon by double clicking on it.
MS-DOS or PC-DOS (with hard drive)	1. Do not put the disk in the external drive. Turn the power on. If the computer is already on, hold down the CTRL (control), ALT (alternate), and DEL (delete) keys at the same time. This procedure restarts the system.
	2. When the computer prompts you to enter the date, key in the date or bypass this by pressing the Enter key. Your teacher will tell you which option to follow.

3. When the computer prompts you to enter the time, key in the time or bypass this by pressing the Enter key. Your teacher will tell you which option to follow.

4. Some computers have a menu from which you may select the program you want by using the arrow keys and then pressing the Enter key. Others have software organized into sections called directories and subdirectories. If you get a C> prompt, your teacher will tell you how to change directories to get into your software. Then follow the start-up procedures required by your software.

Networks

1. Your computer will already be turned on.

2. Log in following your teacher's instructions and select the application from the menu.

3. If you have been told to do so, insert a data disk in the appropriate drive.

PART F
Error Messages

If there is a problem with the computer or your disk, you will get an error message on the screen during the power-up process. If this happens, don't panic. Ask your teacher for help. Sometimes it is a simple matter of starting over and making sure that all steps were followed in the start-up process; or you may need to start over with another disk.

PART G
Powering Down

Turning off the power is called powering down. Procedures for turning off most common computers are listed below. (Your teacher may have other procedures that you should follow at the end of each period to exit your software and make the computer ready for the next person.)

1. Open the disk drive door. Be sure the disk drive light is **off** when opening the door.

2. Remove the disk. If the disk came in a protective cover, replace it in the cover. (See the illustration on the next page.)

3. Turn off the computer and monitor unless instructed otherwise by your teacher.

Follow this procedure if you are using an Apple Mac:

1. Quit the application by selecting quit from the file menu. If on a hard drive, close the application window by single clicking in the upper left-hand corner and taking the application disk to the trash can to eject, or go to the special menu and select eject.

2. Close the application window by clicking in the upper left-hand corner and taking the application disk to the trash can to eject, or go to the special menu and select eject.

Using a Printer

As you work through the lessons in this book, you will frequently need to print the material you have input. How you print this material will depend on the software you are using. Each software program has different instructions that must be followed. Your teacher will explain the printing commands required by your particular software program.

When you get ready to print, follow these guidelines:

1. Be sure the printer is turned on.

2. Be sure the "on line" button is turned on.

3. Check to be sure there is adequate paper.

4. If using "tractor-feed" paper (sheets connected to each other), check to be sure the paper is at the top of the form. Your teacher will explain how to set the paper correctly.

5. If more than one computer is connected to a printer, you may need to dial your position at the switchbox. Your teacher will tell you if this is necessary.

6. If using "tractor-feed" paper, press the "form feed" button to feed the paper out of the printer after printing is finished. Your teacher will explain the proper procedure for doing this.

7. If the printer jams, ask your teacher for assistance.

PART I

Care of Equipment

Your school has spent a lot of money on computer equipment. It is important that you take care of it properly. Computers are sensitive and should be treated carefully. Computers do not like dust, or static electricity, or high temperatures. Your school's custodians will take care of these problems if they arise.

But you can help too. Be careful not to bump the computers. Hard drive computers can be damaged if jostled too much. Also, never take a disk out of the drive when the drive light is on. That could damage the drive.

PART J

Correcting Errors

Remember when you learned to roller skate or ride a bike? You probably made many mistakes when you first started. That's only natural; we all make mistakes when first learning a new skill. The same thing will happen when you learn how to keyboard. But don't worry too much about your early mistakes. Many of the errors you make in the beginning lessons will disappear by themselves as you become more familiar with the keyboard.

In keyboarding, mistakes are also called **misstrokes**. In the early lessons you will probably not want to correct your misstrokes. If you spend a lot of time correcting errors, you will not have much time for keying. Remember, your objective is to learn the touch method of keyboarding, not to correct every error you make. After you learn the location of the keys, that goal will change. Then you will begin to focus more on correcting errors. Your teacher will tell you when you should begin correcting your mistakes. When you do start correcting, there are special keys that make the job of erasing errors an easy one.

One of those keys is the backspace key. On some computers this key has a large left arrow on it. Locate it now on your keyboard. This key moves the cursor one space to the left. The cursor is the dot of light on the screen where the next letter can be entered. Pressing the backspace key wipes out the letter immediately to the left of the cursor.

No. 15   Pity the poor urban youngsters. What do they SI=1.4
do with all their spare time? Two of my relatives
who reside on a farm always say that; and no, they
are not joking. They mean it. Running the dishes
through the washer or vacuuming the rugs is hardly
their idea of work. Guiding a power lawn mower to
cut the grass or taking a garbage pail down to the
curb will never convince them that city youngsters
work. They believe children should be partners in
the household rather than observers.

    If you visit my relatives on the farm, you'll
find children being sent down to the chicken house
to find eggs for their breakfast. Should you want
fruit on top of your cereal, then you must quickly
grab a pail and get on down to the raspberry patch
before the birds get them. Everyone pushes a snow
shovel when it snows, and all hands must help with
stacking firewood for winter.

. . . . 1 . . . . 2 . . . . 3 . . . . 4 . . . . 5 . . . . 6 . . . . 7 . . . . 8 . . . . 9 10

No. 16   I have an aunt who believes in the old saying SI=1.4
of waste not, want not. She finds uses for almost
everything that most people would throw out. Take
cardboard boxes, for example. She fills them with
ashes from her fireplace and in springtime empties
ashes on her gardens. An empty wax milk carton is
filled with water and frozen to use with drinks on
a picnic. A carton filled with ice keeps your pop
cold on a picnic. My uncle likes to use these ice
packs when he goes fishing. In spring old cartons
are cut apart for sowing seedlings, which my aunt
nurses on the windowsill. A glass jar can be used
forever if you are careful. Jars make great gifts
when filled with jams and jelly or candy. Paint a
design on them and use the jars to store dry pasta
or sugar or dried spices from the garden.

. . . . 1 . . . . 2 . . . . 3 . . . . 4 . . . . 5 . . . . 6 . . . . 7 . . . . 8 . . . . 9 10

Another correction key, found on some computers, is the delete key. This key erases the letter where the cursor is located. Your teacher will tell you if your keyboard has this special key.

Some computers have another key used for corrections that places the computer into a typeover mode. This means that wherever you place your cursor in the text and begin keying new words, the new words will replace the old words. Your teacher will tell you if your keyboard has this feature.

Besides using these special correction keys, there are many software packages that check for spelling, grammar, and punctuation errors. Ask your teacher if such software is available to you. If it is, your teacher will determine the proper time for you to begin using it and will show you how to use it when you are ready.

Remember, do not let your early errors bother you. As you gain more control over the keys, your errors will decrease. While correcting errors on the computer is very easy, your teacher will probably want you to ignore errors at first. It is better to spend your time keying rather than correcting errors. When your teacher feels you are ready to begin correcting errors, he or she will tell you.

PART K

Storing and Retrieving Words

One of the advantages of keyboarding on a computer is that your keyed words (usually called documents or files) can be saved on a disk (called storage or **saving**) and brought back to the screen at a later time. When saving words, you must give the document a name. How you name your document depends on the type of computer and software you are using. You can either select a name that helps you recall what the document is or give the document a page or job number. In this book you will have experience using both methods for naming documents. Your teacher will explain the procedure you should follow to save your words.

When you want to bring what you have keyed back to the screen, you simply retrieve it from the disk. This is called **retrieval**. How you retrieve your words depends on the type of computer and software you are using. Your teacher will explain the procedure you should follow to retrieve your words.

PART L

Start-up Routine for all Lessons

After you power up and are into your software, follow these steps before beginning each lesson:

1. Open your textbook to the page indicated by your teacher.

2. Place the book at a 45-degree angle on your desk. This is the best position for ease of reading.

No. 13   Do you ever wonder about how things like cars and computers and video games are made? If you do think about these things, you may want to consider going to a technical school after high school. If you find math and science classes pretty easy, you may want to pursue a career where your talents are used. Are you the person who hooks up the stereo? Do you prefer to learn by doing rather than from a book? Perhaps you like to figure out what makes a certain piece of machinery tick. If so, technical training is probably for you. SI=1.4

People who take job training after they leave high school will earn more money per hour and have more opportunities than those who do not get extra schooling.   Your earnings will not only increase, you will also meet many people with similar career interests. The more training you have, the better prepared you will be for your future.

. . . . 1 . . . . 2 . . . . 3 . . . . 4 . . . . 5 . . . . 6 . . . . 7 . . . . 8 . . . . 9 10

No. 14   If you are wondering what career is right for you, there are a number of things that can be done now to help you decide. A great activity that you can do is job shadowing. For the better part of a day you watch someone on the job. You can ask the person observed as many questions as you like. If you listen carefully, you gain lots of information about the job. SI=1.4

School clubs are excellent ways to learn more about your future career interests. Try joining a club that relates to your field of interest. Then you may hear guest speakers, go on tours, and even get hands-on experience with your career. Besides all this, you will get to meet other students who, like you, are interested in the same career.

Doing volunteer work for a hospital or school is another way to find out about some occupations. Many child care and senior citizen centers in your city or town may be looking for students who would be willing to donate some time.

. . . . 1 . . . . 2 . . . . 3 . . . . 4 . . . . 5 . . . . 6 . . . . 7 . . . . 8 . . . . 9 10

3. Because raising the copy makes it easier to read, use a bookstand if one is available. Insert your book into the stand so it is vertical or almost vertical. If no stand is available, prop the book up with something else, such as other books stacked together.

4. If your software has a default margin setting of 1 inch and single spacing, you are ready to begin typing. These default settings by the manufacturer of the software determine where the words will be printed on the paper and if there will be any blank lines between each printed line. If your software does not have these defaults, your teacher will show you how to make changes.

PART M

Quiz on Lesson 1

The following questions will help you review the information in this lesson. On a separate sheet of paper, write T if the statement is true, or F if it is false.

1. It will not harm a floppy disk if you place it in the sun.

2. You can write on a 5.25-inch floppy with a ball-point pen.

3. The brains of the computer are located in the Central Processing Unit.

4. To get a permanent copy of what is keyed on the screen you must use the printer.

5. The monitor displays the words that are keyed.

6. The part of a computer into which a disk is inserted is called the disk unit.

7. Dual-floppy computers have at least two disk drives.

8. Never take the disk out of the drive if the light is on.

9. Do not touch the exposed areas on a disk.

10. The touch method of keyboarding refers to the light way the keys are struck.

No. 11   If you visit a county or state fair, you will SI=1.3
not want to miss the stock exhibits where you will
see judges looking over hogs and cattle. Watch as
the lucky person who raised them receives a ribbon
or cash prize. Besides judging, other things that
might interest you are the cut flower arrangements
or garden vegetables. Look at the needlework. If
you like crafts, check out the knitted mittens and
socks made from sheep's wool. Don't miss the rock
collections or dozens of yeast breads fresh from a
farmer's oven. On one table you will find cookies
and on another cakes. If neither of these tickles
your fancy, check out the pies with a blue ribbon.
Be sure to look at the stacks of homemade clothing
and macrame with house plants. Next, watch horses
pulling in teams and handlers urging them on. One
day at the fair is never enough to see everything.

. . . . 1 . . . . 2 . . . . 3 . . . . 4 . . . . 5 . . . . 6 . . . . 7 . . . . 8 . . . . 9 10

No. 12   The first pens were fingers dipped in colored SI=1.4
liquid such as berry juices. Cave people used the
broken ends of twigs to paint cave walls. Ancient
people made pens from twigs which were dipped into
wet clay tablets that were hardened in ovens. The
early writing tools were reeds that grew along the
Nile. These were later replaced by feathers taken
from the wings of birds such as turkeys, swans and
geese. These feathers were called quills and were
dried by slowly applying heat to prevent them from
becoming brittle.
    Early ink used with reed pens was black. The
ink was made from ashes mixed with lamp oil and it
was boiled with gelatin obtained from donkey skin.
This gave it a bad odor so perfume was added. But
even then people were not satisfied with their ink
because after several weeks the ink faded to muddy
brown.

. . . . 1 . . . . 2 . . . . 3 . . . . 4 . . . . 5 . . . . 6 . . . . 7 . . . . 8 . . . . 9 10

Introducing Home Row Keys

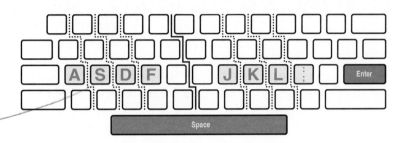

Objectives:

- To learn the proper height for the keyboard
- To learn the position of the home row keys
- To learn how to hold your hands when keyboarding
- To learn how far away to sit from the keyboard

Proper Height of the Keyboard

1. Having the keyboard at the proper height is very important. *If it is too high, you will have trouble reaching some of the keys. If it is too low, your shoulders and arms will become tired.*

2. Look at the illustration. Note there is only a slight slant to the forearms, and the elbows are bent and held close to the body. The person's feet are placed flat on the floor.

3. Position yourself at the keyboard so you look like the picture. Your feet should touch the floor. If they do not, you need to adjust either the position of your keyboard or your chair. Ask your teacher for help if you need to make an adjustment.

No. 9   Size is just one consideration when selecting SI=1.3
a dog. If you study different breeds of dogs in a
breed book, you will learn something about how big
a particular dog will get. The height of a dog is
figured from the shoulder to the ground.

Coat is another thing to think about when you
are choosing a pet. Coats that are thick or heavy
will require many hours of combing, which you must
be prepared to do every day or each week. Poodles
are a type of dog that have their coats trimmed to
conform to a pattern. This type of trimming takes
time and effort. If you choose not to do it, then
you must pay a groomer to perform the task.

Some people look for a pet that is especially
smart. Still others want a pet that will be clean
inside the house. Most people forget that pets do
what they have been taught. If you desire animals
that behave well, you must teach them to obey you.

. . . . 1 . . . . 2 . . . . 3 . . . . 4 . . . . 5 . . . . 6 . . . . 7 . . . . 8 . . . . 9 10

No. 10   There is nothing quite like a county fair. It SI=1.3
can be lots of fun for the whole family. There is
something for everyone.

If you like to ride a carousel, then you will
enjoy the midway. Here you can thrill to riding a
roller coaster or a ferris wheel. Your sweetheart
and you can hop on board a boat and sail through a
tunnel of love. If you knock down a bunch of milk
bottles with a ball, you may win a stuffed bear or
a lion. Maybe you would rather try your luck on a
game of chance. Then you should try a booth where
each ticket costs only a dime, and picking out the
right number means you can win an electric shaver,
crock pot, or iron. If you would rather feed your
stomach, there are many selections available. You
might decide to get a hamburger or corn dog. Then
you could buy some cotton candy.

. . . . 1 . . . . 2 . . . . 3 . . . . 4 . . . . 5 . . . . 6 . . . . 7 . . . . 8 . . . . 9 10

Position of the Home Row Keys

1. Look at the diagram at the top of the preceding page. Note that the keys in one row are shown in yellow. These keys are known as the **home row keys** because your fingers must return to these keys after striking other keys.

2. Now position your fingers on the home keys.

3. Remove your hands and drop them at your sides. Place your hands on the home keys again. Your two thumbs should be resting over the Space Bar (see diagram at left) and so close together that you could lock thumbs if you had to.

4. Remove your hands and drop them again at your sides. Cup your fingers. Keeping your fingers well curved, place your hands on the home keys.

5. Check to be sure you are in proper position. Are there two keys, the **G** and **H,** in between your left and right hands? Are your thumbs close together resting above the Space Bar? Do your hands look like the picture below? Good. *Curved fingers are important because they give you the striking power you need to hit the keys*. Now you are ready to begin.

Space Bar Technique

1. With your hands in proper position on the keyboard, strike the Space Bar with your right thumb if you are right-handed or your left thumb if you are left-handed. Stroke downward and quickly release the Space Bar. If you don't release quickly, the cursor will continue to move across the screen and you will have extra spaces in your keyboarding.

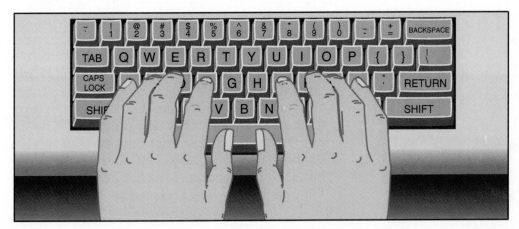

No. 7

When you have a toothache, you go to see your SI=1.3 dentist. In ancient times, if you complained of a toothache, you would be told to eat a mouse. Then if that did not work, your dentist would take some twine or forceps and remove the bad tooth.

Brushing your teeth in ancient times meant to use pieces of root or twigs attached to the end of a thin handle. Early toothpaste was made from oil and herbs and honey. Next, flavoring was added to mask the bitter taste of these pastes and powders. Despite all modern advances, tooth decay remains a problem we must deal with from childhood until the time we are adults.

Today most dentists believe three things will prevent tooth decay. First, avoid sweets; second, visit your dentist frequently. Last but not least is to brush and floss regularly.

```
. . . . 1 . . . . 2 . . . . 3 . . . . 4 . . . . 5 . . . . 6 . . . . 7 . . . . 8 . . . . 9 . . . .10
```

No. 8

Some people make the mistake of bathing their SI=1.3 dog too often. This makes the dog's skin dry out. If you must wash your dog, do it about every eight weeks but not more often than that. To keep a dog comfortable during the bath, experts recommend the ears be loosely plugged with cotton. Be sure that the water is warm, not hot, and use a mild soap to wash the dog.

When the bath is finished, carefully lift the dog out of the water. Rub the coat briskly with a towel or cloth. Do not brush a dog's coat when it is wet; you may pull out too many hairs. Blow dry the coat if you want to make it fluff out. During winter be sure the dog remains inside for at least two hours before letting the animal outside. Much of how the dog regards the bath depends on how you handle the animal. If bath time is pleasant, then future baths will be easy to do.

```
. . . . 1 . . . . 2 . . . . 3 . . . . 4 . . . . 5 . . . . 6 . . . . 7 . . . . 8 . . . . 9 . . . .10
```

2. Complete the exercise below. As you key, watch the cursor as it moves across the screen.

space once, space once, space twice, space once, space once, space twice, space twice, space once, space twice, space once, space twice, space once, space once, space twice, and stop

PART D

Returning to the Next Line

1. To move the cursor to the next line you must use the **Return/Enter** key, which is located at the right side of the keyboard. Find it now. There it is, right next to the little finger on your right hand, your "pinkie." And you will use your pinkie to operate that key. Let's try it now.

2. Place your hands on the home row keys. Keeping all fingers in position, slightly raise your right pinkie and tap the Return/Enter key. Watch the cursor on the screen. What happened to the cursor?

3. Yes, it moved down one line. Try it again. Watch the cursor on the screen.

4. Did it move down another line? If your cursor moved down more than one line, you may be resting your finger on the Return/Enter key. Try it again.

No. 5   When you go to a store to buy some shoes, you SI=1.3 can try them on and see how they fit. Early shoes did not fit people as well as they do today. They were handmade by cobblers who bound the upper part of the shoe to the sole with nails or pegs. There was no right foot or left foot shoe. Either could be worn on any foot with equal discomfort.

Shoppers can choose from numerous shoe styles ranging from clogs to pumps. Prices can vary from less than a dollar for a pair of thongs to several hundred for slippers lined with mink fur. Perhaps the most popular shoe is the sneaker. This shoe's rubber sole is responsible for its name. When you wear rubber soles, you can sneak around and not be heard. Another style that is worn by many persons today is the athletic shoe. However, this shoe is not reserved just for athletes; today many wear it because it is sturdy and comfortable.

. . . . 1 . . . . 2 . . . . 3 . . . . 4 . . . . 5 . . . . 6 . . . . 7 . . . . 8 . . . . 9 10

No. 6   Soccer is one game that is played by athletes SI=1.3 around the world. In most nations it is the major sport. Matches between different teams draw large crowds and soccer players get paid big salaries to play the game. A soccer game requires little more than a ball and a field on which to play.

The rules are fairly simple to learn. Anyone can learn to play the game in no time at all. The players advance the ball by kicking it or touching it with any part of their body except the arms and hands. The team scores a point for a ball that is played into the opponent's net but unlike football or some other games, when the soccer ball goes out of bounds, the match keeps going because the clock does not stop. The only time the clock is stopped is when there is a serious injury. When you watch a game, you may see players wearing knee guards to protect them from injury.

. . . . 1 . . . . 2 . . . : 3 . . . . 4 . . . . 5 . . . . 6 . . . . 7 . . . . 8 . . . . 9 10

5. Did it move down just one line? Good. Now, use your Space Bar and Return/Enter techniques on the lines below.

space once, space twice, space three times, space once, space twice, space once, space once, space three times, space twice, space once, space twice, **press Return/Enter**

space twice, space once, space once, space three times, space once, space twice, space once, space three times, space once, space twice, space once, **press Return/Enter**

Using the Home Row Keys

1. Place your hands in home row position. Check to be sure they are positioned correctly. Key each line below **twice**.

1 fff [space] ddd [space] sss [space] aaa [space] Return/Enter

2 jjj [space] kkk [space] lll [space] ;;; [space] Return/Enter

2. Remove your hands from the keyboard and drop them to your side. Shake your hands. This is a good way to relieve tension in your hands. Now place your hands back in home position. Check to be sure you have two keys between your right and left hand. Are your hands cupped with fingers curved? Good.

3. Key each line below **twice**.

1 aaa [space] ;;; [space] sss [space] lll [space] ddd [space] kkk [space] fff [space] jjj Return/Enter

2 jjj [space] fff [space] kkk [space] ddd [space] lll [space] sss [space] ;;; [space] aaa Return/Enter

No. 3

Some people are wonderful at telling a story. SI=1.3
They know exactly just how much detail to tell the
listener but don't burden their listeners with too
much. They start right at the beginning and avoid
making the listener wade through a number of facts
of little importance. They stick to the point and
do not get off the track. They avoid stories that
are long and strung out; they know that shorter is
better. When telling a joke, they do not laugh at
their own punch line.

A good way to improve your skill at telling a
story is to practice aloud to yourself. Do not be
too concerned if people think this rather strange.
Every person who is skilled achieved that skill by
practicing. Also practice telling stories to your
friends. The more stories you tell, the easier it
will become; soon you will become one of the pros.

. . . . 1 . . . . 2 . . . . 3 . . . . 4 . . . . 5 . . . . 6 . . . . 7 . . . . 8 . . . . 9 10

No. 4

If you own a computer, you have made a fairly SI=1.3
large investment, and you will want to learn about
what should be done to keep it from breaking down.
Since dust is an enemy of computers, you will want
to cover your equipment when it is not in use. To
keep the disk drive clean use a head cleaning kit,
which you can get from your computer dealer. Keep
the computer away from hot, humid and dusty areas.
Make sure that air can move around the computer to
avoid heat building up. Use a clean cloth to wipe
the keys. The monitor can be cleaned with special
pads; always let the screen air dry.

Be careful about how you handle your computer
disks; do not write on the label with anything but
a felt-tip pen. Never force a disk into the drive
and keep it away from magnets. Do not bend a disk
and avoid attaching notes to it with a paper clip.

. . . . 1 . . . . 2 . . . . 3 . . . . 4 . . . . 5 . . . . 6 . . . . 7 . . . . 8 . . . . 9 10

Are you getting the hang of it? Good. *From now on, every time you come to the end of the line, you must press Return/Enter.*

Proper Distance from the Keyboard

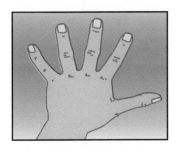

1. Spread out your hand so it looks like the diagram. Your fingers should be as far apart as you can make them. This is called a hand span.

2. A hand span is important because that is the proper distance you should be from your keyboard. *If you sit too far away, you will not be able to reach the keys just above the home row keys. And if you sit too close, you will not be able to reach the keys just below the home row keys.* Although we are not learning these keys right now, it's a good idea to start out with the right distance so it becomes a habit every time you sit down at a keyboard.

3. First, pull the keyboard forward so it is even with the front edge of the desk or table. To determine the proper distance for you, place your thumb on your chest and push yourself forward until the tip of your little finger is touching the edge of the keyboard. Now you are ready to do more work on the home row keys.

Sustained Timed Writings

The following timed writings (for 3- or 5-minute timings) may be used any time after you have completed Lesson 20. If you finish the paragraphs before time is called, start over again from the beginning.

No. 1

SI=1.1

There are many things you can do to prevent a fire from happening in your home. One of the most important things to have on each floor of the home is a working smoke detector. In some towns that's the law. Some people believe if a fire breaks out when they are asleep the smoke or flames will wake them up. This is not true. Smoke is a toxic gas. The smoke will put people into a deeper sleep, and it makes it harder for them to wake up and escape. Even if they do wake up, they are likely to panic.

After installing smoke detectors outside each sleeping area, the next thing to do is plan escape routes on paper and then conduct a dry run. Also, check to be sure that windows open freely. If the window is high off the ground, you may need to get an escape ladder. These are available at hardware stores.

. . . . 1 . . . . 2 . . . . 3 . . . . 4 . . . . 5 . . . . 6 . . . . 7 . . . . 8 . . . . 9 10

No. 2

SI=1.2

If you have ever tried the art of stenciling, then you know how much fun it can be. Only simple tools are needed to transform a dull room into one that is cozy and warm. To begin you need brushes, paints, and stencil plates. After you decide what color paint is best for the job, you must apply it with stencil brushes; these are round brushes with stiff bristles that permit you to apply paint with broad strokes. Stencil brushes come in many sizes so you can handle small details as well as broader patterns and designs.

With just a couple of stencil plates, you can give any room the special look you want. Stencils consist of a certain number of patterns per plate. By painting over one stencil and then over another you can create any kind of interesting design, and you can proudly say you did the job yourself.

. . . . 1 . . . . 2 . . . . 3 . . . . 4 . . . . 5 . . . . 6 . . . . 7 . . . . 8 . . . . 9 10

4. Try to keep the proper distance between you and the keyboard as you work on these lines. *From now on, every time you must press the Space Bar, the textbook will indicate this with a blank space between the letters.* For example, in the first line below, you key **aaa** then strike the **Space Bar,** then **;;;** and then strike the **Space Bar,** and so on. Now, key the lines below **twice**.

```
1 aaa ;;; sss lll ddd kkk fff jjj a;s kdj
2 aaa ddd add add dad dad lll lad lad as;
3 fff fad jjj jal sss sal kkk ask sal las
4 add lad fad as; sad all ask ad; lad ask
5 ads lass fall asks lads fads adds flask
```

Challenge

1. Your teacher will time you for one minute. How many times can you key the line below?

```
1 asdf jkl; asdf jkl; asdf jkl; asdf jkl;
```

2. In one minute how many times can you key the line below?

```
2 a;sldkfj a;sldkfj fjdksla; fjdksla;
```

3. Repeat the two lines above and see if you can improve your score as your teacher times you.

4. Race with a partner on the two lines above as your teacher times you.

No. 36

I have an aunt who is so organized that every little trinket in her home is put away in a drawer or a box. Each box is plainly marked to show what the content is. She believes there is a place for everything and everything in its place. My aunt's problem is she forgets just where she put the box.

. . . . 1 . . . . 2 . . . . 3 . . . . 4 . . . . 5 . . . . 6 . . . . 7 . . . . 8 . . . . 9 . . . .10 SI=1.3

No. 37

Litter is a problem for everyone. We all see the pop cans on the highway. We all step over the newspapers blowing down the street. However, some people try to do something about it. They stop to pick up the waste and put litter where it belongs, and they do it gleefully without ever complaining.

. . . . 1 . . . . 2 . . . . 3 . . . . 4 . . . . 5 . . . . 6 . . . . 7 . . . . 8 . . . . 9 . . . .10 SI=1.4

No. 38

I recently toured an art gallery with a group of people. I was amazed at the reactions of folks who came to look at art. Some gasped while others frowned. A few smiled as if they alone understood what the artist had meant by painting the picture. I just shake my head. It is beyond understanding.

. . . . 1 . . . . 2 . . . . 3 . . . . 4 . . . . 5 . . . . 6 . . . . 7 . . . . 8 . . . . 9 . . . .10 SI=1.4

No. 39

Dogs have been trained by people to perform a number of jobs. Some will herd sheep. Others can warn a person who cannot hear that the doorbell is ringing. Some go along with a hunter to point out game or retrieve it from the pond. Some dogs even do tricks like begging and sitting up and jumping.

. . . . 1 . . . . 2 . . . . 3 . . . . 4 . . . . 5 . . . . 6 . . . . 7 . . . . 8 . . . . 9 . . . .10 SI=1.4

Objectives:

- To review the home row keys
- To practice proper technique at the keyboard

PART A

Warmup

1. Check your position at the keyboard.
   - Are your fingers on the home row keys?
   - Are your fingers curved?
   - Are you sitting a hand span away?

2. This lesson contains no new keys to learn, so you can relax and concentrate on strengthening the reaches to the home row keys. Key the lines below **two times** each. If time permits, repeat the lines. Don't forget that a blank space between letters means you press the Space Bar, and you press Return/Enter at the end of each line.

```
1 a ; s l d k f j a ; s l d k f j a ; d a;
2 jjf kkf llf ;;f jja jjs jjd jjf jf kd ls
3 djj dkk dll d;; kaa kss kdd kff ks la ;j
4 sjj skk sll s;; laa lss ldd lff ls ;a ja
5 ajj akk all a;; ;aa ;ss ;dd ;ff ;a ls kd
```

No. 32   A woman with a seeing eye dog got on the bus. Some children close to her started to pet the dog. The woman told them to stop, but they continued to do it. The children failed to see that by petting the animal they were preventing the dog from doing its job of safeguarding the blind woman from harm.

. . . . 1 . . . . 2 . . . . 3 . . . . 4 . . . . 5 . . . . 6 . . . . 7 . . . . 8 . . . . 9 . . . .10 SI=1.3

No. 33   There is something about the smell of freshly baked bread as it drifts from the kitchen. Mouths start watering. My grandmother baked bread once a week. Sometimes she made dark rye bread rich with molasses. If she had some apples, she would throw them in too. Such are memories from my childhood.

. . . . 1 . . . . 2 . . . . 3 . . . . 4 . . . . 5 . . . . 6 . . . . 7 . . . . 8 . . . . 9 . . . .10 SI=1.3

No. 34   My uncle likes to hide his money. He puts it in the cookie jar and under his bed. Some he will wrap up in paper and freeze. My uncle thinks that no thief will ever look in these places. His best hiding place is a box in the furnace in summer and in the air conditioner in winter. He's so clever.

. . . . 1 . . . . 2 . . . . 3 . . . . 4 . . . . 5 . . . . 6 . . . . 7 . . . . 8 . . . . 9 . . . .10 SI=1.3

No. 35   My mother tries to stay on a diet but most of the time she cheats. She will nibble on a portion of cheese while fixing dinner. She skips dessert, but she snacks on cookies and crackers later on in the evening. Now she is trying a new tactic; when she opens a cabinet or drawer, a mouse trap snaps.

. . . . 1 . . . . 2 . . . . 3 . . . . 4 . . . . 5 . . . . 6 . . . . 7 . . . . 8 . . . . 9 . . . .10 SI=1.3

Left-Hand Home Row Keys

How good are you at striking the left-hand home row keys without looking at them? Let's find out. Key the lines below, **twice** each. As you key, try not to look at the keys.

1 a d f s d f s a d f a f d s d a f d s da
2 fad sad as fad sad as fads dad dads as a
3 a dad a fad sad dad as a sad fad dad f d

Right-Hand Home Row Keys

Now let's work on the right-hand home row keys. Can you key the lines below without looking at the keys? Give it a try. Key each line **twice**.

1 j k l ; l k j ; k j l k ; j k l j ; k l;
2 jj kk ll ;; j; k; l; j; kl lj lk l; k; j
3 jlk kl; l;k ;jk jkl kl; l;j ;jk ;kl; jlk

Both Left- and Right-Hand Home Row Keys

You should be getting pretty good now at these home row keys. See if you can key the lines below, **twice** each, without looking up from the book.

1 all ask fall as fad falls fads asks as a
2 lad; lads; sad; fad; lass; as; ask; sad;
3 ask a lad; ask a lass; ask dad; sad lass

Feet Flat on the Floor

Why are feet important to keying? No, you don't key with your feet, but if they are in proper position they help brace your body for keyboarding. *Crossing your ankles or knees puts a strain on your spine. Keeping your feet flat on the floor, one slightly ahead of the other, is the best way to brace yourself for keyboarding.* Let's see if you can keep your feet flat on the floor as you key the lines below, **two times** each.

1 all ads; add all; all fall; ask a dad; a
2 as all; a ad; as asks; add; fall all; as
3 dad asks; dad falls; dad adds; a lass; a

No. 28   Some students say they study and remember all they read much better if loud music is playing. I find that hard to believe. Research has been done that shows playing music helps cows give more milk and hens lay more eggs, but no study confirms that human beings learn data better with music playing.

. . . . 1 . . . . 2 . . . . 3 . . . . 4 . . . . 5 . . . . 6 . . . . 7 . . . . 8 . . . . 9 . . . .10 SI=1.3

No. 29   My aunt is a collector of antiques. She will travel many miles to a fair or show where antiques are displayed. To me many of these old things are just pieces of junk, but my aunt views them not as old things but articles of value. I guess what is junk to me is valuable prized treasure to another.

. . . . 1 . . . . 2 . . . . 3 . . . . 4 . . . . 5 . . . . 6 . . . . 7 . . . . 8 . . . . 9 . . . .10 SI=1.3

No. 30   When I walk down the aisles at the local drug store to shop for shampoo, I am somewhat confused. There are apple blossom, lemon, and honey flavors. I can purchase the shampoo in a variety of colors. Some of them appear and sound much too good to put on my hair. Maybe I should make some fruit salad.

. . . . 1 . . . . 2 . . . . 3 . . . . 4 . . . . 5 . . . . 6 . . . . 7 . . . . 8 . . . . 9 . . . .10 SI=1.3

No. 31   Every time my neighbor returns from a trip he plans a party to show the rest of us his snapshots from his journey. There is no way to avoid going. He expects all of us to be there. So we just grit our teeth and endure a dull evening of viewing all his pictures and hearing all about his adventures.

. . . . 1 . . . . 2 . . . . 3 . . . . 4 . . . . 5 . . . . 6 . . . . 7 . . . . 8 . . . . 9 . . . .10 SI=1.3

Sitting Up Straight

Are you sitting up straight, with your hips all the way back in the chair? If not, you are putting a strain on your spine. You will be more comfortable if your back is straight. Let's see if you can key the lines below, **twice** each, without slouching in your chair.

```
1 aaa ;;; sss lll ddd kkk fff jjj kkk sss
2 asdf jkl; sdfa kl;j dfas l;jkfasd ;jkl;
3 sad as a lass; sad as dad; dad adds; ad
```

PART G

Hand Span Away from the Keyboard

Check to be sure you are sitting a hand span away from your keyboard. Keep that good position as you key the lines below, **twice** each.

```
1 all fads; ask all; add; dad; ask dad; la
2 lass; as; fall; adds; sad; ask; as; lads
3 ask a dad; sad dad; as a lad; as a lass;
```

PART H

Challenge

1. You may select any section of lines in this lesson for the next exercise. Your goal will be to key those lines without taking your eyes from the book. Your teacher will time you for 30 seconds. Are you ready? Remember, you cannot look at the screen or your fingers during the 30 seconds.

2. Now find a new set of lines in this lesson and repeat the exercise.

No. 24   My friend likes to collect things. If you go to her house, you will see a pile of trading cards here and a box of bottle caps there. The basement has cartons of stuffed animals and model airplanes of every shape and size. Like all good collectors she plans to keep collecting until space runs out.

. . . . 1 . . . . 2 . . . . 3 . . . . 4 . . . . 5 . . . . 6 . . . . 7 . . . . 8 . . . . 9 . . . .10 SI=1.3

No. 25   Next time you go to a circus and watch clowns perform, think about the skill that is required to make other people laugh. These people dress up in funny noses, oversized shoes, and bright red hair. They must take a clown course to learn how to fall down and make others laugh; they are truly giants.

. . . . 1 . . . . 2 . . . . 3 . . . . 4 . . . . 5 . . . . 6 . . . . 7 . . . . 8 . . . . 9 . . . .10 SI=1.3

No. 26   My friend just moved to the city from a rural area. She never stops talking about how wonderful it was in the country. The city has noise, smoke, traffic. The country is quiet and smoke free. It seems you can take the girl out of the country but you can't take the country spirit out of the girl.

. . . . 1 . . . . 2 . . . . 3 . . . . 4 . . . . 5 . . . . 6 . . . . 7 . . . . 8 . . . . 9 . . . .10 SI=1.3

No. 27   My family has a curious custom. Each time we get together for a reunion, someone places one egg on a plate and cuts it into as many parts as there are people. Then everyone takes one of the pieces and eats it. We do this to be sure that next time we meet in someone's home we will all be together.

. . . . 1 . . . . 2 . . . . 3 . . . . 4 . . . . 5 . . . . 6 . . . . 7 . . . . 8 . . . . 9 . . . .10 SI=1.3

Introducing H and E

Objectives:
- To learn the location of the **H** key
- To learn the location of the **E** key
- To learn proper wrist position at the keyboard

Warmup

1. Check your position at the keyboard.
   - Are you sitting a hand span away?
   - Are your feet flat on the floor?
   - Are your fingers curved?

2. Now key the lines below, each line **twice**.

```
1 jjj fff aaa ;;; ddd kkk sss lll;
2 fj a; dk sl aj sl dk lf ks ja ;;
3 ;a la ka ja ;s ks js ;d ld kd jd
```

Proper Wrist Position

1. Place your hands on the home row keys. Are your wrists so far down that your palms touch the keyboard?

2. If they do, raise them slightly so your palms do not touch the rim of the keyboard. Check the diagram on the next page.

3. Be careful. Don't raise your palms so much that your wrists arch. Try to hold your wrists so your hands look like those in the diagram. *Maintaining proper wrist position helps avoid fatigue in your hands.*

4. Key each line on the next page **twice** as your teacher observes your wrist position.

No. 20   Students at our school are planning to hold a talent show. Anyone who can play an instrument or dance or sing is welcome to audition. Tryouts are to be held early next month. If you think you can be part of this show, come and try out. You could be amazed at the hidden talents you might possess.

. . . . .1. . . .2. . . .3. . . .4. . . .5. . . .6. . . .7. . . .8. . . .9. . . .10 SI=1.3

No. 21   When you decide to purchase a pet, whether it be a cat or a dog or a bird, be sure you have time to take care of it. Pets rely on people for their food and water. More important, they also rely on humans for attention. If a parrot gets lonely, he may pluck his feathers and refuse to eat his meal.

. . . . .1. . . .2. . . .3. . . .4. . . .5. . . .6. . . .7. . . .8. . . .9. . . .10 SI=1.3

No. 22   Any time we go on a picnic, we always seem to end up with ants. They are into the potato salad, into the chips, and on the brownies. The only way to deal with ants is to put something in the lunch that will attract them, like honey. Then they all wander over to that and leave your sandwich alone.

. . . . .1. . . .2. . . .3. . . .4. . . .5. . . .6. . . .7. . . .8. . . .9. . . .10 SI=1.3

No. 23   There is a new family who moved in across the street. I want to go over there and meet them but perhaps it is too soon. Moving to a new place can be very stressful. Making new friends, going to a new school, and adjusting to a new environment are not easy. It takes time to call a new place home.

. . . . .1. . . .2. . . .3. . . .4. . . .5. . . .6. . . .7. . . .8. . . .9. . . .10 SI=1.3

```
1 aj sj dj fj sk dk fk al sl dl fl
2 ask jak lads sad all flasks dads
3 ask dad; jak falls; alas; as; a;
4 as a lass; dad falls; dad asks a
```

Key

1. Place your hands in proper home row position. Look at the keyboard chart and locate the **H** key. It's right next to **J** and you will use your **J** finger to key it. Try it now. Key **jh** several times as you watch your fingers.

2. Key each line below **twice**. Be sure to bring your **J** finger back home after you strike the **H** key.

```
1 jhj hjj jhj hjj jhj hjj jhj jhh jhj hjj
2 jjj hhh jjj hhh jjj hhh jjj hhh jjj hhh
```

3. Key each line below **twice**.

```
3 haa hss hdd hff hjj hkk hll h;; has has
4 had has had has ash ask ash ask hall as
5 flash dash halls flash dash halls asks;
```

No. 16   No other animal is so loyal as the dog. Dogs will follow you around all day long. They welcome you home when you have only been gone a few hours. They guard your house and help warm your cold feet on chilly nights by lying across them. By the wag of a tail they show happiness when you are around.

. . . . 1 . . . . 2 . . . . 3 . . . . 4 . . . . 5 . . . . 6 . . . . 7 . . . . 8 . . . . 9 . . . .10 SI=1.2

No. 17   Once we went to a carnival to see a Gypsy who read palms. She took one look at my friend's hand and said she would soon inherit lots of money. We were pleased to hear that. Then she read my palm. She said I would not receive any money, but I will gain power. How can you have power without money?

. . . . 1 . . . . 2 . . . . 3 . . . . 4 . . . . 5 . . . . 6 . . . . 7 . . . . 8 . . . . 9 . . . .10 SI=1.2

No. 18   I went to the doctor complaining of being ill and he gave me some pills. I must take them three times a day. There is just one problem. I cannot open the bottle. It has a cap designed to prevent children from opening it; yet I cannot open it. I guess there is one thing left to do--find a child.

. . . . 1 . . . . 2 . . . . 3 . . . . 4 . . . . 5 . . . . 6 . . . . 7 . . . . 8 . . . . 9 . . . .10 SI=1.2

No. 19   I have a friend who is always in a good mood. Nothing seems to get her down. When it rains, she can only think about tomorrow when the sun will be out again. When it is hot, she reminds me of cool winter air. I wish more people were like her. To her the glass is always half full, not half empty.

. . . . 1 . . . . 2 . . . . 3 . . . . 4 . . . . 5 . . . . 6 . . . . 7 . . . . 8 . . . . 9 . . . .10 SI=1.2

E Key

1. Place your hands in proper home row position. Look at the keyboard chart and locate the **E** key. It's right above the **D** key, so you will use your **D** finger to key it. Try it now. Key **de** several times as you watch your fingers.

2. Key each line below **twice**. Move only the **D** finger up to the next row and be sure to bring your **D** finger back home after you strike the **E** key.

```
1 ded edd ded edd ded edd ded edd ded edd
2 ddd eee ddd eee ddd eee ddd eee ddd eee
```

3. Key each line below **twice**.

```
3 he he she she lash lash sash held sash;
4 shed shed heed heed elf elf elk elk jak
5 jade jade held held shelf shelf sale as
```

Challenge

1. *Pencil Test.* Key the two lines below, **two times** each, as your teacher observes your wrist placement. Your palms should be raised just enough so your teacher can slide a pencil under your hands as you key.

```
1 elk elk lead half sale fad jade all ask
2 desk sled halls sale falls hash fell he
```

2. *Balancing Act.* Place a coin on each wrist and then place your hands on home row. Be careful not to drop the coins. Key the two lines below, **two times** each, as your teacher times you for one minute. If your wrists are held in proper position, you will be able to keep the coins from rolling off your wrists.

```
3 desk sled shelf ask sale lass asked she
4 had hale jell lead half fad elk held he
```

No. 12   People who take vacations can be divided into two groups. The first group spends weeks planning just where they will travel and how long they will stay in each place. The second group picks a spot where they can stay in one place and relax. These groups both have a splendid time talking about it.

. . . . .1. . . .2. . . .3. . . .4. . . .5. . . .6. . . .7. . . .8. . . .9. . . .10 SI=1.2

No. 13   I have a friend who is never on time. It can be morning or evening; it matters not. She always has an excuse for being late. The car broke down, or her alarm clock never went off. To solve this, I now ask her to meet me at seven o'clock when the real time is eight o'clock, and then she is early.

. . . . .1. . . .2. . . .3. . . .4. . . .5. . . .6. . . .7. . . .8. . . .9. . . .10 SI=1.2

No. 14   When my uncle talks about how he walked every day to school in the freezing sleet and cold rain, I want to scream. We are not in the good old days any more. This is the modern age. Sure he had it rough, but so do I. After all, waiting outside on the corner for a bus at seven is no picnic either.

. . . . .1. . . .2. . . .3. . . .4. . . .5. . . .6. . . .7. . . .8. . . .9. . . .10 SI=1.2

No. 15   Perhaps you have a friend like mine who can't wait to tell you about a movie he just saw, but he does not stop there. He must then review the plot for you step by step. If you should nod your head to encourage him, he even tells you the ending. I must beat him to it by depicting the ending first.

. . . . .1. . . .2. . . .3. . . .4. . . .5. . . .6. . . .7. . . .8. . . .9. . . .10 SI=1.2

Introducing G and U

Objectives:
- To learn the location of the **G** key
- To learn the location of the **U** key
- To practice the technique of keeping elbows in while keyboarding
- To practice the technique of keeping eyes on copy while keyboarding

Warmup

1. Check your position at the keyboard.
   - Are you sitting a hand span away?
   - Are your fingers curved?
   - Are your wrists in proper position?

2. Good. Now key the lines below. Do each line **twice**.

```
1 a ; s l d k f j e h a ; s l d k f j e h;
2 has he asked; he fell; she asks; he asks
3 she fell; he fell; he led; she led; sale
4 she asked a lad; he has a sale desk; elf
```

 Key

1. Place your hands in home row position. Look at the keyboard chart and locate the **G** key. It's right next to **F**, so you will use your **F** finger. Try it now. Key **fg** several times as you look at the keyboard.

2. Now key the lines on the next page. Do each one **twice**. Remember to keep your eyes on the book.

No. 8   Every time our family takes a trip by car, we get lost. My dad always wants to take short cuts, which he says will get us there quicker. Mom says we should stick to the main roads and not take one of those deserted country roads, but Dad drives on the back roads until he finally admits he is lost.

. . . . 1 . . . . 2 . . . . 3 . . . . 4 . . . . 5 . . . . 6 . . . . 7 . . . . 8 . . . . 9 . . . .10 SI=1.2

No. 9   There is a cat who meows outside our house at night. My mother opens a window and yells for the cat to keep quiet, but then Dad complains that she is making more noise than the cat. We have solved the problem by leaving a saucer of milk out on the patio for the cat. Now we all can get some sleep.

. . . . 1 . . . . 2 . . . . 3 . . . . 4 . . . . 5 . . . . 6 . . . . 7 . . . . 8 . . . . 9 . . . .10 SI=1.2

No. 10   I have friends who will shop until they drop. Going from store to store they search for bargains and discounts. It does not matter what time it is or how warm or cold the weather is. Nothing stops them from wandering through the mall in pursuit of a superior deal; only tired feet bring them home.

. . . . 1 . . . . 2 . . . . 3 . . . . 4 . . . . 5 . . . . 6 . . . . 7 . . . . 8 . . . . 9 . . . .10 SI=1.2

No. 11   The people who make road maps surely must not know how much trouble they have caused those of us who cannot fold things. No matter how hard I try, and how much I struggle, that road map never seems to look as it did when it was new. However, there is one solution; buy only maps that come in books.

. . . . 1 . . . . 2 . . . . 3 . . . . 4 . . . . 5 . . . . 6 . . . . 7 . . . . 8 . . . . 9 . . . .10 SI=1.2

```
1 fgf gff fgf gff fgf gff fgf gff fgf gff
2 fff ggg fff ggg fff ggg fff ggg fff ggg
```

3. Now key the lines below, **two times** each. Remember, you are not going to look at the screen until you complete each line. Keep your eyes on the book.

```
3 gas gas gad gad keg kegs leg legs heads;
4 gull gull dull dull sag sag gag gag lags
5 lug lugs jug jugs slug slugs sages gages
```

PART C

Elbows In

1. Let's talk about elbows. Yes, elbows! Of course, you don't key with your elbows, but they're important. If you let your elbows stick out when you key, your **F** and **J** fingers come off home row. And when your fingers come off home row, you then have trouble striking the other keys from home position.

2. Try it now. Place your hands on home row. Stick out your elbows and watch what happens to the **J** and **F** fingers. The farther you stick out your elbows, the more your **J** and **F** fingers come off the keys. See why keeping your elbows at your sides is important? *Keeping elbows close to your sides prevents your fingers from coming off home row.*

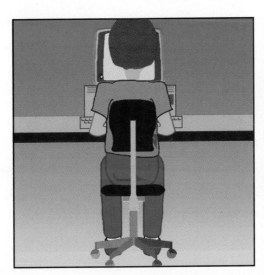

No. 4   A friend of mine has a problem every night he tries to fall asleep. He will climb into his bed, but sleep does not come. He has tried many cures. It seems the problem is noise from the street. So now he turns on the fan to cover up any noise. It matters not what time of year it is; the fan runs.

. . . .1. . . .2. . . .3. . . .4. . . .5. . . .6. . . .7. . . .8. . . .9. . . .10 SI=1.1

No. 5   My friend and I decided to hike up a mountain trail. When we came to a fork in the road, we had to decide which trail to take. He wanted the left trail and I wanted the one on the right. We could not agree, so we tossed a coin. My friend got his way. Now I grasped why. That coin had two heads.

. . . .1. . . .2. . . .3. . . .4. . . .5. . . .6. . . .7. . . .8. . . .9. . . .10 SI=1.1

No. 6   Some people go on a diet because they want to look thin. They stop eating or skimp on breakfast or lunch. Then when dinner time rolls around they are starved and consume everything in sight that's not tied down. This is not the proper way to drop a few pounds. Weight lost slowly should stay off.

. . . .1. . . .2. . . .3. . . .4. . . .5. . . .6. . . .7. . . .8. . . .9. . . .10 SI=1.2

No. 7   When my dog hears thunder booming from above, he gets scared and tries to hide behind the stove. Sometimes he will squeeze himself behind the sofa. If we happen to have a bad storm during the night, he will simply crawl up into bed with me to sleep. I like having him sleep with me; he keeps me warm.

. . . .1. . . .2. . . .3. . . .4. . . .5. . . .6. . . .7. . . .8. . . .9. . . .10 SI=1.2

3. Practice keeping your elbows close to your body as you key the lines below. Do each line **twice**.

1 heed heeds feed feeds head heads sage he
2 she has legs; he asks sad dad; she gags;
3 dead eels shelf legs sags kegs asks hall

 Key

1. Place your hands in home row position. Look at the keyboard chart and locate the **U** key. There it is in the third row, just above the **J** key. So you will use your **J** finger to strike **U.** Try it now. Key **ju** several times as you watch your fingers. Be sure to bring your **J** finger back home after striking the **U** key.

2. Now key the lines below, *keeping your eyes on the book as you key.*

1 juj ujj juj ujj juj ujj juj ujj juj ujj
2 jjj uuu jjj uuu jjj uuu jjj uuu jjj uuu

3. Let's try some more lines with **U** in them. Do each line **twice**.

3 due dues hue hues dude dudes use duke us
4 dull duds head lull fuss flush hash hush
5 he has a uke; a fluke; sue us; used ukes

PART E

G and **U** **Keys Combined**

Type each line below **twice**. Remember to bring your fingers back to home row after striking the new keys.

1 hugs gus hull dudes flukes jugs hugs use
2 sages dues fuss guss lugs jade dude jude
3 he fled; she hugs; safe lull; he lugs a;

The following timed writings may be used any time after you have completed Lesson 20. If you finish the paragraph before time is called, start it over again from the beginning.

Short Timed Writings

No. 1

     I have often heard it said when it rains hard that it is raining cats and dogs. Now, I ask you, why cats and dogs and not pigs and cows? Or lambs or horses or mules? Perhaps it could rain buttons and bows. Or turtles and fish, or ducks and hens. Next time try saying it is raining deer and geese.

. . . . 1 . . . . 2 . . . . 3 . . . . 4 . . . . 5 . . . . 6 . . . . 7 . . . . 8 . . . . 9 . . . .10 SI=1.1

No. 2

     Training a dog to walk on a leash and to stay when told is what is taught in dog school. I took my dog to school to learn these things, but he did not pass the test. He sat when I told him to heel and he downed when he was to stand. Apparently it is true; you can't teach an old canine new tricks.

. . . . 1 . . . . 2 . . . . 3 . . . . 4 . . . . 5 . . . . 6 . . . . 7 . . . . 8 . . . . 9 . . . .10 SI=1.1

No. 3

     I have a friend who likes to ride in the back seat of the car. She feels that it is her duty in life to help whoever is driving. When lights turn green, she makes it a point of announcing it. One day she gave her message to deaf ears. The driver could not hear a word through those big ear muffs.

. . . . 1 . . . . 2 . . . . 3 . . . . 4 . . . . 5 . . . . 6 . . . . 7 . . . . 8 . . . . 9 . . . .10 SI=1.1

Eyes on Copy

Keeping your eyes on the copy (looking at the letters you are keying) is so important that we're going to practice that now. Key the lines below, **two times** each. Don't look at the screen or your hands until you've keyed the entire line. Can you do it? Let's see.

1 sage keg sad fad lad led lull sale hales
2 fuel duel sue duke heed gage feeds leads
3 fed dead head seed leads lugs huge flash

Review

The lines below review all the keys you've learned thus far. Do each line **twice**. Can you key them without hesitation? Let's see.

1 half a glass; a lull; use seeds; a duel;
2 she fell; half fuel; she shakes; due us;
3 hug dug sale fluke suds gas he she flake

Challenge

Your teacher will time the class for 30 seconds as everyone keys the lines below. Your goal is to key without looking at your keyboard or your screen for half a minute. If your teacher sees anyone looking, the clock stops and is reset. You must continue the exercise until all students in the class can key for 30 seconds without taking their eyes off the book. If your teacher sees anyone looking at his or her hands, the clock stops and the timing begins again with zero seconds. Keep repeating the lines below until your teacher stops you. Ready?

1 sad lad fad fade fuss guss lull see uses
2 dad dude lake safe hugs head ask duke us
3 guss hug dug sale dale fluke suds gas he

SECTION 8

Timed
Writings

LESSON 6

STOP! and Review

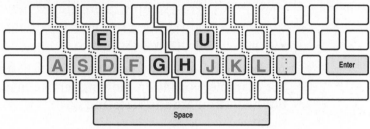

Objectives:
- To review keys learned in previous lessons
- To practice technique pointers learned in previous lessons

Warmup

1. Check your position at the keyboard.
   - Are you sitting a hand span away?
   - Are your fingers curved?
   - Are your wrists in proper position?

2. This lesson contains no new keys to learn. So you can relax and concentrate on strengthening the reaches to those keys you have learned thus far. Key the lines below, **two times** each. If time permits, repeat the lines.

```
1 asedf jukl; asedf jukl; fedsa jukl; gheu
2 fed keg lug hug elk dead head uke hue us
3 he fed us eggs; she has seeds; feed elks
4 see all; feed us; lug a jug; a safe lake
```

PART B

Eyes on Copy

Key the lines on the next page, **twice** each. As you key, force yourself to keep your eyes on the book. Do not look at the screen or your hands until you have finished the set of lines. Can you do it? Let's try.

Application 117: Sales Plan

Directions:

To increase your business, you have decided to send your workers to make door-to-door sales calls at houses in your neighborhood. Before beginning these calls, you need to develop a sales plan. After checking several sources, you decide your sales plan should include the three points listed to the right.

Compose a one-page report, double spaced, explaining these points, and arrange it attractively on the page. Use the file name Ap117.

1. A description of the best feature of your business. For example, you may be the first one out in the morning shoveling snow so your customers' driveways will be clear before they have to leave for work.

2. The customer's needs and wants and how your business can meet these needs. For example, there are two advantages if you walk someone's dog. The dog owner is free to do something else and the dog gets much-needed exercise.

3. An explanation of why your business is better than the competition. For example, your lawn mowing service may not just cut the grass but hand trim around trees and bushes where the mower cannot reach.

Application 118: Sales Plan Cover Sheet

Directions:

Compose and arrange attractively a cover page for the sales plan you completed in Application 117. Use the file name Ap118.

Application 119: Sales Plan References

Directions:

Compose and arrange attractively a reference page for the sales plan you just completed. Use the file name Ap119. You used the following sources:

Owning and Operating Your Own Business by Charles W. Taylor; published by Vinton Press, New York, 1989.

Competition in Business by Mary Larson; published by Quicken Publishing Company, Chicago, 1990.

Why Some Businesses Fail by Bart Walker; published by Underhill Publishing Company, Boston, 1991.

"Getting Started in Your Own Business" by Shana Avery; published in Business Monthly, June, 1991, pages 89-91.

```
1 head feed dead kegs lad sad deed ages us
2 jell deal seal guff lull dull gull feels
3 she has flu; she dug a lake; a fake seal
```

Palms off the Keyboard

Palms resting on the keyboard can cause you to make extra spaces where you don't want them because your hands may accidentally hit the Space Bar. Let's try the lines below, **two times** each, and see if you can keep the palms of your hands from resting on the keyboard.

```
1 sue led he lead use hug eke uke due sage
2 lakes fake sake head dead seal deal jell
3 she has flu; he leads; shake a safe; ah;
```

Feet on the Floor

Keeping your feet flat on the floor, one slightly ahead of the other, is the best way to brace yourself for keyboarding. Let's see if you can keep your feet flat on the floor as you key the lines below, **two times** each.

```
1 jug fed seed lake jell head feed gas sad
2 use has lake asked halls eggs hulls fell
3 ashes flash duke lake lash seeds fad lad
```

Distance from the Machine

Are you a hand span away from your keyboard? If you sit too close, you will have trouble reaching the bottom row keys; if you sit too far away, you will have trouble reaching for the top row keys. Place yourself the correct distance from the keyboard and then key the lines on the next page, **twice** each.

Application 116: Running a Business

Directions:

Your business is so successful that you have been asked to speak to the high school business class about the topic of owning your own business.

You plan to talk from an outline. Arrange it attractively on the page. Name the file Ap116.

```
Running Your Own Business

I.    Personal traits needed to succeed

      A.  Risk taker

      B.  Creative

      C.  Flexible

      D.  Energetic

      E.  Persistent

      F.  Self-starter

      G.  Decisive

II.   How to set up the business

      A.  Expenses

          1.  Supplies

          2.  Advertising

      B.  Risks

      C.  Profit or loss

III.  How to deal with the competition

      A.  Price

      B.  Service

      C.  Location

IV.   How to hire workers

      A.  Newspaper ads

      B.  Bulletin board notices

V.    Some problems encountered

      A.  Lazy workers

      B.  Price competition

      C.  Rush periods
```

```
1 half fuel dead fed sad hale gag sage age
2 lead flea gash aghast dash lugs dull use
3 ash flash skull fed asked hall sale lake
```

Return/Enter
Key

1. How you return to the next line is important. If you take your eyes off the book to do that, you lose valuable time finding your place in the book again. *That loss of time takes away from your speed development. Also, whenever you take your eyes off the book you risk the chance that you may not find the right line when you continue keying. You may skip words or repeat a line.* The best technique is to keep eyes on the book, use the finger that controls the semicolon key, your "sem" finger—to strike Return/Enter, and quickly bring that little pinkie back home. Do not space before striking Return/Enter; that would be a waste of time.

2. Let's practice that technique on the lines below. When you see R/E, press your Return/Enter key. Repeat if time permits.

```
flash gush dash hall R/E due us fuss dull use R/E
head seeds hash dash R/E half duel dull gulls R/E
sad dead deeds hulls R/E he she lead dash hug R/E
deaf ashes jell lake R/E fade shade dude jade R/E
```

Elbow Position

Are you a bird? You are if you let your elbows stick out when you keyboard. From the rear, you look like a bird getting ready to flap its wings and take off. Let's try keying the lines below, **twice** each, and see if you can keep your elbows at your sides. Remember, no birds allowed in keyboarding class!

```
1 sad sale; dead lake; she dug; a hall; ah
2 he leads; she feeds us; sad lad; he hugs
3 ash desks; all add; lead us; a fall sale
```

Challenge

Your teacher will time the class for one minute as everyone keys the lines on the next page. Your goal is to key without looking at your keyboard or your screen for a whole minute. If your teacher sees anyone

Application 113: Interview Questions

Directions:

Your business is doing so well that you will need to hire a few temporary part-time workers to help you handle the work when it is too much for you to do alone. Since the reputation of your business depends on the kind of work these people do, you want to hire people who will represent your business well. Compose a list (enumeration) of at least ten questions you would ask prospective workers before allowing them to work for you. Arrange the list attractively on the page. Name the file Ap113.

Application 114: Prospective Customers

Directions:

Now that you have other people working for you, you have decided to expand your business. Compose a three-column table titled Prospective Customers. The first column should contain the customers' names; the second column, their street addresses; and the third column, their phone numbers. You want to have at least ten of your neighbors on this list. Arrange it attractively on the page. Name the file Ap114.

Application 115: Order Letter

Directions:

You need to write a letter ordering merchandise for your business. You decide what you need. Perhaps you need more snow shovels or lawn mowers. Maybe you need to get some more toys or playground equipment so the children you baby-sit will have things to play with. Or perhaps you need more collars and leashes for the dogs you are walking. Compose the letter to West Wind Supplies, 87 W. Redwing Avenue, [Your City, State, Zip Code]. Explain what your needs are and ask them to send you a catalog of their merchandise. Arrange the letter attractively on the page and sign your name. Name the file Ap115.

looking, the clock stops and is reset. You must continue the exercise until all students in the class can key for 60 seconds without taking their eyes off the book. If your teacher sees anyone looking at his or her hands, the clock stops and the timing begins again with zero seconds. Keep repeating the lines below. Ready?

```
1 safe lake; he led; fuel due; lush lakes;
2 dull head; she hugs; safe eggs; all heed
3 a lull; she feels; a jade egg; ask a lad
```

LESSON
7

Introducing R and I

Objectives:
- To learn the location of the **R** key
- To learn the location of the **I** key
- To practice proper techniques when keyboarding

PART A

1. Check your position at the keyboard.
   - Are you sitting a hand span away?
   - Are your elbows close to your body?
   - Are your palms off the keyboard?

2. Now key the lines below, each line **twice**.

```
1 dull deaf kale sale sage huge jugs halls
2 use fee jugs flee keg jade head ask gash
3 duel hash jell half ashes safe dashes ah
4 jade lake; he has a gash; huge desk; flu
```

Application 111: New Business Plans

Directions:

Compose a personal note to a relative (cousin, aunt, uncle, grandmother, grandfather, etc.), telling them of your new business venture. Explain what your business is called, what service you provide, how much you charge, how much you hope to make, and what plans you have for the money. Name the file Ap111.

Application 112: Advertisement in Rhyme

Directions:

The poem at the right is an advertisement. Arrange it attractively on a full page so it can be reproduced on a copy machine and tacked up at local supermarket and church bulletin boards. Insert the appropriate information where needed. Name the file Ap112.

A NEW BUSINESS IN TOWN
Owned and Operated by [Your full name]

There's a new business in town,
    No kidding, it's true.
No need for you to frown,
    I'll take care of your _____ for you.

I'll get the job done,
    No matter how big or small,
For me hard work is really fun.
    So please, give me a call.

If you wish, references I am happy to provide.
    My work record is nothing but great.
I have nothing to hide,
    So call now for my rate.

My number is _____; phone any time.
    My prices are so low
That you'll think it's a crime.
    I'm anxious to start; give me the "go."

Key

1. Place your hands in home row position. Look at the keyboard chart and locate the **R** key. It's right above the **F** key, so you will use your **F** finger to strike it. Try it now. Key **fr** several times as you watch your fingers make the reach.

2. Now try the lines below, **twice** each.

1 frf rff frf rff frf rff frf rff frf rff
2 fff rrr fff rrr fff rrr fff rrr fff rrr

3. Key each line below **twice**. Remember to bring your **F** finger back home after striking the **R** key.

3 jar fur far lark rake jerk hear dear are
4 shear deer fear jeer drags rah hark dark
5 red freed sear lure ark shark gear dread

Eyes on Copy

As you key the lines below, **twice** each, try to keep your eyes on the book. Do not look at the screen or your hands until you have keyed the entire line.

1 her fur; a red desk; she jeers; fur sale
2 he has a hard desk; she reads; all shall
3 she has a gash; rush her; use a jade egg

 Key

1. Place your hands in home row position. Look at the keyboard chart and locate the **I** key. It's just above **K,** so you will use your **K** finger. Try it now. Key **ki** several times as you watch your fingers do the keying.

2. Now try the lines below. Do each line **twice**. Be sure to bring your **K** finger back home after striking the **I** key.

1 kik ikk kik ikk kik ikk kik ikk kik ikk
2 kkk iii kkk iii kkk iii kkk iii kkk iii

LESSON 75

Formatting Documents for a Business

Objectives:

■ To keyboard documents required to run a part-time student business
■ To review the format for documents covered in previous lessons

In this lesson, you will not be doing any drills. Instead, you will do the keyboarding required to run your own part-time business. You must decide what that business will be. You could mow lawns, shovel snow, walk dogs, or baby-sit younger children. Think about it now and make a choice from one of the four options. Then decide on a name for your business. It could be as simple as Pat's Baby-Sitting Service or Teri's Lawn Mowing Service or a more creative name such as Collar and Leash Walkers (dog walking service) or Snow Birds (snow shoveling service). Once you have decided on a business and its name, you are ready to begin.

Do the applications in the order given. You will want to print and save each application. Work independently at your own pace. If you get stuck on a problem, try to figure it out yourself. Use your textbook as a reference; turn back in the book to where that particular document was first presented and study the model and directions.

Application 110: New Business Flyer

Directions:

Your first application is to advertise your new business. Key the flyer at the right, arranging it attractively on the page. The flyer should be one page so you can reproduce it on a copy machine and distribute it door-to-door within your neighborhood. Name the file Ap110.

[NAME OF YOUR BUSINESS]

[Describe the service you provide]

[Give the days and time you are available for this service]

[State your hourly fee]

[Give your name and a phone number where you can be reached]

[Add whatever additional information you feel is necessary to convince people to use your service. For example, you could provide references upon request, or you could state what past experience you have had in this type of work]

3. Key the lines below, **two times** each. Keep your eyes on the book!

```
3 if is hill fill ail dial sail said jails
4 die did side fish hide kids lid dial ski
5 his gill dish like dike hike fish dishes
```

I and R Keys Combined

Key the lines below, **two times** each. Remember to bring your fingers back to home position after striking the **R** and **I** keys.

```
1 rail fir rides figs jig frail lies frill
2 gills rill shrill drill sill arf dark hi
3 he said; he dials; free dishes; he fried
```

Body Erect

Do you sit up straight when you keyboard? Slouching puts a lot of strain on your spine. Let's see if you can key the lines below, **twice** each, and keep good posture all the way through.

```
1 she drills; he digs; fresh fish; her rig
2 hide a ski; ride her red rig; dark hulks
3 he said; she dials; free dishes; fish is
```

Application 108: Chicago Fire References

Directions:

- Key the reference page for the two-page report completed in Application 107. Arrange the entries attractively and in alphabetical order on the page.

- Number the page appropriately
- File name: Ap108

REFERENCES

Trenton, Jill. The Great Chicago Fire. Chicago: DeKoven Publishing Company, 1988.

Potter, Horace. "The Swamp That Grew Up," Traveler, March, 1990, 41-43.

Clark, Amanda. Illinois History. Boston: Marr and Denison, 1988.

Kelly, Wayne. "Historical Places to Visit," Guide to Illinois. Springfield: Illinois Department of Tourism, 1991.

Application 109: Chicago Cover Page

Directions:

- Below is the cover page for the two-page report completed in Application 107. Arrange it attractively.

- File name: Ap109

THE HISTORY OF CHICAGO

From Its Beginning to 1900

Prepared for Mrs. Jacob's Social Studies Class

Fifth Period

[Your Name]

[Current Date]

Palms off the Keyboard

You already know how important it is to keep your palms off the keyboard. Let's try the lines below, **twice** each, and see if you can keep your palms from resting on the keyboard.

```
1 his kid; if she is; deer rides; red side
2 he hides; she has a dark shelf; rush all
3 dear sir; a salad; half salsa; he drills
```

Challenge

1. Your teacher will time you for one minute. How many times can you key the double-letter words in the line below?

```
1 ill gills deeds see jells dull glee frees
```

2. Now find a partner. As your teacher times you for one minute, race with your partner to see who can key the most words in the line below.

```
2 sill all jell deer heed deed steers kiss
```

3. Try again with your partner on this line.

```
3 free dill; a lull; a drill; a reel; sees
```

from Indians, and Chicago started to grow. Eight years later the fort was destroyed by an attack, but it was rebuilt.

In 1818 Illinois became a state. Chicago consisted of a few cabins, swamp land, forest, and wild onions. It was not until 1833 that Chicago became an official village with a population of 150. The town was described as "wild" because its citizens hunted wolf and bear in the streets.

By 1837 the town had grown to over 4,000 people. Many of the new arrivals came from the East via the Erie Canal. In ten years its population increased five times. By 1870 the population had grown to 300,000. Almost every building was made of wood. This proved to be Chicago's downfall a year later.

In 1871 a cow kicked over a kerosene lantern and started what later was called The Great Chicago Fire. Feeding on the wooden buildings that were everywhere, the fire roared through the southern part of town. Then a shift in the wind sent flames northward. People jumped in Lake Michigan to escape the heat of the fire. When it was all over, 300 people were dead; 100,000 were homeless; and 17,000 buildings had been destroyed.

After the fire, the people of Chicago rebuilt their city. By 1874 all signs of the fire were gone. By the turn of the century Chicago was a booming town once again. It proudly hosted the Columbian Exposition, which demonstrated for the first time a new invention--electricity. Chicago was on its way to becoming a thriving city.

LESSON 8

Introducing T and Right Shift

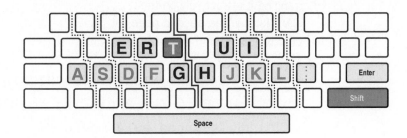

Objectives:

- ■ To learn the location of the **T** key
- ■ To learn the location of the **Right Shift** key
- ■ To learn proper shifting technique
- ■ To practice proper keyboarding techniques

PART A

Warmup

1. Check your position at the keyboard.
    - ■ Are you sitting a hand span away?
    - ■ Is your body erect?
    - ■ Is your body centered opposite the **J** key?

2. Now key the lines below **two times** each. If time permits, repeat the lines.

```
1 like leaks dear gulls sir jerk dark hair
2 air fair jeer deer sea see rig fig drill
3 dear sir; free fish; guide her; sea gull
4 she is sad; dark desk; free air; hides a
```

PART B

 Key

1. Place your hands in home row position. Look at the keyboard chart and locate the **T** key. It's above and a little to the right of **F,** so you will use your **F** finger. Try keying **ft** now. Watch your fingers as you strike this combination several times.

2. Now key the lines on the next page, **twice** each. Be sure to bring your finger back to home position after striking the **T.**

Application 107: History of Chicago

Directions:

- Key the two-page report below, arranging it attractively on the page. Number the second page in the top right-hand corner.

- File name: Ap107

THE HISTORY OF CHICAGO

From Its Beginning to 1900

Chicago started as a mound of ice creeping slowly from the North Pole. As the ice slowly moved south, it gouged out the land. When the glacier was gone, there was a large depression that we now call the Great Lakes. Runoff from the melting ice formed many rivers, among them the Illinois, Chicago, Des Plaines, and Mississippi Rivers.

The land that would become Chicago was inhabited by several Indian tribes--Winnebagos, Potawatomi, Foxes, Sacs, Shawness, Miami, and Mascoutens. For thousands of years these native Americans lived in harmony with each other and the land.

Then people landed on the continent in search of a shorter route to the Orient. Samuel de Champlain was the first explorer to hear about the Chicago area. When he founded the city of Quebec, he was told about people who lived by the "Great Stinking Water." Lake Michigan was surrounded by wild onions, which gave it this name.

Chicago's first permanent settler was Jean Baptiste Point du Sable, a Canadian trader. He lived on the banks of the Chicago River between 1784 and 1800. In 1804 Fort Dearborn was built as protection

(continued on next page)

```
1 ftf tff ftf tff ftf tff ftf tff ftf tff
2 fff ttt fff ttt fff ttt fff ttt fff ttt
```

3. When you are first learning the location of a new key, it's okay to look at your hands. But after that you should keep your eyes on the book as you key. Now key the lines below, **twice** each. Keep your other fingers on the home keys as you reach for **T.**

```
3 fit jet at eat ate tree the sat huts gut
4 lift it the sit at gate rate hates tarts
5 hat late dart seat alert dirt shirts the
```

Sitting Back in the Chair

When you sit at your keyboard, are your hips all the way back in the chair? If you sit on the edge of your chair, you're not only likely to fall but you put a strain on your spine. So get comfortable and sit all the way back in the chair. Try it now as you key the lines below, **twice** each.

```
1 trite fried high dried site rug ruts the
2 hid hide side aside sift drift gist seat
3 hide the desk; she is a kid; if he is at
```

He called his sleeping car the pioneer. It was an
instant success. It was even used as part of the
funeral train that brought President Lincoln form
Washington, D.C., to his home in Springfield,
Illinois.

Mr. Pullman decided to build his sleeping-car
plant in Chicago because the city was on Lake
Michigan. He reasoned that his workers could get
more work done in the summer because of the breezes
off the lake. Mr. Pullman bought 3,000 acres of land
and built his plant in 1879. In 1881 he built a town
forall his workers. The town was named after him.
It had shops, a library, a theater, churches,
schools, and parks. The town of Pullman became part
of Chicago in 1889. Many ofthe original buildings
still stand today.

Application 106: Class Officers

Directions:

- Key the table below, arranging it attractively on the page. Leave ten spaces between the columns.
- File name: Ap106

CLASS OFFICERS FOR 19--
[Name of your teacher's class]

Name	Office Held
[Your Name]	President
Molly Saunders	Vice President
Arthur Cruz	Treasurer
Sandra Johnville	Secretary
Emily Tseng	Historian

Right Shift Key

1. Place your hands in home row position. Look at the keyboard chart and locate the **Right Shift** key. It's in the bottom right-hand corner of the keyboard. This key is used to key capital letters struck with the left hand. For example, to key a capital **e** or a capital **r,** you must hold down the Right Shift key while you key the **e** or **r.**

2. Let's try using that shift key. Shifting is a three-step process: First, keeping your other fingers in home position, stretch your little pinkie to the Right Shift key and hold down that key. Second, strike the letter you want capitalized. Third, bring both fingers back to home position. Try it now to key these capital letters:

1 A; S; F; D; R; Al Sl D; Fl Rl Ak Sk

3. Key each line below **two times** each. Remember to bring your little finger back home after striking the shift key.

2 Sis is ill; Sal is full; Dad agrees; eat
3 Dale ties the kite; Gail tries; Sasha is
4 Ed asked Duke; Art tried; Sue dashed; Ru

Shifting Technique

Key the lines on the next page, **twice** each, as your teacher observes your shifting technique. Good technique means two things: (1) you reach down to the shift key with your pinkie or "sem" finger while keeping the other fingers in home position, and (2) after making the capital letter, you return your sem finger back home.

A. Displays images on screen

B. May be monochrome or colored

V. Input Devices

A. May be a keyboard

B. May be a mouse

VI. Printer

A. May be a dot matrix

1. Makes characters and graphics out of dots

2. Prints near-letter quality

B. May be a laser

1. Makes characters by moving laser beam across drum

2. Prints superior quality to dot matrix

Application 105: The Pullman Sleeper

Directions:
- Key the one-page report below, arranging it attractively on the page. Make all corrections
- indicated by the proofreader's marks.
- File name: Ap105

THE PULLMAN CAR

By [Your Name]

When George m. Pullman took a sixty-mile trainride and did not get a good night's sleep, he decided to do something about it. He would improve the railroad sleeping car so it would be comfortable and convenent.

Mr. Pullman moved to Chicago where he proceeded to redo two day coaches into sleeping cars. The cars, however, were not a success. Pullman started over and designed new plans. he worked on his plan for four years. The car was finally ready in 1865.

(continued on next page)

1 Fred likes salsa; Sue likes jade dresses
2 Derek digs; Gretta said she likes salads
3 Ask Shasta if Duke is free; Ed uses fuel

PART F

T and
Right Shift
Keys Combined

Key the lines below, **two times** each. As you key, remember to bring your fingers back to home position.

1 Fat Fred fried the fish; Tess gets tired
2 Sue ate the salsa; Derek shall ask Eddie
3 Rita fasts; Elsie edits; Duke tries hard

PART G

Eyes on Copy

As you key the lines below, **twice** each, try to keep your eyes on the book; do not look up from the text until you finish the each line.

1 if the hat fits; it is true; he did ride
2 she slides; he glides; see the red rugs;
3 he strides; she had a jar; see the trees

PART H

Challenge

Find a partner. As your teacher times you for one minute on each line below, see who can type the most words. Be sure you capitalize every word.

1 Fast Asks Desk Grad Sage Edges Take Rage
2 Fled Ashes Dishes Treats Did Said Rear A
3 Fluid Great States Drake Eats Seats Reef

and Review

Objectives:

- To review formats for the following documents:
  - outlines
  - one-page reports
  - tables
  - two-page reports
  - reference page
  - cover page

Application 104: Personal Computer Outline

Directions:

- Key the outline below, arranging it attractively on the page.
- File name: Ap104

BASIC ELEMENTS OF A PERSONAL COMPUTER SYSTEM

I.   System Software

A.   Installed on hard disk drive

B.   Required before any application can be used

II.   Application Software

A.   Also called programs

B.   Divided into three categories

1.   Word Processing

2.   Spreadsheets

3.   Data Bases

III.   Central Processing Unit (CPU)

A.   Contains memory

B.   Contains hard disk drive

IV.   Monitor

(continued on next page)

LESSON 9

STOP! **and Review**

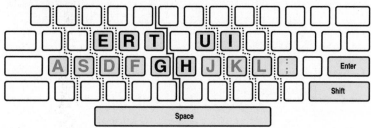

Objectives:
- To review keys learned in previous lessons
- To practice technique pointers learned in previous lessons

Warmup

1. Check your position at the keyboard.
   - Are you sitting all the way back in your chair?
   - Are your wrists in proper position?
   - Are your elbows close to your body?

2. This lesson contains no new keys to learn. So you can relax and concentrate on strengthening the reaches to those keys you have learned thus far. Key the lines below, **two times** each. If time permits, repeat the lines.

```
1 Al tried; she dried the dishes; he fried
2 Duke is alert; Gretta dresses like Elsie
3 Shasta said she rakes the seed; Ed talks
4 Did she ride; Al hides Ed; tie this kite
```

PART B

Eyes on Copy

You already know the importance of keeping your eyes on the book when keyboarding. Let's practice that now with the lines on the next page. Key each one **twice**. Do not look up from the book until you have finished each line.

On Sunday we'll be taking a ride to Honey Bear Farm
for brunch. They have fabulous food there, and you
can eat all you want from the buffet.

I can hardly wait for the weekend.
Sincerely

[Your Name]

Application 103: Personal Letter

Directions:
- Key the personal letter below
  and arrange it attractively on the
  page.
- The / means to start a new line
- File name: Ap103

Current Date

Grover's Market/286 W. Main Street/Your City, State,
Zip Code/Dear Mr. Grover My brother, Tom, works
part-time for you in the produce department. On
Saturday my family is planning a surprise birthday
party for him.
In order for the party to be a real surprise, we need
to have Tom come home one hour later than usual.
That will give all our relatives time to get here.
Could you please make up some excuse to keep him
there later than usual on Saturday? My family will
really appreciate your cooperation in helping us pull
this off. Sincerely [Your Name], [Your Address]

```
1 due sue fur jet jut hut the jar has she;
2 used just high free said dire hire seats
3 skiff lakes drake stake stark disks flea
```

Palms off the Keyboard

Now let's practice keeping your palms off the keyboard. As you key the lines below, be especially alert to this technique. Do each line **twice**.

```
1 Their jade jar takes fluid; she has fuel
2 The kite flies high; the elf has a treat
3 Take the skiff at the lake; use the desk
```

Shifting Technique

Shifting is not an easy technique to master. Let's practice it now. Remember, always bring your fingers back to home row position after shifting for a capital letter and be sure to keep all the other fingers at home. Key each line **twice**.

```
1 Take a ride; Get a tire; Shake the fries
2 Dead lake; Red skiffs; All the girls did
3 Also dust; Free fruit is there; Sift it;
```

Proper Distance from the Computer

Do you hug your computer? If you sit too close, you are a hugger. You need to sit the right distance away so you can reach all the keys properly. Let's practice that right now. Make a hand span and place yourself a hand span away from the edge of the keyboard. Now key the lines below, **two times** each, while staying in that good position.

```
1 use that tie; take that jet; hire her if
2 did he get the desk; get the ad address;
3 tight dress; silk tie; fir tree; is free
```

Return/Enter Key

Key the lines on the next page **once**. When you come to **R/E,** press the **Return/Enter** key. As you key, avoid looking up at the end of each line and always bring your little finger back to home position after returning/entering. Repeat if time permits.

any special music tapes you would like to play, bring them. The Tolers will bring their stereo equipment. The Meyers will bring two grills, but we could use a few more as well as some bags of charcoal. The Gustoffs have kindly donated hotdogs and the Frenches have donated bratwurst. If you would like some other meat, you will have to bring your own and cook it on the grill. Our cook this year is Mr. Yarby.

Application 102: Personal Note to Cousin

Directions:
- Key the personal note below and arrange it attractively on the page.
- File name: Ap102

[Current Date]

Dear Cousin
I'm very excited that you are coming to visit next weekend. On Saturday we will go to Knock Park for the dog Frisbee contest. Yes, my dog, Bingo, is competing this year. He is getting pretty good at catching those flying disks. Wait till you see how high he jumps. I'll explain the competition rules when you get here.

Saturday night my school is having a Mardi Gras Night. There will be booths where we can play different games. Last year I went with a friend, and we had lots of fun. I'm sure you'll enjoy it too. There is only one requirement, and that is that everyone wear a mask. Don't worry; I have lots of masks left over from Halloween.

(continued on next page)

```
The fir tree is free; R/E Take her red dresses; R/E
She hates fried fish; R/E Rush the right fees; R/E
She ate half the salsa; R/E Sue said the salad
fits the dish; R/E Tad has a silk tie; R/E There is
a safe hut; R/E Ella is the first rider;
```

The Space Bar

Let's work on your Space Bar technique. Do you sometimes get extra spaces between words? If you do, you may be letting your thumb lean on the Space Bar, which produces extra spaces. Try to use a *down and in* motion when spacing. See if you can do that now as you practice the lines below. Do each line **once**. Repeat if time permits.

```
1 air tar far jar get fit fig dig jig rigs
2 rude just rush dust gusts dash rash kale
3 grasses greed greets freed agreed juggle
```

Challenge

Can you key with your eyes closed? Let's find out. Your teacher will dictate the words below. Key each word **once**. At the end of the line, your teacher will ask you to open your eyes and read back the words. Now, close your eyes, and no peeking!

```
1 sit fit get jet air did ask gas fur gate
2 gift huge rugs jerk desk said ride glide
3 sifts freed fried earth first glue stiff
4 there three that dread sheds agreed jest
5 takes ashes fresh fruit kisses guess set
```

Application 100: Wrigley Field Poem

Directions:
- Key the poem below, arranging it attractively on the page.
- File name: Ap100

WRIGLEY FIELD IN THE LIGHTS

By Richard Nelson

It was Sunday at the ballpark.

The Cubbies lost again.

I'm sure they once won five in a row.

But I can't remember when.

As a Cub fan for many years

I've suffered in the light.

But now with illumination

I can suffer too at night!

Application 101: Block Party Flyer

Directions:
- Key the flyer below, arranging it attractively on the page.
- File name: Ap101

BLOCK PARTY

SATURDAY, JULY 16

4:30 Until It Gets Dark

Bring a Dish to Pass, Eating Utensils, and Lawn

Chairs

RSVP Call 555-3491 (The Andersons)

Note: The city will block off our street to eliminate

all traffic during the scheduled time. If you have

(continued on next page)

LESSON 10

Introducing O and C

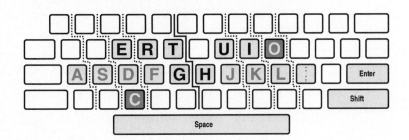

Objectives:

- To learn the location of the **O** key
- To learn the location of the **C** key
- To practice proper keyboarding techniques

PART A

Warmup

1. Check your position at the keyboard.
   - Are you sitting a hand span away?
   - Are your palms off the keyboard?
   - Are you bringing your fingers back to home row after striking other keys?

2. Now key the lines below, each line **twice**.

```
1 dug keg sad fad lad ear sit tar far eggs
2 fruit great dead head jute flute sear ah
3 fragile frugal gratitude altitude steers
4 Al used a skiff at the lake; that is all
```

PART B

O Key

1. Place your hands in home row position. Look at the keyboard chart and locate the **O** key. It's above the **L** key, so you will use your **L** finger. Try it now. Key **lo** several times as you watch your fingers make the reach. Be sure to keep your **J** and **K** fingers at home.

Application 99: Computer Tips

Directions:

- Key the enumeration below, arranging it attractively on the page.
- File name: Ap99

TIPS TO KEEP YOUR COMPUTER PARTS HEALTHY

If you want your computer mouse to live a long and healthy life, there are a number of things you should do to ensure its health. Turn the mouse over and twist off the ring. Take out the little ball that is inside. Blow into the opening. Wipe the ball, the bar, and the rollers inside the mouse with a cotton swab dipped in alcohol.

Here are some other tips for the rest of your computer:

1. Wipe down the surface of the terminal and the printer at least once a month.

2. Vacuum the keyboard to get rid of dust and other particles that may be caught under the keys.

3. Keep food away from the work area. Unless your disks are teflon coated, a spill on a floppy could damage your data.

4. Clean your read-write head with a cleaning kit. These are available from most computer stores.

5. When not in use, cover your hardware with a dust cover. Computers work better in a dust-free environment.

2. Now key the lines below, **twice** each.

```
1 lol oll lol oll lol oll lol oll lol oll
2 lll ooo lll ooo lll ooo lll ooo lll ooo
```

3. Let's practice some words with the letter **O** in them. Key the lines below, **twice** each, keeping your eyes on the book as you key.

```
3 so of do foe old toe to off for oaks doe
4 soot root good foot hoot look rose hoses
5 sold took rode door food rods fork hooks
```

Eyes on Copy

Let's practice keeping your eyes on the book as you key the lines below. This time key each line only **once**, but *key the words from right to left* instead of left to right as you usually do. Keying this way will force you to concentrate on the book.

```
1 told gold old oaks sold rode holds dolls
2 loaf goof fog frogs rolls tolls soul oar
3 Al asked for half a filet of sole for Ed
```

 Key

1. Place your hands in home row position. Look at the keyboard chart and locate the **C** key. It's in the bottom row, below **D,** so you will use your **D** finger. At first this reach may seem a little awkward to you, but with practice you will be able to do it just fine. Try it now. Key **dc** several times as you watch your fingers make the reach. Try to keep your **A** and **S** fingers at home as you make this reach. If that seems awkward, then try to at least keep **F** at home.

2. Now key the lines below, **twice** each.

```
1 dcd cdd dcd cdd dcd cdd dcd cdd dcd cdd
2 ddd ccc ddd ccc ddd ccc ddd ccc ddd ccc
```

LESSON 73

STOP! and Review

Objectives:

- To review formats for the following documents:
    - announcements
    - enumerations
    - poems
    - flyers
    - personal notes
    - personal business letters

In the next two lessons, you will be reviewing the formats introduced in previous lessons. The directions have purposely been omitted; all you are told to do is arrange the document attractively on the page. If you are not sure about how to set up a particular document, you may wish to refer back to the part of the text where the document was first introduced. There you will find a full-page model of that type of document. Check the index to help you locate the particular document you want.

Application 98: Dance Announcement

Directions:

- Key the announcement below, arranging it attractively on the page.

- File name: Ap98

```
TURN-AROUND DRESS-UP DANCE

Girls Ask the Boys

Friday, April 17, 19—

7:30 p.m. to 9:30 p.m.

Gymnasium
```

3. Let's try some words with **C** in them. Remember, keep your eyes on the book as you key. Do each line **twice**.

```
3 cot ice cut cue cud cuds cuts cues cats;
4 cake cure clue cite call creek cell cast
5 cause create clash cedar clad click cues
```

PART E

 **C and O Keys Combined**

Here are some words that contain both of the new keys. Key each line **twice** as you keep your eyes on the book.

```
1 coat code cods cash coils coed ice crack
2 for luck; to dock; old coed; lots of ice
3 She tore the slot; Fred sells old coats;
```

PART F

Return/Enter Key

Let's practice your Return/Enter technique. As you key the lines below, **once** each, avoid looking up as you press the Return/Enter key. Taking your eyes off the copy to return/enter wastes valuable time because you must then find your place in the book to resume keying. Those few wasted seconds not only take away from your speed but can cause you to make such errors as skipping a word or even a whole line! So don't look up as you key the lines below. If time permits, repeat the lines.

```
Cut the cake; curl her hair; R/E Cook a duck; if
it is due us R/E Dock the skiff; lots of luck to
her R/E Call for cracked ice; he cites the code R/E
The clock goes tic toc; R/E Check the fuel gauge
R/E Sue cuts the cake; did he go to the dock R/E
```

PART G

Shifting Technique

Let's work on your shifting technique. When you shift for a capital letter do you
- Stretch your pinkie down to the shift key and keep the other fingers at home?
- Bring all fingers back to home position after making the capital letter? Practice those two things as you key the lines on the next page, **twice** each.

SECTION 7

Review
and
Simulation

1 Fred Ed Gracie Gretta Susie Sol Al Carol
2 Alice Carr; Duke Ducas; Derek Gross; Cal
3 Sue Shoots; Rudie Skools; Freddie Frick;

Challenge

Can you key with your eyes closed? You did this in Lesson 9, but this time your teacher will dictate phrases. Key each phrase **once** and put a space between each phrase. At the end of the line, your teacher will ask you to open your eyes and read back the phrases. Now, close your eyes, and no peeking!

1 cut the cake/leads the class/talks a lot
2 four lakes/creates a fuss/touch the fork
3 lots of luck/curls her hair/off the cuff
4 at the hour/cuts the fir tree/get it all
5 take a cue/uses the old desk/kick off at
6 just cause/first dock/sick kid/oak trees

LESSON

11

Introducing B and .

Objectives
■ To learn the location of the **B** key
■ To learn the location of the period (.) key
■ To practice proper keyboarding techniques

Application 96: Teacher Roster

Directions:

Compose and arrange attractively a two-column table titled TEACHERS IN _____ SCHOOL. (Insert the name of your school in the blank.) The first column should have the names of the teachers and the second should show the grade(s) or subject(s) they teach. Label the first column with the heading, *Name* and the second column with the heading, *Grade or Subject*. Estimate how many spaces to leave between columns. Name the file Ap96.

Application 97: Important Birthdays

Directions:

Compose and arrange attractively a three-column table titled IMPORTANT BIRTHDAYS. Your table should have at least five entries. The first column should include the names of the birthday people; the second column should show their relationship to you—brother, sister, friend, cousin, etc.; and the third column should show the dates of their birthdays. Label the first column with the heading *Name;* the second, *Relationship;* and the third, *Date.* Estimate how many spaces to leave between columns. Name the file Ap97.

Warmup

1. Check your position at the keyboard.
   - ■ Are you sitting a hand span away?
   - ■ Is your body erect?
   - ■ Are your feet flat on the floor?

2. Now key the lines below, each line **twice**.

```
1 ace ice dud oar rods cud for the sod fog
2 face frog hogs cafe goes toad roads seek
3 crater sheets tootsie jello secure hoods
4 Flo has sold oak desks; Al rides the jet
```

 Key

1. Place your hands in home row position. Look at the keyboard chart and locate the **B** key. It's in the bottom row to the right of the **F** key, so you will use your **F** finger. Try it now. Key **fb** several times as you watch your fingers make the reach. Be sure to keep all the other fingers at home.

2. Now try keying the lines below. Keep your eyes on the book as you key each line **twice**.

```
1 fbf bff fbf bff fbf bff fbf bff fbf bff
2 fff bbb fff bbb fff bbb fff bbb fff bbb
```

3. Let's try keying some words with **B** in them. Remember, keep your eyes on the book as you key and don't let your **A, S,** and **D** fingers come off home row. Key each line **twice**.

```
3 bud big but rob rib fib buff bid lob bat
4 brat brags beef bead cubs grab bit curbs
5 scrubs blurb brash beasts breads bridges
```

Keying from Script

Key the paragraph below **once.** Then go back and do it again.

Parrots like to eat bird food and bits of fresh fruits and vegetables, but they can be messy. A parrot will kick out of the cage leftover food and old feathers. Cages need to be cleaned weekly and disinfected. Also, to stay happy, most parrots need either another parrot for company or contact with their owners. Otherwise, they will resort to screaming and feather plucking.

Keying with Proofreader's Marks

Key the paragraph below exactly as it is shown; *do not make any corrections.* Then print a copy. Correct the errors on the printed copy using proofreader's marks. Then check your marks with your teacher.

     People who complian constantly can be annoying. For the complainer nothing goes right. Theyare either sick or tried or bored. They had a terible night or a bad day. Most complainers try to get satisfaction by draging the spirits of others donw with them. One of the best way to deal with complainers is to joke with th em about how tough life is.

Composing Tables

Application 95: Top Ten TV Shows

Directions:

Compose and arrange attractively a two-column table titled MY TOP TEN TELEVISION SHOWS. The first column should have the names of the shows and the second column the days of the week they are scheduled in your area. Include a by-line. Double space the body of the table. You will have to estimate how many spaces to put between columns. If your key line wraps, you have left too many spaces between columns. Name the file Ap95.

Phrases

Key the phrases below, each line **twice**. Try to key the short words quickly.

```
1 to be; for the; he is; be at; if she is;
2 of it; all for; if the; as if; to be the
3 to a; for it; is the; go to it; be sure;
4 to be here; there is; here is; let us go
5 but the; at the; if the; for us; go to a
6 take this; take the; go for it; take her
```

 Key

1. Place your hands in home row position. Look at the keyboard chart and locate the **period key.** It's in the bottom row below **L,** so you will use your **L** finger on it. Try it now. Key **l.** several times as you watch your fingers make the reach.

2. Now try the lines below, **two times** each. As you key, keep your eyes on the book and reach for the keys without looking at them.

```
1 l.l .l. l.l .l. l.l .l. l.l .l. l.l .l.
2 lll ... lll ... lll ... lll ... lll ...
```

3. Now try these lines, **two times** each. Remember to keep your **J** and **K** fingers at home when reaching down for the period key.

```
3 dr. sr. jr. rd. ct. st. ft. ed. br. hr.;
4 bio. bar. fed. obj. drs. crt. cir. alt.;
5 add. adj. agr. agt. bar. ack. dec. col.;
```

Spacing After a Period Ending a Sentence

1. Here's a spacing rule you need to remember: Space *twice* after a period that ends a sentence. The exception to the rule is when the period comes at the end of a line and you are going to press Return/Enter. Then you would not space because that would be wasted motion. In all other cases, though, space twice after a period ending a sentence. Let's practice correct spacing on the lines on the next page. Key each line **once**.

Warmup

Key each line **twice.**

1 His hobby is collecting coins, buttons, and books.
2 Jogging through the woods we noticed many animals.
3 Read the comic book after finishing your homework.
4 Ask for Model 2381; if they are out, ask for 6094.

. . . .1. . . .2. . . .3. . . .4. . . .5. . . .6. . . .7. . . .8. . . .9. . . .10

Speed Building

The lines below contain words followed by punctuation marks. Take a one-minute timing on each line to determine your base rate. Then practice the lines before taking another one-minute timing to see if you have improved. Compare your rates.

1 gems; desks; radios; stoves; drawers; bulbs; jets;
2 trees, twigs, leaves, rakes, bushels, shovels, ax,
3 first-class, second-class, third-class, self-will,
4 example: profit: island: proverbs: illustrate:

. . . .1. . . .2. . . .3. . . .4. . . .5. . . .6. . . .7. . . .8. . . .9. . . .10

Numbers

Get ready to decode. Be sure you put five spaces between each word.

23-8-1-20   23-15-18-4   15-6   15-14-12-25
20-8-18-5-5   19-25-12-12-1-2-12-5-19
3-15-13-2-9-14-5-19   20-23-5-14-20-25-19-9-24
12-5-20-20-5-18-19?   1-12-16-8-1-2-5-20

1 She likes to eat cake.[2 spaces]Ed shall ask Al.

2 Cal ate salad.[2 spaces]Grace is ill.[2 spaces]Al hides.

3 Derek has dead frogs.[2 spaces]Sal rides horses.

4 Bo reads books.[2 spaces]Flo takes the old road.

5 Sue has big feet.[2 spaces]Al hurts.[2 spaces]Sis cried.

6 Get the hose.[2 spaces]Rush the job.[2 spaces]Face Fred.

2. Now check your work. Use your arrow key to cursor through each line and make sure you have two spaces where a period ends a sentence inside a line.

Spacing After a Period Used in Abbreviations

1. Here is another rule to remember: Space *once* after a period used in an abbreviation or with initials. Let's practice correct spacing on the lines below. Key each line **once**.

1 Sgt. Rice lost his job; Sat. he goes So.

2 The tech. book is good; the ed. is Dale.

3 F. R. Gar got a ck. Fri. for a huge car.

4 She goes to the acad. for biol. courses.

5 Al gets lg. shoes but Ed gets sm. shoes.

6 Frieda E. Foggerty got fresh choc. cake.

2. Now check your work. Use your arrow key to cursor through each line and make sure you have one space where a period is used after an initial or abbreviation.

Key the lines below, **twice** each. As you key, remember to bring your fingers back to home position after striking the B and period keys.

1 The big bed is here. Take it to Freddie.

2 Bessie bakes big cakes. Be sure to sell.

3 The blue fish is good food. Bo likes it.

Application 94: Noted Scientists

Directions:

- Use the key line to determine horizontal placement
- Center top to bottom
- Double space the body
- Center the title and subtitle; double space twice after the subtitle
- Put five spaces between each of the three columns
- Double space after the column headings and the title
- File name: Ap94

```
NOTED SCIENTISTS OF THE PAST
(1700 to 1900)

Name                  Occupation       Discovery

Henry Bessemer        Engineer         Steel-Making Process

Marie Curie           Chemist          Radium

Charles Darwin        Naturalist       Theory of Evolution

Thomas Edison         Inventor         Phonograph

Alexander Fleming     Bacteriologist   Penicillin

William Herschel      Astronomer       Uranus

Edward Jenner         Physician        Vaccination

Louis Pasteur         Chemist          Pasteurization

Joseph Priestley      Chemist          Oxygen
```

LESSON 72

Composing Tables

Objectives:

- To improve speed on alphabet keys
- To improve accuracy of numbers
- To key copy from script
- To use proofreader's marks
- To compose and format tables containing column headings

Challenge

Find a partner. You are going to play Beat the Clock. When your teacher says, "Get Ready," each of you should look through the lessons in the book that you have covered thus far and select a line that you think you can key faster than your partner. Each of you will have your turn in keying the line you selected. When your teacher says, "First Round," you and your partner turn to one of the pages selected. When your teacher says, "Ready, Go," begin keying the selected line. *Whoever is the first to finish the line **twice** with perfect accuracy is the winner.* When your teacher says, "Second Round," you and your partner turn to the other page selected. Continue playing to determine the winner—the one who gets the best out of six rounds (six timings).

LESSON 12

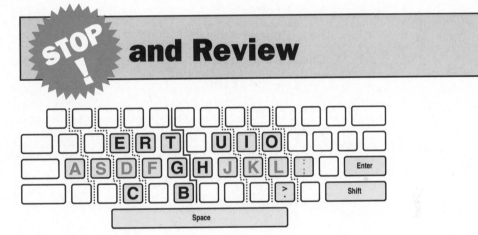

STOP ! and Review

Objectives:

- To review keys learned in previous lessons
- To practice technique pointers learned in previous lessons

Warmup

1. Check your position at the keyboard.
   - Are you sitting a hand span away?
   - Are your palms off the keyboard?
   - Are your feet flat on the floor?

Application 93: American Cartoonists

Directions:

- Use the key line to determine horizontal placement
- Center top to bottom
- Single space the body
- Center the title and subtitle; double space twice after the subtitle
- Put 15 spaces between the two columns
- Double space after the column headings and the title
- File name: Ap93

```
NOTED AMERICAN CARTOONISTS

(1880 to Present)

Artist                       Cartoon

Walt Disney                  Mickey Mouse

Bud Fisher                   Mutt and Jeff

Hal Foster                   Tarzan

Chester Gould                Dick Tracy

George Herriman              Krazy Kat

Walt Kelly                   Pogo

Bob Montana                  Archie

Alex Raymond                 Flash Gordon

Charles Schultz              Peanuts

Elzie Segar                  Popeye

Mort Walker                  Beetle Bailey

Chic Young                   Blondie
```

2. This lesson contains no new keys to learn. So you can relax and concentrate on strengthening the reaches to those keys you have learned thus far. Key the lines below, **two times** each. If time permits, repeat the lines.

1 brute brags bath buff bugs brig buss bus
2 brother bridge bother broke sobs buffalo
3 bribe brides bright brood broiler bruise
4 Dr. Blake is good. A. T. Berk is bored.

Eyes on Copy

Let's practice eyes on copy technique. As you key the lines below, **twice** each, try not to look up from the text until you have completed each line.

1 fill a dish; grab the books; bake a cake
2 sail a boat; fish at the lake; ask if he
3 aid for her; use the desks; about a date

Space Bar Technique

How is your Space Bar technique? Do you sometimes get extra spaces where you don't want them? Let's work on that now. As you key each line below **one time**, try to use a down-and-in motion with your thumb. Avoid leaning on the Space Bar because that will produce extra spaces.

1 at for the us is if off go goes has buds
2 hi jet die sis ate ear eat sir hid slide
3 fir hue due bob bog fog dog sag rag drag
4 cut but gut jut kid fib sod rug bugs cud
5 hit fit sit as ah ho foe fig rig rut fur
6 had bad fad ere irk uke beds did gas has

Formatting Tables with Subtitles and Column Headings

Application 92: American Presidents

Directions:

- Use the key line to determine horizontal placement
- Center top to bottom
- Double space the body
- Center the title and subtitle; double space twice under the subtitle
- Put 15 spaces between the two columns
- File name: Ap92

Refer to page 202 in Lesson 47 if you have forgotten how to format a table using a key line.

```
               FIRST TEN AMERICAN PRESIDENTS
                  Washington through Tyler


     Order                    President

     First                    George Washington

     Second                   John Adams

     Third                    Thomas Jefferson

     Fourth                   James Madison

     Fifth                    James Monroe

     Sixth                    John Quincy Adams

     Seventh                  Andrew Jackson

     Eighth                   Martin Van Buren

     Ninth                    William Henry Harrison

     Tenth                    John Tyler
```

Spacing After the Period

Let's see if you can key the lines below, **once** each, with proper spacing after the periods. When you finish keying, your teacher will check your work.

1 F. E. Duke is scared. Dr. Cook is here.
2 She has a Fri. date. The horse is fast.
3 Al adds starch to the cake. Fred cries.
4 Ed is ed. of that. Gretta does like it.
5 The race starts at four. Al cheers her.
6 Take Fred for a ride. Russ likes salsa.
7 G. R. shoots geese. Derek calls Debbie.

Elbows In

As you key the lines below, **twice** each, keep your elbows close to your body.

1 bugs are bad; jet before four; it is far
2 there is also; take to the road; be sure
3 a just cause; fed the flock; food is hot

Return/Enter

1. Your teacher will time you for one minute as you key the lines below. Be sure to press Return/Enter whenever you see **R/E.** Your goal is to keep your eyes on the book; do not look up when returning/entering until the minute is over.

Flu is bad. She is sick. R/E Sue goes to court.
R/E Ed likes this state. She also likes this
state. R/E Be sure to dot the i. Be careful. R/E
Ask Carol to ski at the lake. R/E Call off the
dogs. Sue is scared.

2. Now repeat the lines above, starting where you left off, and try again to keep your eyes on the book when you are returning/entering. If you finish, start over from the beginning.

PART C

Numbers

Get ready to decode. Be sure you put five spaces between each word.

23-8-25   1-18-5   15-21-18   12-1-23-19

12-9-11-5   20-8-5   15-3-5-1-14?

2-5-3-1-21-19-5   20-8-5   13-15-19-20

20-18-15-21-2-12-5   9-19   3-1-21-19-5-4

2-25   20-8-5   2-18-5-1-11-5-18-19

PART D

Keying from Script

Key the paragraph below **once.** Then go back and do it again.

The Amazon parrot has brilliant feathers, high intelligence, and makes an excellent pet. Buy your bird from a pet shop that specializes in domestically raised parrots. Avoid birds that sit with their feathers puffed out and eyes closed. They are sick. Also stay away from birds that are screechy or appear nervous; they have not adjusted to living with humans and probably never will.

PART E

Keying with Proofreader's Marks

Key the paragraph below exactly as it is shown; *do not make any corrections.* Then print a copy. Correct the errors on printed copy using proofreader's marks. Then check your marks with your teacher.

Perfectionists cannot tolreate errors. Even though mistakes happen, to a perfectoinist there is noroom for error. Experts beleive these people may be that way because (1) they were severely penalized for mis takes made when children, or (2) they have to do this convince themselves they are improtant.

Body Erect

You will be more comfortable if your back is straight. If you sit hunched over your keyboard, you put a strain on your back. Let's see if you can key the lines below, **twice** each, without slouching in your chair.

```
1 free tree agrees dread ahead about trash
2 stash gash fast last dash dust rust just
3 fruit suit glue fluid liter busses fills
```

Challenge

1. Pack your bags with your best keyboarding technique and get ready to travel across the country. You begin in Los Angeles. To win the game you must travel around the country, city to city, until you are back in Los Angeles. You travel from city to city by keying each line on the next page during a 30-second timing.

2. Your teacher will decide if you are playing for accuracy or speed. If you are playing for accuracy, you must key perfect lines during the 30 seconds. It doesn't matter how many lines you key, but there should be no errors. If you are playing for speed, you must finish the line; when playing for speed, errors are ignored.

3. If you don't reach your goal during the timing, you must stay on the same line and try it again.

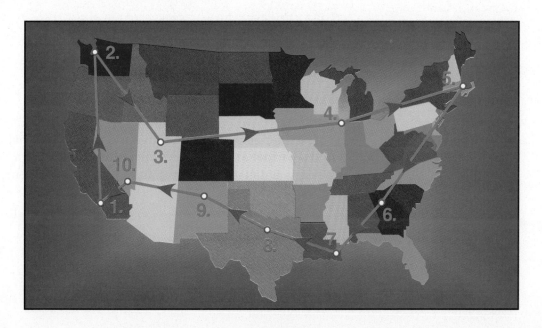

Robert E. Berkley. It is called *Theories of Solar Disturbances* and was published by Mackinrow Publishing Company in Milwaukee in 1986. A second book is *Our Star, the Sun.* It is copyrighted 1988 and was written by Gayle Morrow and Frank E. Whittier. The publisher is Mammoth Publishers located in New York. A third source was published by Villa Press located in Los Angeles. The book is called *Our Solar System* and was written by Sylvia Witt. It is copyrighted 1989. The reference page is page 5 of your report. Name the file Ap91.

LESSON 71

Formatting Tables

Objectives:
- To improve accuracy on alphabet keys
- To improve accuracy of numbers
- To key copy from script
- To use proofreader's marks
- To format tables containing subtitles and column headings

PART A

Warmup

Key each line **twice.**

1 Don takes a nap before dinner while Natalie cooks.

2 That hockey team won every game in the tournament.

3 They were attracted to the neon signs on the wall.

4 Steven quoted us $359 for the furniture, not $452.

. . . . .1. . . . .2. . . .3. . . .4. . . .5. . . .6. . . .7. . . .8. . . .9. . . .10

PART B

Accuracy Building

The lines below contain one-hand words. Key each one **twice.** Then find a partner and take turns dictating and keying a line of the words. When you dictate, try giving the words in a different order than they appear in the book.

1 no we are at set you get tax my in on date rate ad

2 free rate date case only area best rest sets after

3 great state only up average him water extra garage

4 pump lollipop car dearest fear mink noon seed moon

4. The winner is the first person to make a round trip.

Los Angeles to Seattle

1 Gretta is a good cook. She flakes fish.

Seattle to Salt Lake City

2 The blue cloth for the suit coat is good.

Salt Lake City to Chicago

3 Frieda looks at the old desks for her brother.

Chicago to Boston

4 The site for the ski race is the old oak tree.

Boston to Atlanta

5 She did tests to see if the old oak desk is better.

Atlanta to New Orleans

6 The girl has fried foods for the tests at the lake.

New Orleans to Dallas

7 The skiers did a lot of great tricks for the late girls.

Dallas to Santa Fe

8 At school he teaches good skill classes for the boaters.

Santa Fe to Las Vegas

9 There is little cause for the court suit if her old cat dies.

Las Vegas to Los Angeles

10 Three sets of rules are good but four for the race are hard.

Dogs have been fol lowing people around for centuries. In fact, it was about fitfeen to twenty thousand years aog that man was first domesticated them. today there are many different shapes, size, colors, and breeds; but all these dogs can traced back to thesame animal group.

Application 89: Good Nutrition References

Directions:

Compose and arrange a reference page for the report you wrote for Mrs. Hanson's first period Home Economics class titled "Good Nutrition." You used a book written by Jessica Stewart called *Good Eating Habits.* The book is published by Tinkerman Publishing House located in New York and is copyrighted 1986. You also used a magazine article, "Why Teenagers Need a New Diet," in *Teen Magazine.* The issue was March of 1990, pages 27 to 30. The article was written by Dr. Mark Pitcher. Your third reference was written by Dr. Elizabeth Curry. The book is called *Do Fad Diets Really Work?* It is published by Grove Press located in Chicago and is copyrighted 1991. The reference page is page 4 of your report. Name the file Ap89.

Application 90: Skin Care References

Directions:

Compose and arrange a reference page for a report you wrote titled "Taking Care of Your Skin." You used all magazine articles for this report. One came from *Teen Magazine.* It was written by Charles Turkell and titled "Eat Well To Be Beautiful." The issue was May, 1989, page 45. Another article came from the February, 1988 *Your Health* magazine on pages 18–20. It was written by Mary E. York and was titled "Good Skin and Vitamins Go Together." The third source was written by Dr. Wayne Grossman in the August, 1991 issue of *Good Health.* The article is titled "Pimples and Goosebumps" on page 5. The reference page is page 3 of your report. Name the file Ap90.

Application 91: Sun Spots References

Directions:

Compose and arrange a reference page for a report you wrote called "Sun Spots." You used all books for this one. One book was written by

LESSON 13

Introducing N and Left Shift

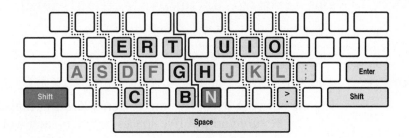

Objectives:

- To learn the location of the **Left Shift** key
- To learn the location of the **N** key
- To practice proper keyboarding techniques

Warmup

1. Technique Quiz: Key **T** if the statement is true, **F** if it is false.
   a. Elbows should be held in close to the body.
   b. Sitting too close to the keyboard means you cannot reach the bottom row keys properly.
   c. Sitting too far away from the keyboard means you cannot reach the top row keys properly.

2. Now key the lines below, each line **twice**.

```
1 to go ho if at of as off too so hi area;
2 just jute fish dish side rides hide dead
3 she salutes; he rides; she studies hard;
4 Black clouds cause dark halls at school.
. . . . .1. . . . 2. . . . 3. . . . 4. . . . 5. . . . 6. . . . 7. . . . 8
```

PART B

Figuring Speed

1. Did you notice the scale below the warmup lines? Now you can determine your keyboarding speed. This scale will appear from now on in upcoming lessons so you and your teacher can use it to determine how your keyboarding speed is progressing.

```
1 pan panels panic pants pandas panelists pantry pan
2 pen penny pencils penthouses peninsula penguin pen
3 air airports airplanes airmail airway airstrip air
4 aut automobiles autumn authors automatic autos aut
  ....1....2....3....4....5....6....7....8....9....10
```

Numbers

Take out your decoding sheet. Here's another message to key and decode. Be sure you put five spaces between each word.

```
23-8-1-20        9-19        20-8-5
4-9-6-6-5-18-5-14-3-5        2-5-20-23-5-5-14        1
8-9-12-12        1-14-4        1        16-9-12-12?        1
8-9-12-12        9-19        8-1-18-4        20-15        7-5-20
21-16        1-14-4        1        16-9-12-12        9-19
8-1-18-4        20-15        7-5-20        4-15-23-14
```

Keying from Script

Key the paragraph below **once.** Then go back and do it again.

Some people enjoy bird watching as a hobby. One of the most interesting things to observe is a bird taking a bath. First, it gets itself all wet. Then it takes oil from one of its glands and rubs it into the feathers all over its body. Then the bird goes over each feather. That not only makes the bird fluffy but helps insulate the bird from winter cold.

Keying with Proofreader's Marks

Key the paragraph on the next page exactly as it is shown; *do not make any corrections*. Then print a copy. Correct the errors on the printed copy using proofreader's marks. Then check your marks with your teacher.

2.   When figuring speed, English words are not counted as words. Instead, every five strokes (an alphabetic, numeric, or punctuation character or a space) equals one word.

3.   Let's see how you would use the scale to figure speed. Suppose you were keying for one minute on the first and second lines and you stopped after the word "rides" in the second line. Your speed would be 8 words for the first line and 6 words completed in the second line, which would equal 14.

4.   See if you can figure out the speed for each situation below:
   a.   You keyed the first line and stopped after the word "jute" in the second line. What is your speed? If you said 10, you are correct.
   b.   You keyed the first two lines and stopped after the word "he" in the third line. What is your speed? If you said 19, you are correct.

PART C
Left Shift Key

You already know how to shift with your right hand. Now you will learn how to use the Left Shift key to make capital letters that are controlled by your right hand.

1.   Place your hands in home row position. Look at the keyboard chart and locate the **Left Shift** key. It's in the bottom left-hand corner of the keyboard. This key is used to key capital letters struck with the right hand. For example, to key a capital **k** or capital **i**, you must hold down the Left Shift key.

2.   Try it now to key the following capital letters:

1 Ja Ka La Ur Ot La Id Or La Ha Od Is Kr Ug

Fisher, Clark. Early American Schools. Chicago: Markham Press, 1987.

Ketchan, Judy. Pioneer Teachers. New York: Harkin Publishing Company, 1985.

Blithe, Donald. The Little Red School House. Cincinnati: Troven Publishing Company, 1988.

Simon, Roberta. Diary of a School Teacher. New York: Markham and Row Publishing Company, 1984.

Benchley, Rudolph R. Encyclopedia of Education. New York: Markham and Row Publishing Company, 1983.

Walker, William A. The Good Ole Days. Chicago: University Press, 1982.

LESSON 70

Composing a Reference Page

Objectives:
- To improve speed on alphabet keys
- To improve accuracy of numbers
- To compose and format a reference page for a multi-page report

PART A

Warmup

Key each line **twice**.

1 Use the maps to avoid getting lost on the highway.
2 Lauren is making a huge pot of sizzling beef stew.
3 In the fall, we plan to plant lots of tulip bulbs.
4 Mark machine 354 and machine 81 as needing repair.

. . . . 1 . . . . 2 . . . . 3 . . . . 4 . . . . 5 . . . . 6 . . . . 7 . . . . 8 . . . . 9 10

PART B

Speed Building

The lines on the next page contain alternate-hand word patterns. Key them, **three times** each. The first time, go at a moderate pace; the second time, go much faster; and the third time, go as fast as you possibly can.

3. Key each line below, **two times** each. Remember to bring your little finger back home after striking the shift key.

2 Jill is late; Jeff catches fish for food.

3 Sue likes old dolls; Katie likes her dog.

4 Ira has a book due; Lois takes the trail.

Shifting Technique

Key the lines below, **twice** each, as your teacher observes your shifting technique. Good technique means two things: (1) you reach down to the shift key with your pinkie or **A** finger while keeping the other fingers in home position, and (2) after making the capital letter, you return your **A** finger back home.

1 Joe flies a jet; Jo is sick; I like cake;

2 Jake tries to ski; Ora studies; Ida asks;

3 Hal likes to ride; I get sick; It breaks;

 Key

1. Place your hands in home row position. Look at the keyboard chart and locate the **N** key. It's on the bottom row just to the left of **J**, so you will use your **J** finger to strike it. Try it now. Key **jn** several times as you watch your fingers make the reach.

2. Key each line below **twice**. Be sure to bring your **J** finger back home after you strike the **N** key.

1 jnj njj jnj njj jnj njj jnj njj jnj njj
2 jjj nnn jjj nnn jjj nnn jjj nnn jjj nnn

3. Now key each line below **two times.** Keep your eyes on the book as you key.

3 ant end nor and inns on not nuts an no in

4 aunt fang hunt bunt dents rent sent sends

5 fender gender anti found round sound tone

Application 87: Computer Piracy References

Directions:

- 2-inch top margin
- 1-inch side margin
- Wordwrap each entry
- Center the title; four single spaces after it
- Single space each entry; double space between entries
- Place quotation marks around magazine articles
- Underline names of magazines and books
- Use Tab on second line of each entry
- Insert page No. 3 in upper left-hand corner
- File name: Ap87

REFERENCES

Chevez, Mary. "Computer Piracy in Corporate Offices." Bytes and Bits, October, 1990, 13-17.

Golinka, George. Computer Problems. New York: VanBuren Press, 1989.

Nichols, Carl F. Computers in our Society. Boston: Martin Publishing Company, 1991.

Patterson, Jane. "Piracy on the Computer Seas." Computer Age, February, 1990, 57-59.

Van De Warker, Vera. "Software Copyright Violations." Chips, November, 1991, 90-92.

Application 88: Colonial Schooling References

Directions:

- 2-inch top margin
- 1-inch side margin
- Wordwrap each entry
- Single space each entry; double space between entries
- Arrange entries in alphabetical order
- Center the title; four single spaces after it
- Insert page No. 3 in top center
- File name: Ap85

REFERENCES

Enders, Amy B. Colonial America. New York: Harkin Publishing Company, 1986.

(continued on next page)

Left Shift and N Keys Combined

Now let's practice using both new keys in the lines below. Key each line **twice**. As you key, try to keep your eyes on the book and do not look at the screen until you have completed the whole line.

```
1 Nick has a fine.  Joe needs to see Karen.
2 Jake has knots in his shoe.  I like nuts.
3 Kate nags Joe.  I can sign it for Noreen.
```

Palms off the Keyboard

As you key the lines below, **twice** each, try to keep your palms off the keyboard. Your teacher will observe to see if you are following this technique.

```
1 catch the train; look at the junk; I see;
2 four hours; three steel cans; one cookie;
3 lend a hand; she has gone; cat was taken;
```

Challenge

You and your teacher are going to play a game of keyboarding tag. For this game, your teacher will select lines from a lesson you have already done and will tell you how many times to key each line. When told to begin, start keying. Your teacher will be watching for good technique and will tag the first person observed making a technique error, such as not keeping eyes on the book or crossing ankles or knees or resting palms on the keyboard. The person tagged must then rise and walk around the room to observe technique and try to tag someone else. Tagged players may take their seat only after tagging another player. At the end of the game, each player should add up the total number of lines keyed. The winner is the person with the most lines.

Formatting Reference Pages

Application 86: Superstition References

Directions:

- 2-inch top margin
- 1-inch side margin
- Wordwrap each entry
- Center the title; four single spaces after it
- Single space each entry; double space between entries
- Place quotation marks around magazine articles
- Underline names of magazines
- Use Tab on second line of each entry
- Insert page No. 4 in bottom center
- File name: Ap86

REFERENCES

Higgins, Ruth. "Why We Do Things for Luck," <u>Socialite</u>, January, 1989, 34-35.

Jacoby, James. "Do You Fear the Dark?" <u>Highlights</u>, Spring, 1990, 89-91.

Sylvester, Wayne. <u>Silly Superstitions.</u> Boston: Grossman Publishing House, 1987.

Underhill, James. "Four Leaf Clovers," <u>Traveler,</u> December, 1991, 26-30.

Introducing V and Y

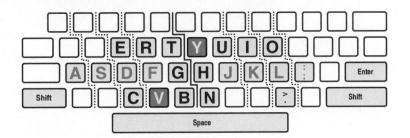

Objectives:
■ To learn the location of the **V** key
■ To learn the location of the **Y** key
■ To practice proper keyboard techniques

PART A

Warmup

1. Technique Quiz: Key **T** if the statement is true, **F** if it is false.
   a. It's a good idea to look up from the copy to rest your eyes.
   b. If reaching for a particular key seems awkward, you should develop your own fingering pattern.
   c. Stabbing the keys with straight fingers makes for faster keying.

2. Now key the lines below, each line **twice**.

```
1 nuts gnat enter send sent bent rent cent
2 binge bingo trains gains brink sink rink
3 not an inch; bunch of junk; just a hunch
4 Nathan joins Janice to sing a fine duet.
  . . . . . 1 . . . . . 2 . . . . . 3 . . . . . 4 . . . . . 5 . . . . . 6 . . . . . 7 . . . . . 8
```

PART B

 Key

1. Place your hands in home row position. Look at the keyboard chart and locate the **V** key. It's just below **F,** so you will use your **F** finger on it. Try it now. Key **fv** several times as you watch your fingers make the reach.

Model Reference Page

REFERENCES

Bartlett, John. <u>Civil War Battleground</u>s. New York: Lester
    Publishing Company, 1990.

Hughes, Carol E. <u>President Ab</u>e. Chicago: Amber Light Publishers,
    1991.

Miller, Donald E., and Brett Nelson. <u>Slavery Revisit</u>ed. Boston:
    Carlton Publishing Company, 1988.

Turk, Grace. <u>The Blue Versus the Gra</u>y. St. Paul: West Publishing
    Company, 1988.

2. Now key the lines below, **twice** each, without looking at your hands.

1 fvf vff fvf vff fvf vff fvf vff fvf vff

2 fff vvv fff vvv fff vvv fff vvv fff vvv

3. Next, key the lines below, **two times** each. As you key, be sure to bring your **F** finger back home after striking the **V** key.

3 via five have live via vie vise veal via

4 verb vain vein vale vast veil veer value

5 velvet virtues vantage valor valet verbs

6 Vera vents her anger; Vic likes venison.

Spacing After Periods

Key the lines below **once**. Pay special attention to proper spacing after the periods.

1 Her cert. is dated in June. Al is late.

2 Fri. I can attend. Sat. Duke is acting.

3 F. A. Jones can take J. K. Sill fishing.

4 Sue is sec. to Dr. Klink. Good for her.

Eyes on Copy

The sentences below are designed to force you to concentrate and keep your eyes on the book. As you key, fill in the blanks with the appropriate letter. If time permits, repeat the lines.

The ni_ht is _ark. I cann_t s_e the ro_d.
It co_ld t_ke hou_s to f_nd th_t dog _n t_e
fog. B_th of us sea_ch nea_ the _ld oak tr_e.
Bingo is n_t the_e. I thi_k he is lo_t.
J_hn and I loo_ at _he dock. N_ d_g to b_
fou_d. Joh_ lo_ks be_ind th_ barn. He s_outs
he h_s f_und Bi_go. Go_d o_d Bin_o. He is a
s_ght. He ne_ds a b_th b_t I d_ n_t care.
He i_ a g_od do_ be_ause he is n_t lost.

Numbers

Take out your decoding sheet. Here's another message to key and decode. Be sure you put five spaces between each word.

15–14   23–8–9–3–8   19–9–4–5   15–6   1

16–9–20–3–8–5–18   9–19   20–8–5

8–1–14–4–12–5?   15–14   20–8–5

15–21–20–19–9–4–5

Reference Page

Anytime you use resources for a report, it's a good idea to list them at the back of the report on a reference page. This page is sometimes called a bibliography. There are a number of different ways to list references. The example on the next page shows one way. Generally, sources used for a report are listed alphabetically according to the last name of the author. The side and bottom margins are the same as for the rest of the report. The title is centered 1½ or 2 inches from the top followed by four single spaces. Each entry is single spaced. Double spaces are used between entries. The first line of each entry begins at the left margin with subsequent lines indented. The reference page should have a page number placed in the same position as it was for other pages of the report.

Keying a Reference Page

Key the model reference page on the next page. Use wordwrap when keying each entry. *Be sure to space twice after each period and colon.* After all entries have been keyed, position your cursor at the beginning of the second line of each entry and press Tab. Remember, be consistent and number this page in the same place you numbered all other pages of the report.

Key

1. Place your hands in home row position. Look at the keyboard chart and locate the **Y** key. It's in the third row, to the left of **J**, so you will use your **J** finger on it. Try it now; key **jy** several times as you watch your fingers make the reach.

2. Now try the lines below, keeping your eyes on the book as you key. Do each line **twice**.

```
jyj yjj jyj yjj jyj yjj jyj yjj jyj yjj
jjj yyy jjj yyy jjj yyy jjj yyy jjj yyy
```

3. Key the lines below, **twice** each. As you key, be sure to bring your **J** finger back home after striking **Y.**

```
3 yes jay joy lay day boy hay say toy bays
4 eye dye fry dry boy ahoy fryer foyer jay
5 fish fry; hay day; forty; fifty; several
```

PART F

V and **Y** **Keys Combined**

Key the lines below, **twice** each. As you key, be sure to keep your eyes on the book.

```
1 Joy is very vocal.  Jay buys horses hay.
2 He can be vulgar.  Joe mails dry boards.
3 You say only five voters can vote today.
```

PART G

Return/Enter Key

As you key the lines below, press the Return/Enter key every time you see **R/E.** Your goal while keying is to keep your eyes on the book and not look up until you have finished *all* the lines. Can you do it? Let's find out.

```
Val vouched for Ray.  Her visit is vital. R/E Her
sign is Virgo.  The floor is vinyl. R/E The case
is Jones versus Vinton. R/E Roy likes a verse that
has a villain. R/E Joy takes violin lessons on
Friday. R/E She learns vintage songs. R/E Ray loves
to travel to Vt. for the ski season. R/E In his
vest he has toys for the children. R/E Jay drives
to the city not the village.
```

Formatting a Reference Page

Objectives:

- To improve speed on alphabet keys
- To improve accuracy of numbers
- To format a reference page for a multi-page report

PART A

Warmup

Key each line **twice.**

1 I picked several bushels of apples in the orchard.

2 Her favorite motion picture will be on television.

3 Al is the class clown; when will that boy grow up?

4 I plan to meet Flight 8192 at Gate 11 on April 27.

. . . .1. . . .2. . . .3. . . .4. . . .5. . . .6. . . .7. . . .8. . . .9. . . .10

PART B

Speed Building

The lines below concentrate on punctuation marks. Take a one-minute timing on each line to determine your base rate. Then practice the lines before taking another one-minute timing to see if you have improved. Compare your rates.

1 I did the work; she was absent. Try a bit harder.

2 If the train is early--which I doubt--we can talk.

3 Order sixty-one panels for the mobile-home owners.

4 For example: Take tab a and insert it into tab b.

. . . .1. . . .2. . . .3. . . .4. . . .5. . . .6. . . .7. . . .8. . . .9. . . .10

Challenge

Remember playing Beat the Clock in Lesson 11? Get ready to play again, but this time you must choose a *different* partner to play with. If you forget how to play, turn back to Part H on page 51 and review the rules.

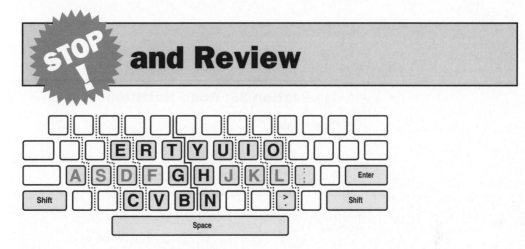

STOP! and Review

Objectives:
- To review keys learned in previous lessons
- To practice technique pointers learned in previous lessons

Warmup

1. Technique Quiz: Key **T** if the statement is true, **F** if it is false.
   a. You should always sit at least two hand spans away from the machine.
   b. It is all right to slump down in your chair.
   c. Palms should not rest on the keyboard.

2. This lesson contains no new keys to learn. So you can relax and concentrate on strengthening the reaches to those keys you have learned thus far. Key the lines below, **two times** each. If time permits, repeat the lines.

```
1 verse five jerky hives city villages gay
2 thirty forty fifty eighty ninety seventy
3 by the bay; goodbye; eyes front; vandals
4 No.  Vanilla is not her favorite flavor.
. . . . .1. . . . .2. . . .3. . . .4. . . .5. . . .6. . . .7. . . .8
```

Composing and Formatting a Cover Page

In the jobs that follow you will be creating cover pages for various reports. You may wish to save some of your printouts as models for reports for other classes.

Application 83: Good Nutrition

Directions:

Compose and format an attractive cover page for a report titled "Good Nutrition." It was written for your first period Home Economics class taught by Mrs. Hanson. Name the file Ap83.

Application 84: Ghosts Everywhere

Directions:

Compose and format an attractive cover page for a story written for your English class taught by Mr. Markle. The story is titled "Ghosts Everywhere" and is a joint effort by you and another classmate. Be sure to include both names. Name the file Ap84.

Application 85: Computer Club Report

Directions:

Compose and format an attractive cover page for a committee report for the computer club. The report covers a proposal for a fund-raising project to purchase additional computers and software. Four people, besides you, served on the committee: Mary Clarke, Chuck Zimmerman, Jorge Santiago, and Sue Chen. Since everyone on the committee worked equally hard, what would be a good way to list everyone's names on the cover page? Name the file Ap85.

Eyes on Copy

The lines below have words that contain missing letters. As you key, fill in the blanks with the appropriate letters. You will have to keep your eyes on the copy to do this. If time permits, repeat the lines.

```
V_c st_rted sch__l ye_terday. H_ go_s to col_ege
in Vt. st_te.  H_ is st_dying fo_ds and busine_s
b_cause h_s go_l is to sta_t a deli.  B_t t_is
sto_e is goi_g t_ b_ di_ferent f_om al_ t_e oth_r
del_s.  H_s st_re_s f_r d_gs.  In h_s s_ore d_gs
c_n g_t dog co_kies, bon_s, stea_, a_d c_ndy
cr_ated ju_t f_r canines.  Also V_c s_ys h_ i_
goi_g to st_ck d_g cloth_s.  A_ter a_l d_gs n_ed
ra_n sl_ckers, bo_ts, and coat_ ju_t li_e bo_s
and gir_s do.
```

Spacing After Periods

Do you remember the rules about spacing after periods that end a sentence and an abbreviation? Let's find out. Key the lines below, **once** each, and pay special attention to your spacing after the period. Hint: When a sentence ends with an abbreviation, space twice if the period is in the middle of a line.

1 Jack lives in N. Y. City. He likes cats.
2 He skis in Vt. Kathy is hot by the fire.
3 Stay very close. Katie is too far ahead.
4 The J. I. Strand Co. sells baseball bats.

Shifting Technique

1. Below are some first names for boys and girls. Key them as they should be, with the first letter capitalized. As you key, remember to bring your fingers back to home position after striking the shift key.

1 rita frances daniel conchita janet karen
2 susan ajay jack lionel rajesh jill luisa
3 anita judy jorge douglas juan ali anjali
4 rudy lee jay joy lois ursula jose robert

Numbers

Take out your decoding sheet. Here's another message to key and decode. Be sure you put five spaces between each word.

23-8-25	9-19	1	12-1-18-7-5	3-15-1-20
12-9-11-5	1	2-1-14-1-14-1	19-11-9-14?	
2-15-20-8	1-18-5	5-1-19-25	20-15	
19-12-9-16	15-14			

Keying from Script

Key the paragraph below **once.** Then go back and do it again.

Littering in national parks has become a big problem, according to officials. Not only does litter mar the beautiful scenery for other visitors, but it can be dangerous to the animals as well. Tabs from cans can cut through the foot of an animal who steps on them. To put litter in its place, always carry a litter bag wherever you go.

Keying with Proofreader's Marks

Key the paragraph below exactly as it is shown; *do not make any corrections.* Then print a copy. Correct the errors on the printed copy using proofreader's marks. Then check your marks with your teacher.

Beautfiul skin does not come from out of ajar. It comes from protein, iron, and vitamins. skin that glows gets an adequate sup ply of oxygen from the blood, which gets its power from iron. Vitamin A keeps your skin from drying out. vitamin B helps elimintae blemishes and too much oil, and Vitamin C helps the skn resist infection.

2. Now see if you can key them again, but this time put them in alphabetical order within each line. And of course, you will capitalize the first letter of each name, using your best shifting technique.

Elbows In

You know how important it is to keep elbows close to your body. Let's work on that technique now as you key the lines below, **twice** each.

```
1 Barbara asks Joan to take the toll roads.
2 Al and Stan ride their bikes to the hill.
3 This bulletin says you have canary birds.
```

Palms off the Machine

Let's work on keeping your palms from resting on the keyboard. Key the lines below, **twice** each. As you key, try not to rest your palms on the machine. Remember, your teacher should be able to slip a pencil between your hands and the keyboard.

```
1 Lu tried to knit a scarf for her friend.
2 Al jogs each day.  He is a good athlete.
3 I bought the shoes on sale at the store.
```

The Space Bar

Below are several lines containing short words so you can practice your Space Bar technique. As you key each line **once**, strike the Space Bar with a down-and-in motion. Try to avoid extra spaces between words.

```
1 go to of as is in so ho do it if as hi a
2 got get set bet fad lad sad had due does
3 lug bug hub gut hut nab bob rod cob sobs
4 her his fit fir sir are eat ate jug kegs
5 nuts suds hugs rugs cogs jogs fog for oh
6 ah oat jot dot got hot ace boys face yes
. . . . 1 . . . . 2 . . . . 3 . . . . 4 . . . . 5 . . . . 6 . . . . 7 . . . . 8
```

Composing a Cover Page

Objectives:
- To improve speed on alphabet keys
- To improve accuracy of numbers
- To key copy from script
- To use proofreader's marks
- To compose and format a cover page for a multi-page report

PART A

Warmup

Key each line **twice.**

1 Max whizzed by on his new bicycle as we looked on.
2 He latched the door shut before the big wind came.
3 We are taking a trip to the coast to see Aunt May.
4 Please order 758 boxes of No. 231 and 90 of No. 4.
. . . . 1 . . . . 2 . . . . 3 . . . . 4 . . . . 5 . . . . 6 . . . . 7 . . . . 8 . . . . 9 10

PART B

Speed Building

The lines below contain more alternate-hand letter combinations. Key them, **three times** each. The first time, go at a moderate pace; the second time, go much faster; and the third time, go as fast as you possibly can.

1 la last large labor laboratory lakes land lamps la
2 an another anger and angels angry anklet annual an
3 wh while when what where whim wheel whiff whine wh
4 em emit emerge emergency ember lemon stems gems em
. . . . 1 . . . . 2 . . . . 3 . . . . 4 . . . . 5 . . . . 6 . . . . 7 . . . . 8 . . . . 9 10

Challenge

Your teacher will time you for one minute on the first line below. When time is called, use the scale to compute your keyboarding speed. Then on the next timing on that same line, see if you can increase your speed by one word. On the third timing on the same line, see if you can add yet another word to your speed. Follow this routine for each of the four lines below. See if you can increase your speed on all four lines.

1 All the girls cooked food for the choir.
2 She can get the job done by trying hard.
3 Jeff did take a ride on your bike today.
4 I have salad ready but you are too late.

. . . . 1 . . . . 2 . . . . 3 . . . . 4 . . . . 5 . . . . 6 . . . . 7 8

LESSON 16

Introducing M and W

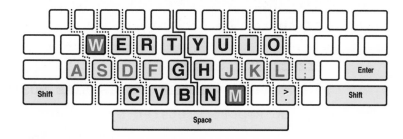

Objectives:

- To learn the location of the **M** key
- To learn the location of the **W** key
- To practice proper keyboarding techniques

Warmup

1. Technique Quiz: Key **T** if the statement is true, **F** if it is false.
   a. Lift your whole hand up from the keyboard when pressing the Return/Enter key.
   b. Do not arch your wrists when keying.
   c. Always bring your fingers back to home after striking another key.

Application 81: Civil War Battles

Directions:

- Use good judgment in arranging data vertically
- Center each line

- Boldface where indicated
- File name: Ap81

FAMOUS BATTLES OF THE CIVIL WAR

Social Studies

Period 4

Mr. Jackson

[Current Date]

[Your Name]

Application 82: Science Experiment

Directions:

- Use good judgment in arranging data vertically
- Center each line

- Boldface where indicated
- File name: Ap82

SCIENCE EXPERIMENT

TO DETERMINE WHETHER PLANTS LIKE MUSIC

A Group Report Prepared by: [Your Name]

[Your Friend's Name]

[Another Friend's Name]

[A Third Friend's Name]

For Mr. Calvert's 2nd
   Period Class

[Current Date]

2. Now key the lines below, each line **twice**.

```
1 sure true blue fuss touch hutch fudge uh
2 are they; can you; should he; of course;
3 do this; five cents; they said; do join;
4 Al flies big kites every chance he gets.
```
`. . . . 1 . . . . 2 . . . . 3 . . . . 4 . . . . 5 . . . . 6 . . . . 7 . . . . 8`

Key

1. Place your hands in home row position. Look at the keyboard chart and locate the **M** key. It's in the bottom row below **J,** so you will use your **J** finger to strike it. Try it now. Key **jm** several times as you watch your finger make the reach.

2. Now key the lines below, **twice** each, as you keep your eyes on the book.

```
1 jmj mjj mjm mjj mjm mjj jmj mjj mjm mjj
2 jjj mmm jjj mmm jjj mmm jjj mmm jjj mmm
```

3. Key these lines, **twice** each. As you key, be sure to bring your **J** finger back home after striking **M.**

```
3 jam ham mit moss mass mod mum met arm ma
4 mom moat mood moan meet him gym dim rims
5 march much mint munch muck firm trim aim
```

Shifting Technique

1. Below are some state names. Key them as they should be, with the first letter capitalized. As you key, remember to bring your fingers back to home position after striking the shift key.

```
1 new jersey; minnesota; montana; illinois
2 oregon; connecticut; new york; oklahoma;
3 missouri; rhode island; kansas; nebraska
```

Formatting a Cover Page

Application 80: Camp Waubonsee

Directions:
- Use good judgment in arranging data vertically
- Center each line
- Boldface where indicated
- File name: Ap80

ROUGHING IT AT CAMP WAUBONSEE
(A composition)

Prepared for Mrs. Burton's 5th Period English Class

Student Name

Current Date

2. Now see if you can key them again, but this time put them in alphabetical order within each line. Do not key the semicolon this time; just space once between states. And of course, you will capitalize the first letter of each word, using your best shifting technique.

 Key

1. Place your hands in home row position. Look at the keyboard chart and locate the **W** key. It's above **S,** so you will use your **S** finger on it. Try it now. Key **sw** several times. As you key, be sure to keep your **D** and **F** fingers at home.

2. Now key the lines below, **twice** each. Remember to keep your eyes on the book as you do them.

```
1 sws wss sws wss sws wss sws wss sws wss

2 sss www sss www sss www sss www sss www
```

3. As you key these lines, **twice** each, be sure to bring your fingers back to home position.

```
3 we way was woo wad waf wow cows owes low

4 win won how sow show own town jaw owl we

5 will wise were wilts want when where who
```

 **and** **Keys Combined**

Key the lines below, **twice** each. See if you can do all of them without taking your eyes off the book.

```
1 Wes went away today; we must search now.

2 Wilma marks time while the band marches.

3 Will has the mumps; he must miss school.
   . . . . 1 . . . . 2 . . . . 3 . . . . 4 . . . . 5 . . . . 6 . . . . 7 . . . . 8
```

**Model
Cover Page**

MY SUMMER VACATION (2 1/4inches from top)

[Your Name] (20 lines below last line)

English (20 lines down)

[Current Date] (2 lines down)

Eyes on Copy

The lines below will not make much sense unless you key them, word by word, in order from *right to left*. Try it now as you keep your eyes on the book. Key each line **once**.

```
1 dry. to towels wet their for waits Louis
2 wind. for out watch west travel you When
3 holes. of wallet his with money lost Ned
4 milk. and meat on sale a has market This
5 away. flew umbrella new a day windy a On
6 fowls. water found Morgan fog misty a In
```

Spacing After the Period

Key the lines below **once**. As you key, pay special attention to proper spacing after the period.

```
1 Mr. Chen will make chow mein for J. Lee.
2 Al goes to Ms. Tuf for swimming lessons.
3 Eat your food.  You need the energy now.
4 Willie runs races daily.  On Fri. I run.
5 Betty made jam.  The county fair is Sat.
6 Juan takes tennis lessons.  So does Ted.
```

Challenge

How fast can you unscramble and key the sentences below? Each line is a separate thought. You will have to keep your eyes on the book to avoid getting mixed up. Hint: The word with a period after it is the last word in the sentence, and one of the capitalized words is the first word. When you finish unscrambling all the lines, signal your teacher that you are finished by raising your hand.

```
1 led scouts the Mike long very hike. on a
2 him. chased was when scared Lee the bear
3 land farm Mr. owns Benson Creek. Salt by
4 to her sew the Lu clothes. own has skill
5 together They geo. study the test in for
```

Accuracy Building

The lines below contain hyphenated words. Key them, **twice** each. Strive for perfect accuracy.

```
1 double-wide load; mobile-home owners, self-reliant
2 toe-stubbing limb; duo-coated tape; six-inch strip
3 left-hand corner; tricks-of-the-trade; self-denial
4 jack-of-all-trades; letter-size paper, self-taught
```

Numbers

Take out your decoding sheet. Here's another message to key and decode. Be sure you put five spaces between each word.

```
23-8-25        19-8-15-21-12-4        1       13-1-14
14-5-22-5-18        20-5-12-12        19-5-3-18-5-20-19
9-14      ·1      3-15-18-14-6-9-5-12-4?
2-5-3-1-21-19-5        9-20        8-1-19        5-1-18-19
```

Cover Page for Multi-Page Reports

If you do a report that is more than one page, its appearance can be improved if you put a cover sheet on it. There is no one right way to do a cover sheet. Generally the information is centered horizontally and arranged vertically so it is attractive to the eye but not necessarily centered top to bottom. Thus the number of spaces left between each line is left to your good judgment. See the example in Part E on the next page.

Some teachers may request specific information be placed on the cover page. If your teacher does not mention this, you will probably want to include the following items on the cover page:

■ The title of the report
■ The name of the class for which the report was written
■ Your name
■ The date the paper is turned in

Keying a Cover Page

Make an exact copy of the model cover page on the next page. Do not key the information in brackets, but key in your name and the current date where indicated.

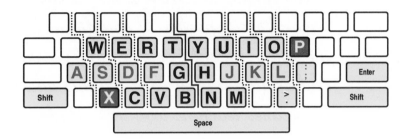

Introducing P and X

Objectives:
- To learn the location of the **P** key
- To learn the location of the **X** key
- To practice proper keyboarding techniques

PART A

Warmup

1. Technique Quiz: Key **T** if the statement is true, **F** if it is false.
   a. Keep both thumbs resting lightly on the Space Bar.
   b. Key the capital letter and press the shift key with the same hand.
   c. Watch your fingers when keying to be sure you are striking the right keys.

2. Now key the lines below, each line **twice**.

```
1 much with war mules was mighty weds milk
2 mink when multi weave wet weeds mom wads
3 much ado; win the lottery; we waste not;
4 Mickey wants to make widgets out of tin.
. . . . 1 . . . . 2 . . . . 3 . . . . 4 . . . . 5 . . . . 6 . . . . 7 . . . . 8
```

PART B

 Key

1. Place your hands in home row position. Look at the keyboard chart and locate the **P** key. It is above the **semicolon** key, so you will use your "sem" finger on **P**. Try it now. Key **;p** several times as you watch your fingers making the reach.

Both you and your family would look forward to Friday night. That's when everyone would come from miles around to see the students compete in a spelling bee and recite poetry. If you did well and out-spelled all the other students, you would be rewarded with a medal and applause from your parents and neighbors. Sometimes teachers took their students on a field trip. You and your classmates would pile into horse-drawn wagons donated by some farmers and travel to another town to attend their spelling bee.

Life as a Colonial student was not easy. Next time you think school is not so good, remember how it was back in the "old days."

LESSON 67

Formatting a Cover Page

Objectives:

- To improve accuracy on alphabet keys
- To improve accuracy of numbers
- To format a cover page for a multi-page report

PART A

Warmup

Retrieve your Journal file. Add to your journal what you learned in the previous lesson about this topic:

- the commands for numbering pages
- three different places page numbers are usually placed

2. Now key the lines below, **twice** each. As you key, be sure you keep your **J** and **K** fingers in home position and your elbow close to your side.

```
1 ;p; p;; ;p; p;; ;p; p;; ;p; p;; ;p; p;;
2 ;;; ppp ;;; ppp ;;; ppp ;;; ppp ;;; ppp
```

3. Here are some more lines with **P** in them. You have probably noticed that this is not an easy reach to make. It's because your little pinkie is your weakest finger. But don't get discouraged. With practice, the reach to **P** will become easier. Key the following lines **twice**. As you key, be sure to keep your eyes on the book and your elbows close to your sides.

```
3 pep up dip sip rip nip mop apes naps pop
4 prey cape tape gaps keep weep laps packs
5 pegs parts prices pride prune party pens
6 dirty paws; back pack; prime meat; pulse
```

PART C
Eyes on Copy

Key the phrases below **once**. As you key, replace the dash with the proper letter. You will have to keep your eyes on the book to do this efficiently.

```
t_ke a n_p; pi_k the li_ter up; a bot_le of p_p;
p_t yo_r be_t fo_t fo_ward; p_ck of t_e litte_;
pa_ks a p_nch; pea_e of m_nd; a p_p as_embly; a
j_r of p_ckles; p_sh or pul_; p_nch of sa_t; tr_m
the bush_s; pa_se and ref_ect; picn_c par_y; p_p
go_s _he wea_el
```

PART D
 Key

1. Place your hands in home row position. Look at the keyboard chart and locate the **X** key. It's in the bottom row, just below **S**, so you will use your **S** finger for it. Try it now. Key **sx** several times as you watch your fingers make the reach.

community water pail and a dipper. Everyone drank from the same dipper. If you were one of the lucky students chosen to walk down to the creek to fill the pail, you could enjoy a few minutes' recess from studying. Of course, in winter when the creek was frozen, you had to brave the freezing cold outside as you filled the pail with snow and then wait for it to melt before you could drink.

When you returned from this errand, you could be called to come up to the teacher's desk and recite your lesson. You were expected to learn everything by memory. If you forgot a part, the teacher might help you, but more often the teacher would admonish you for not studying and send you back to your seat, if you were lucky. If you were not lucky, you might have your knuckles rapped with a stick or be told to sit in the corner wearing a dunce cap as punishment for not knowing your lessons.

Your textbooks would be the ones your family owned. Not every child in the school would be learning out of the same book. Each child brought to school the books he or she had at home. These books were passed down from one child to another. You would not get to start another book until you showed your teacher that you had memorized the first book from cover to cover.

(continued on next page)

2. Key the lines below, **twice** each. Be sure you keep your **A** finger at home when making the reach to **X.** If this feels too clumsy, then you may want to lift up your **A** finger slightly and keep your **F** finger on **F.** You have four anchors—the **F** and **A** on your left hand and the **J** and **;** on your right hand. These anchors help guide your other fingers back to home row. When keying the **X** key, it's important to keep either **A** or **F** anchored to home row so you can quickly guide your fingers back to home position.

1 SXS XSS SXS XSS SXS XSS SXS XSS SXS XSS

2 SSS XXX SSS XXX SSS XXX SSS XXX SSS XXX

3. Now key these lines, **two times** each. After you make the reach to **X,** be sure to bring your finger back to home position.

3 six axes fix fox tax lax ox mix sox oxen

4 boxes next exist exit excel exam excuses

5 exhale extreme hex exercises lox extract

PART E

P and X Keys Combined

As you key the lines below, try to keep your eyes on the book. Do each line **twice**.

1 expand expense expect export express pox

2 experts explain exposes exposure expires

3 expense account; export tax; extra exam;

4 He explained why the oxen were examined.

PART F

Spacing After the Period

You already know that a period that ends a sentence requires two spaces, and a period used after an abbreviation requires one space. Here is another rule to remember about the period: Do not space after an internal period in an abbreviation, such as Y.M.C.A. On the next page are some lines for you to key, **one time** each, with proper spacing after the periods.

Application 79: Colonial Schooling

Directions:

- 1-inch side and bottom margins
- 2-inch top margin; 1-inch top margin on continuing pages
- Wordwrap
- Center the title and by-line;
- double space twice after by-line
- Double space
- Number the second page in the top center
- File name: Ap79

GOING TO SCHOOL IN COLONIAL DAYS

By [Your Name]

You may complain about going to school today, but you don't know how lucky you are. Children going to school during Colonial Days walked many miles. They left home in the morning darkness and came home in the dark.

School was usually a one-room building with rough sawed planks for benches and desks. All grades were together in one room. The teacher would work with one group while the others studied by themselves.

Where you sat depended upon how much firewood your parents had donated to the school. Those whose parents were generous with their wood were seated close to the fire. Those whose parents were not so generous or donated green wood, which did not burn very well, found themselves seated far away from the warmth.

If you got thirsty, you would have to ask permission to get a drink. There was no water fountain, just a

(continued on next page)

1 I live in the U.S.A. and am proud of it.
2 Her new dentist is Jorge Salinas, D.D.S.
3 Martha will have her Ph.D. from college.
4 Marvin also belongs to the A.F.L. union.
5 Bret took his dog to Bob Cortesi, D.V.M.
6 His degree is a B.A. from Evans College.

Placement of the Wrists

Let's work on another technique that will help you develop good skill at the keyboard. It's called *quiet hands*. How can your hands be quiet if they are busy striking keys, you ask? Quiet hands means that your fingers, not your arms, are doing all the work. Keyboarding experts (those who can key at more than 150 words per minute) demonstrate how quiet their hands are by placing a small glass of water on each wrist. And you know what? When the experts key, they don't spill a drop! As you key the lines below, **twice** each, pretend you have a glass of water sitting on each wrist. Try not to spill one drop.

1 A fox went up to the ox who was napping.
2 Fix Pam some oxtail soup; she is hungry.
3 Ed mixed up two answers on the map exam.
4 Bo Cox is lax about jogging in the park.

made. When the count reaches zero, no more copies can be made.

Other methods use passwords and codes. A password requires a secret word to get into the program. Programs that use codes rely on the different serial number of each computer. That number is read by the program the first time it is used. Thereafter, the same number must be read or the program will not run. While this seems like a foolproof method, not all computer manufacturers have electronically numbered their computers.

The effects of software piracy are several. First, companies who produce software and people who write the programs lose money. They can only make money by selling. Less money coming in means the company will spend less on developing new software. That means the people who use software are the losers. The pirates are losers as well as honest people because there will be less new software developed.

Challenge

Here are some phrases for you to unscramble. You can accomplish this by simply switching the words around until they make sense. For example, "hair your part," would be "part your hair." How quickly can you finish this list and still get all of them correct?

1 mayo the hold
2 apart comes seams at the
3 eat I horse a could
4 ways both look
5 sides till your ache laugh
6 body my over dead
7 fast in life lane the
8 coming keep them
9 with room view a
10 risk your at enter own
11 two easy over eggs

LESSON 18

STOP! **and Review**

Objectives:

■ To review keys learned in previous lessons
■ To practice technique pointers learned in previous lessons

law states that the owner of the copyright has exclusive rights to the software. But the law is not enforced, and there is nothing to stop someone from developing a program that does exactly the same thing that a copyrighted program does. Copyright protects only the form of an idea, not the idea itself.

Games are one of the prime targets for software piracy. Games are easy to learn and operate. Because you don't need to read a manual first, just about anyone can pick up a game and play it. Application programs, such as word processing and spreadsheets, are also targets for illegal copying, but the more complicated the program, the less likely it will be pirated. Most people need to read a manual to understand a complicated program, and manuals only come with the original software.

Software manufacturers have come up with a number of ways to protect their programs. One is to copy-protect a disk. They do this by placing an error on the disk, such as an improperly formatted sector. This doesn't interfere with the running of the program but causes a disk-copy command to report an error.

Another protection method is to limit the number of back-up copies that can be made by putting a count on the disk that is decreased by one each time a copy is

(continued on next page)

Warmup

1. Technique Quiz: Key **T** if the statement is true, **F** if it is false.
   a. You should cross your ankles when keying.
   b. Your wrists should be level.
   c. You should cross your knees when keying.

2. This lesson contains no new keys to learn. So you can relax and concentrate on strengthening the reaches to those keys you have learned thus far. Key the lines below, **two times** each. If time permits, repeat the lines.

```
1 pop tax ox oxen steps tips taxes fox lox
2 expects preps expire extra proper pieces
3 fix the property; pinch an inch; popover
4 Peggy prepares apple dumplings and pies.
  . . . . 1 . . . . 2 . . . . 3 . . . . 4 . . . . 5 . . . . 6 . . . . 7 . . . . 8
```

PART B

Eyes on Copy

In the lines below, key the words in order from *right to left,* instead of the way you usually key from left to right. That will force you to keep your eyes on the book.

```
1 yesterday. fish a catch to tried Patrick
2 sick. pretty got and pop cold drank Rita
3 bike. broken old his fix to tried Steven
4 dogs. their with foxes hunt Roni and Vic
5 high. is clips paper of cost the think I
6 you. phone will Judy stops rain the When
```

PART C

Palms off the Keyboard

Key each paragraph on the next page **once**. As you key, try to keep your palms from touching the keyboard. Be sure to press Return/Enter at the end of each line. After the first paragraph, press Return/Enter twice before starting the second paragraph. This will leave a blank space between the two paragraphs.

of water, they thought the reflection was their soul. If that image was disturbed, the person would be injured in some way. The number _seven_ comes from the Romans who thought it took seven years for life to renew itself.

Application 78: Software Piracy

Directions:

- 1-inch side and bottom margins
- 2-inch top margin; 1-inch top margin on continuing pages
- Wordwrap
- Center the title and by-line;
- double space twice after by-line
- Double space
- Number the second page in the top right-hand corner
- File name: Ap78

SOFTWARE PIRACY

By [Your Name]

Pirates in the old days attacked sailing ships and stole their merchandise. Today's pirates don't have to get their feet wet. If someone gives you a floppy containing a program, and you make a copy of it, you are a modern-day pirate.

I have a friend whose father buys him all kinds of software. My friend gladly shares his software with his computer friends. He copies each new program and hands it out to whomever wants it. I call my friend Robin Hood because he "shares the wealth with the poor."

All software is protected by the copyright law. That

(continued on next page)

```
My father bought a new wood chipper.  It
works very well except sometimes it jams
up.  Then I poke inside it with a stick.

Lu asked Al to the dance but he refused.
Then she asked Roberto who said he would
be delighted to go to the Harvest Dance.
```

Shifting Technique

1. The lines below contain boys' and girls' first names. They *all* need to be capitalized. Let's see your best shifting technique as you key each line **once**.

```
1 melanie kirk derek paco pablo kathy alex
2 alejandro ruchir raol maria sudip louise
3 evan pete faye gretta karen munif walter
```

2. Now see if you can alphabetize the *entire* list of names above. Key one name per line. Hint: Key the names in the first line, one name per line. Then use your cursor movement keys to insert the other names in the list. Of course, you will capitalize each name using your best shifting technique.

Spacing After Periods

Remember the rule about no spaces after an internal period used in an abbreviation? As you key the lines below, **once** each, pay special attention to how many spaces you put after the period.

```
1 The Y.M.C.A. team won four soccer games.
2 Dr. J. Berk mailed his tax to the I.R.S.
3 I. T. Brindle Co. just hired Mr. Franke.
4 Kate wrote N.A.S.A. for some moon rocks.
5 I know.  Juan can do it.  Try very hard.
6 The N.A.A.C.P. lawyer spoke to our class.
```

avoid danger. The spirit on the left would get salt in his eyes and would not be able to do you any harm.

Opening an Umbrella Inside Is Unlucky. For many centuries the umbrella was used as protection from the sun, not rain. Opening the umbrella inside was considered an insult to the sun and would bring bad luck. It was not until 1700 that people started using the umbrella to keep rain off their heads.

Knocking on Wood Three Times Stops Something from Happening. In olden days people knocked on wood to keep from being punished for bragging. They believed if you talked about your good fortune, evil spirits would become jealous and take it away. Knocking three times was additional good measure; they believed the noise would prevent the spirits from hearing about your good fortune.

The Night Air Is Bad for You. Long ago people believed that air after sundown was harmful because evil air rose up from the ground and floated around poisoning the atmosphere. Those who worshiped the sun did not go out after dark because when the sun was gone they had no protection.

Breaking a Mirror Is Seven Years' Bad Luck. Before there were mirrors, people used shiny surfaces to reflect images. When people looked at their reflection in a pool

(continued on next page)

Keeping Elbows In

Are there any "birds" in your class? Let's find out. As you key the lines below, **twice** each, try to keep your elbows close to your body.

1 Randy tried out for the basketball team.
2 Too bad Eduardo ate the cake by himself.
3 Nina is sad because she failed the test.

The Space Bar

How is your Space Bar technique? Do you sometimes get extra spaces where you don't want them? Let's work on that now. Key each line **twice**; as you key, strike the Space Bar with a quick, down-and-in motion.

1 of to go ox it if is on up do us as ax I
2 toe rip fig get hug dig sop mop hop tops
3 win can our now old the for pay you eats
. . . . 1 . . . . 2 . . . . 3 . . . . 4 . . . . 5 . . . . 6 . . . . 7 8

Challenge

Have you ever participated in a marathon? You have probably heard about marathons where people run for many miles. You are going to be in one now so get ready. No, you don't have to put on your running shoes. This is a key-a-thon where keyboarding speed and endurance count. Here, and in the Challenge sections of the next two lessons, you will compete with your classmates to see who can key the most lines. Your teacher will time you. Do not begin until told to start. You may want to clear your screen and keep your key-a-thon lines in a separate file. The winner of the key-a-thon is the person who has keyed the most number of lines. If you finish all the lines below, start them over again.

1 Alecia always asks about average apples.
2 Bob brings books and bright bookmarkers.
3 Clo Claus caught cold cooking cucumbers.
4 Doug Dirkson dug down deeper and deeper.
5 Edith Earthington exercises excessively.
6 Fetch a frazzled frock for the frontier.

all that changed in the Middle Ages when the cat was considered to be the pet of witches. From that time on, if a black cat crossed your path, it meant bad luck.

Walking Under a Ladder Is Bad Luck. In olden days many people believed that a triangle or a pyramid was the symbol of life. A ladder leaning against something formed a triangle. Anyone walking through that sacred triangle would be punished. In some Asian countries criminals were hung under ladders. Some people in these countries believed that anyone walking under that ladder would see the ghost of death there and die themselves.

A Rabbit's Foot Is Lucky. To be lucky the foot must be from the rabbit's hind legs, which touch the ground ahead of its front ones as it hops along. When ancient people observed how a rabbit moves about, they decided its hind feet must have magical powers because it walked in this unusual way.

Throw Salt Over Your Left Shoulder. Primitive man used salt to preserve food. Because it could preserve food, it was thought salt could preserve people too. When salt was spilled, a special guardian spirit was supposed to be warning against upcoming danger. Because good spirits lived on the right and bad ones on the left, throwing salt over your left shoulder was an attempt to

(continued on next page)

Introducing Z and ,

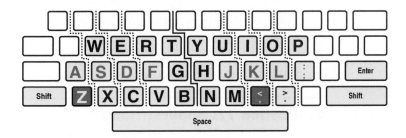

Objectives:
- To learn the location of the **Z** key
- To learn the location of the comma (,) key
- To practice proper keyboarding techniques

PART A

Warmup

1. Technique Quiz: Key **T** if the statement is true, **F** if it is false.
   a. Wrists should be arched when keying.
   b. Keep eyes on the copy.
   c. Sit a hand span away from the edge of the keyboard.

2. Now key the lines below, each line **twice**.

1 fax flax max tax axe pip gip pig put ape
2 exams excerpt exceeds exhibits exercises
3 a wise owl; a tough exam; a fine exhibit
4 Max slipped on the soap and broke a leg.

. . . . . 1 . . . . 2 . . . . 3 . . . . 4 . . . . 5 . . . . 6 . . . . 7 8

PART B

Z Key

1. Place your hands in home row position. Look at the keyboard chart and locate the **Z** key. It's down in the bottom left corner of the keyboard, under **A**, so you will use your **A** finger on it. Try it now. Key **az** several times as you watch your fingers make the reach.

Inserting Page Numbers

Using the command(s) for your software, place page numbers as instructed below. Keep pressing the Return/Enter key until you reach a new page.

1. Put *3* in the upper right-hand corner.

2. Put *16* in the bottom center.

3. Put *9* in the top center.

Formatting Multi-Page Reports from Script

Application 77: Superstitions

Directions:

- 1-inch side and bottom margins
- 2-inch top margin; 1-inch top margin on continuing pages
- Wordwrap
- Center the title and by-line; double space twice after by-line
- Double space
- Number the second and third pages in the bottom center
- Underline where indicated
- File name: Ap77

SUPERSTITIONS

By [Your Name]

A superstition is the belief that something we do, say, or see may change our luck. Superstitions are not based on reason or fact, but some people regard them as rules to follow. Here are some common beliefs and how they came about.

<u>A Black Cat Crossing the Street Is a Sign of Bad Luck.</u> In ancient Egypt cats were worshiped. If a person's cat died, all the people in the household were expected to shave their eyebrows and mourn the cat's death. Black cats were considered a lucky symbol, but

(continued on next page)

2. Now try the lines below, **two times** each. As you make the reach to the new key, be sure to keep your **F** and **D** fingers at home and keep your eyes on the book.

```
1 aza zaa aza zaa aza zaa aza zaa aza zaa
2 aaa zzz aaa zzz aaa zzz aaa zzz aaa zzz
```

3. Now key each line below **twice** each. Try to *keep your eyes on the book as you reach to the new key.*

```
1 zoo zap zig zag zip zoos zigs zags zips;
2 hazy lazy pizza zoom zonk zipper zircons
3 a pizza; a zipper; a zircon; a lazy boy;
```

PART C
Eyes on Copy

As you key the lines below, **one time** each, try to keep your eyes on the book for the entire time. Do not look up until you have completed all three lines. Then repeat if time permits.

```
1 Ziggy zigged and zagged.  Zippers stick.
2 Zip is zero; zero is zip.  Zigger zooms.
3 Zoos have zebras who zig and zag around.
```

PART D
, Key

1. Place your hands in home row position. Look at the keyboard chart and locate the **comma** key. It's right below **K,** so you will use your **K** finger on it. Try it now. Key **k,** several times as you watch your fingers make the reach.

2. Key the lines below, **twice** each. As you make the reach to the new key, remember your anchors—**J** and **;** and **F** and **A.** Keep either your **J** or **;** finger firmly anchored on home row so you can find your way back to home position quickly.

```
1 k,k ,kk k,k ,kk k,k ,kk k,k ,kk k,k ,kk
2 kkk ,,, kkk ,,, kkk ,,, kkk ,,, kkk ,,,
```

Numbers

Take out your decoding sheet. Here's another message to key and decode. Be sure you put five spaces between each word.

8-15-23   4-15   2-5-5-19   7-5-20   18-9-4

15-6   20-8-5-9-18   8-15-14-5-25?   20-8-5-25

3-5-12-12   9-20

Numbering Pages

Page numbers can be placed in several different places on a page. They are most commonly found (1) centered at the bottom of the page, (2) centered at the top of the page, or (3) placed in the upper right-hand corner. Look at the diagram below.

Most word processing software packages have a command for inserting page numbers on the page. Your teacher will explain the command(s) to you and how to tell when you have come to the end of a page on the computer. Depending on your software, you may be able to include the word *Page* or you may use the figure alone.

If your software does not have a page number command, you can easily insert a page number by simply centering the number *2* on the first line of the second page, *3* on the first line of the third page, and so on. (Usually the first page of a multi-page report is *not* numbered, but all other pages are.)

Whichever position you choose for your page number, it is important to be consistent. Pick a position and stick with it for the whole paper.

Page # Bottom Center

Page # Top Center

Page # Top Right Corner

3. Now key the lines below, **twice** each, keeping your eyes on the book. Space once after each comma.

```
3 six cats, four dogs, five pigs, two bats
4 two pies, five tarts, four rolls, a cake
5 sky blue dress, brown pants, black boots,
```

PART E
Z and , Keys Combined

As you key the lines below, **twice** each, remember to bring your fingers back to home position after striking the bottom row keys.

```
1 quiz or test, zip with zeal, pizza pies,
2 zero zircons, zinc is zilch, zany Ziggy,
3 Zelda Jo zips over to the zoo for pizza.
```

PART F
Shifting Technique

Key the lines below **once** using your best shifting technique. Your teacher will be observing. If time permits, repeat the lines.

```
1 Marla Zerk will travel to Zurich Sunday.
2 The Burlington Zoo imported a new zebra.
3 You must copy ZIP Codes with great care.
4 Bixby Zipper Company is out of business.
5 Martin Martinez moved to the Canal Zone.
6 The Daughtrey Store sells Zenith radios.
```

PART G
Spacing After Periods and Commas

As you key the lines below, **once** each, pay special attention to your spacing after the periods and commas. Check your work with your teacher.

```
1 A gift was sent c.o.d. by their nephews.
2 My plane landed Sat. morning.  Hurry up.
3 Add one oz. of water, mix well, and fry.
4 J. Soo drinks one gal. of milk each day.
5 Do journey with us to Miss. this summer.
6 Good.  She bought eggs, milk, and bread.
```

Formatting Multi-Page Reports from Script

Objectives:
- To improve speed on alphabet keys
- To improve accuracy of numbers
- To learn how to number pages
- To format multi-page reports from script

Warmup

Key each line **twice.**

1 Block out failures; concentrate on your successes.

2 Gavin will trim the hedge while I weed the garden.

3 We plan to move when school closes for the summer.

4 (1) math; (2) science; (3) English; (4) geography;

....1....2....3....4....5....6....7....8....9....10

Speed Building

The lines below contain alternate-hand letter combinations. Key them, **three times** each. The first time, go at a moderate pace; the second time, go much faster; and the third time, go as fast as you possibly can.

1 fo fort form forbid force food found fork foggy fo

2 le lend lean left lead leap least leaf leapfrog le

3 di diner dinner dishes dimes digger diary ditch di

4 co coach comb coat comic color cough cords corn co

....1....2....3....4....5....6....7....8....9....10

Challenge

Retrieve your key-a-thon file. Get ready to continue the race. This is the second day of the race. Do not start until your teacher tells you. Key the lines below as many times as you can in the time period.

1 Grasp the glorious grand gelatin gently.
2 Hubert hitched his horses to a Holstein.
3 Iodine Igloo Ice is ideal imitation ice.
4 Jack justly judges the jitterbug jargon.
5 Kevin keeps knackwursts in his knapsack.
6 Lois loves luxurious light lilac lotion.

LESSON 20

Introducing Q and ?

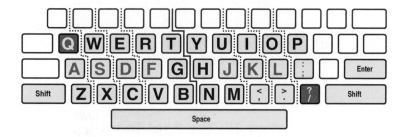

Objectives:
- To learn the location of the **Q** key
- To learn the location of the question mark (**?**) key
- To practice proper keyboarding techniques

Warmup

1. Technique Quiz: Key **T** if the statement is true, **F** if it is false.
   a. Do not bounce your wrists when keying.
   b. Always keep your feet flat on the floor.
   c. Do not arch your wrists when keying.

Keying with Proofreader's Marks

Key the paragraph below **once,** using wordwrap. Make all the corrections indicated as you key.

> There is nothing like a picnic in the woods to enjoy Nature. Once you locate your site sight, you need to scout for twigs to make a fire. When the fief is going, poke some hotdogs on a stick and grill them in the fire. Later, when the fire dies down, use that same stick for your marshmellows. Then sit around the campfire and tell ghost stories.

Composing One-Page Reports Using Proofreader's Marks

Application 74: Inventions or Products

Directions:

Compose at the computer, *without correcting any errors,* a one-page, double-spaced paper explaining a new product or invention that the world really needs and why. The title is WHAT THE WORLD NEEDS NOW. Print a copy of your first effort. Then use proofreader's marks to correct and edit the copy. Using your edited copy, make the changes indicated and print a copy of the revision. Note: you will have two copies of this problem to turn in—the original and the edited version. Name the file Ap74.

Application 75: The Best Teacher

Directions:

Following the same procedure as described above, prepare a one-page paper titled, THE BEST TEACHER I EVER HAD. Name the file Ap75.

Application 76: Making Some Changes

Directions:

Following the same procedure as described above, prepare a one-page paper titled, THERE'LL BE SOME CHANGES MADE. Explain in your paper things you would like to see changed in your school and why. Name the file Ap76.

2. Now key the lines below, each line **twice**.

```
1 zebras, zeros, zippers, pizzas, zircons,
2 zephyr, zinc, zillion, zoo, zones, zest,
3 more zucchini, zooms in, plant a zinnia,
4 Zed and Zelda write zip codes with zeal.
  . . . . 1 . . . . 2 . . . . 3 . . . . 4 . . . . 5 . . . . 6 . . . . 7 . . . . 8
```

 Key

1. Place your hands in home row position. Look at the keyboard chart and locate the **Q** key. It's in the upper left-hand corner of the keyboard just above **A,** so you will use your **A** finger on it. Try it now. Key **aq** several times as you watch your fingers make the reach. Keep your left elbow close to your side.

2. Now key the lines below, **twice** each. As you key, try to keep your **F** and **D** fingers at home. Try to make the reach without looking at your hands and keep your left elbow near your side.

```
1 aqa qaa aqa qaa aqa qaa aqa qaa aqa qaa
2 aaa qqq aaa qqq aaa qqq aaa qqq aaa qqq
```

3. Now key these lines, **twice** each. As you key, remember your anchors and try to *keep your eyes on the book.*

```
3 quad quarts quick quints quiet quit quiz
4 quantity qualify quadrangle quince quill
5 a quart of quince, two questions, quartz
6 Jo was quite quick at the race in Quebec.
```

Eyes on Copy

1. If you have a problem keeping your eyes on the book, a good remedy to try is keying foreign language material. Here's the first paragraph from Caesar's Gallic Wars speech. It is in Latin. Key it **once**. If time permits, repeat the paragraph. To get it right, you will have to concentrate and keep your eyes on the book because the word patterns will probably be unfamiliar to you.

Accuracy Building

The lines below contain "weak finger" words. Key them, **twice** each. Strive for perfect accuracy.

1 quarts quills quaint quid quipped pop props preppy
2 zapped zipped dizzy prized pizza wasp quiz swapped
3 tax lax quite zoologist wasp pep squad lazy woolly
4 quite quick poplar poplin popular populate quietly

PART C

Numbers

Take out your decoding sheet. Here's another message to key and decode. Be sure you put five spaces between each word.

23-8-1-20   16-1-18-20   15-6   1   6-9-19-8
23-5-9-7-8-19   20-8-5   13-15-19-20?
20-8-5   19-3-1-12-5-19

PART D

Keying from Script

Key the paragraph below **once.** Then go back and do it again.

Feeding birds is easy and a great pastime. Most birds will eat anything that is not spicy or too salty. Suet is one of the best things to feed, either plain or as a base for a seed cake. Hang suet out of the sun or rain. Or try feeding peanut butter mixed with seeds. If you want to prevent squirrels and cats from eating your food, set your feeding station off the ground.

Gallia est omnis divisa in partes tres, quarum
unam incolunt Belgae, aliam Aquitani, tertiam,
qui ipsorum lingua Celtae, nostra Galli
appellantur. Hi omnes lingua, institutis,
legibus inter se differunt. Gallos ab
Aquitanis Garumna flumen, a Belgis Matrona et
Sequana dividit.

2. Now key the translation below **once**.

All Gaul is divided into three parts, one of
which the Belgae inhabit, another the
Aquitani, the third those who in their own
language are called Celts, in ours Gauls. All
three differ among themselves in language,
institutions, and laws. The River Garonne
divides the Gauls from the Aquitani, the Marne
and Seine from the Belgae.

PART D

 Key

1. Place your hands in home row position. Look at the keyboard chart and locate the **question mark** key. It's down in the bottom row, right-hand corner. Since it's just below the **semicolon,** you will use your "sem" finger on it. Try making the reach now *without striking the keys*. Keep your **J** and **K** fingers at home as you reach to the new key.

2. To operate the question mark key you will have to use the Left Shift key. Move your **A** finger down to the shift key and depress the shift. Now move your sem finger down to the question mark key and depress that key. Try it several times as you key the question mark.

3. Now try the lines below, **twice** each. Be sure to bring all fingers back to home position after striking the new key.

1 ;?; ?;; ;?; ?;; ;?; ?;; ;?; ?;; ;?; ?;;
2 ;;; ??? ;;; ??? ;;; ??? ;;; ??? ;;; ???

width of the computer screen by only moving the#mouse
a few inches. Early mice did not last long, but
today modern mice tested on tread⌢mills have lasted
for about as long as 50 miles. Since the average
mouse user ~~only~~ moves the mouse 60 feet a day, (stet)
most#mice will probably outlive their owners.

Today's mouse owner may not bee satisfied with
just a mouse. The well-cared-for computer mouse has
a mouse house for storagƐe; a duƵs cover complete
with eyes, nose ~~snout~~, and tail; and little rubber pads on
which the mouse is used.

LESSON 65

Composing Reports Containing Proofreader Marks

Objectives:
- To improve accuracy on alphabet keys
- To improve accuracy of numbers
- To key copy with proofreader's marks
- To key copy from script
- To compose and format one-page reports containing proofreader's marks

Warmup

Key each line **twice.**

1 Jane has a cut on her eye and needs first aid now.
2 Adrian caught a giant fish down by Swanson's Lake.
3 The chairman of the committee will be seeing them.
4 Take a 10% discount; then deduct still another 5%.

. . . . 1 . . . . 2 . . . . 3 . . . . 4 . . . . 5 . . . . 6 . . . . 7 . . . . 8 . . . . 9 10

4. A question mark requires the same spacing as a period that ends a sentence. Remember how many spaces that is? That's right, two spaces. Space twice after a question mark, unless it appears at the end of the line; no space is required if the question mark falls at the end of the line. Now key these two lines, **twice** each. Try to keep your eyes on the book as you key.

1 Who came late? Why say no? Did I know?
2 Is it yours? Can you ask? Did they go?
3 What time? When did you leave? Why me?

PART E

Spacing After the Question Mark Key

Here are some more lines containing question marks. As you key them **once**, pay special attention to your spacing after the question mark.

1 Did Mary ask you to the dance? Oh, yes.
2 What time do we meet? How about twelve?
3 Is there time? Can we do it? Maybe so.
4 Forget it. Why? I do not remember now.
5 Does he jog much? Yes, he does. Where?
6 Do you like my school? Are you kidding?

PART F

 Q and ? Keys Combined

Now practice using both of the new keys from this lesson. Key each line **twice**. As you key, try to keep your eyes on the book.

1 quart? quince? quicksand? quiz today?
2 step quickly? a quantity? two quiches?
3 Are they hunting quail? Yes. Be quiet.

PART G

Palms off the Keyboard

Key the lines below, **twice** each. As you key, concentrate on keeping your palms from resting on the keyboard.

1 Skipping breakfast makes me very hungry.
2 This hobby shop stocks the kit you want.
3 Listening is a skill we need to develop.

My mom explained on the way home # why that was such a wonderful present. ₌candy was his first seeing-eye dog. She served Bill for many years until # she too went blind and was sent to a farm in Wisconsin to retire. This was their first re union since Bill's tearful goodbye.

Application 73: A Better Mouse

Directions:
- 1-inch side and bottom margins
- 1.5-inch top margin
- Wordwrap
- Center the title and by-line; double space twice after by-line
- Double space
- Make all corrections indicated by proofreader's marks as you key
- File name: Ap73

BUILDING A BETTER MOUSE

By [Your Name]

In 1951 ₌douglas Englebart had # a vision. He saw mice sitting next to computers. Not the kind that eat che e se, the kind whose tails are plugged into the computer. In 1963 he started working on his dream. He carved a 2- by 3- by 4-inch wo o den box, which had wheels. As you moved the mouse around the desk, sensors on the two whe e ls moved the screen cursor in the same directoin. ¶ The first mice cost around $300 and were plugged into separate power supplies. Microsoft ₌word was the first ^company to sell a # mouse in 1984. If you look at a mouse today, you will not see a wooden box on wheels. Mice have undergone a change.

The two wheel s were replaced with a steel ball and then later with a rubber ball. The mouse has also become more sensitive. Now you can navigate the

(continued on next page)

Challenge

Retrieve your key-a-thon file. Get ready to continue the race. This is the last day of the race. Begin keying the lines below when your teacher tells you to start.

1 My monkeys mindlessly minced a mothball.
2 Natalie navigated a narrow new nautilus.
3 Observe Opal obstruct the odd officials.
4 Peters is a practical, precise preacher.
5 Quenela has quarts of quince and squash.
6 The rushing river resisted at the ridge.
7 Su Sims sorts seashells at the seashore.

Application 72: The Best Gift

Directions:

- 1-inch side and bottom margins
- 1.5-inch top margin
- Wordwrap
- Center the title and by-line; double space twice after by-line
- Double space
- Make all corrections indicated by proofreader's marks as you key
- File name: Ap72

THE BEST GIFT

By [Your Name]

It was Dec. 24 and Mom asked me to go with her to the office. When we got there, Mom introduced me to the people she works with. The one person I remember was Bill. He was blind and he had a seeing-eye dog, Tammy, who lay by his feet.

As the morning went on, people got happier and merrier. Everyone was eating and drinking and laughing. No one but Bill was working. Then someone stopped Bill and told him he had a visitor in the lobby. They helped Bill make his way to the elevator. Everyone in the office gathered round to see. As the elevator doors opened, a big collie dog gingerly stepped forward and started sniffing the floor. You could tell the dog was old; it's muzzle was gray and it's eyes were no longer bright and clear. Everyone stopped talking and watched. The dog kept sniffing until it found bill. Then Bill cried out, "Candy, Candy, is it you? Oh, what a wonderful present." Bill started to cry as he hugged the old dog. Everyone else had tears in their eyes two, including me.

(continued on next page)

SECTION 2

Building Speed and Accuracy on Alphabet Keys; Learning Punctuation and Operation Keys

Keying One-Page Reports with Proofreader Marks

Application 71: Friends Till the End

Directions:

- 1-inch side and bottom margins
- 1.5-inch top margin
- Wordwrap
- Center the title and by-line; double space twice after by-line
- Double space
- Make all corrections indicated by proofreader's marks as you key
- File name: Ap71

FRIENDS TILL THE END

by Todd Strasser, Delacorte , 1981

By [Your name]

The Author

    Mr. Strasser writes about topics of interest to young adults. His book, ROCK 'N ROLL NIGHTS, was about a teenager and his band and how they tried to break into the rock scene.

The Story

    David Gilbert is on the school's soccer team. During the first week of school David makes friends with a new student, Howie Jamison, who has leukemia. Howie is hospitalized and David visits him. David learns that Howie has a love of soccer. When Howie gets out of the hospital, David invites him to a victory soccer party. His mother protests but Howie goes anyway. when he comes home, he is so sick that he must be hospitalized. The soccer team organizes an emergency blood drive to help Howie. David leaves with the team to attend the state tournament. While he is gone, Howie is transferred to a hospital in his old home town. Later david learns that Howie's condition is very bad. He writes Howie many times but never recieves an answer.

Comments

    I would recommend everyone read this book. It makes you think about death and dying. All soccer fans would also enjoy this book because it has lots of soccer action.

LESSON 21

Introducing Tab

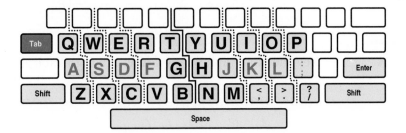

Objectives:
■ To develop keyboarding speed and accuracy
■ To compose at the computer
■ To learn the location of the **Tab** key
■ To review language arts principles

PART A

Warmup

Key each line **twice**. Try to key the lines without pausing between words.

1 if we go; she may see; why can they; on top of the
2 if it is; for an end; at the; there is; as she may
3 She gave Fred the facts that most art is not free.
4 If Bud stops by, quench his thirst with an orange.

. . . . 1 . . . . 2 . . . . 3 . . . . 4 . . . . 5 . . . . 6 . . . . 7 . . . . 8 . . . . 9 10

PART B

Speed Building

Here is a chance for you to work on improving your keyboarding speed. On the next page is a speed pyramid. Your goal is to begin at the top and work your way down. You will be timed on each line. Your teacher will decide which column to use, either 30 seconds or 20 seconds. If 30 seconds is used, your goal is to complete each line **twice** in a minute. If 20 seconds is used, your goal is to complete each line **three times** in a minute.

After 20 or 30 seconds, your teacher will say "Return" to indicate that you should be returning and starting a new line. If you are ahead of your teacher's call, that's fine. But if you are not yet ready to return and start a new line when your teacher says "Return," you are

23-8-1-20   3-1-14   25-15-21   14-15-20

8-15-12-4   20-5-14   13-9-14-21-20-5-19

2-21-20   9-19   12-9-7-8-20   1-19   1

6-5-1-20-8-5-18?   25-15-21-18   2-18-5-1-20-8.

Keying from Script

Key the paragraph below **once.** Then go back and do it again.

Ear piercing dates back to the days of the pyramids. Scientists have found huge golden earrings in the shapes of links and circles inside the tombs. Today gold earrings come in a variety of sizes, shapes, and materials. Most gold jewelry contains at least two other metals. For example, 14-karat gold is 14 parts gold with 10 parts some other metal. "Gold-filled" or "gold-plated" means a layer of gold has been bonded to a metal base.

Keying with Proofreader's Marks

Key the paragraph below exactly as it is shown; *do not make any corrections.* Then print a copy. Correct the errors on the printed copy using proofreader's marks. Then check your marks with your teacher.

Albert schweitzer was born over 100 years ago in the north eastern part of Frence. He ewas taleneted in a numberof areas. As a youngster he was a n accomplished church and concert organist. When he was 30, he felt a special calling and decided to study medicine. After finishing his medical traniing, he gave concerts toraise money for a trip to africa. When he got to Africa, he set up a hospital. At 72 he ewas givne the Nobel Peace prize.

falling behind and need to speed up your keying. The numbers in each column show your keyboarding speed if you finished the line the required number of times. Since this is a speed drill, do not be concerned about how many errors you make.

		30 sec	20 sec
1	They may take the fish down to the lake.	16	24
2	It is major work to make the bike paths firm.	18	27
3	The title for lake land owned by the town is good.	20	30
4	Pay them for the good work they did on our six mantles.	22	33
5	Both girls did rush to box the city ornaments and ship them.	24	36

Composing at the Computer

Your teacher will call on a student to select a letter of the alphabet. Your job is to compose as many words as you can think of that start with that particular letter. You have three minutes to do it. If time permits, repeat the exercise with another letter of the alphabet.

Accuracy Building

Accuracy is really a matter of keying at the proper speed. Below are four sentences that contain mostly *one-hand* words. These kinds of words will slow you down because all letters are struck by the same hand. Your goal is to key each line, **three times** in a row, with 100% accuracy. If you make a mistake, you must start all over from the beginning on that particular line. Can you do it? Let's find out.

1 Are you aware Dave gave Rex a great pumpkin bread?
2 Look at Holly eat fat free onions, milk and bread.
3 Only pupils and staff were eager to start jumping.
4 Data bases keep nouns, verbs, and facts with ease.

Tab Key

The most frequent use of the Tab key is to indent lines at the beginning of a paragraph. Most computer software uses tabs that are preset every five spaces. If your software does not have this feature, your teacher will show you how to set a tab.

Formatting Reports Containing Proofreader Marks

Objectives:
- To improve speed on alphabet keys
- To improve accuracy of numbers
- To key copy with proofreader's marks
- To key copy from script
- To format one-page reports containing proofreader's marks

PART A

Warmup

Key each line **twice.**

1 Forty-six people were hurt by the big forest fire.

2 That tornado touched down for just a brief moment.

3 Let's go for a long walk on the path in the woods.

4 (1) Prepare the food (2) Keep it hot (3) Serve it.

. . . . 1 . . . . 2 . . . . 3 . . . . 4 . . . . 5 . . . . 6 . . . . 7 . . . . 8 . . . . 9 10

PART B

Speed Building

Below are alternate-hand words. Your teacher will time you on each line to determine your speed. After practicing the lines, **three times** each, your teacher will time you again to see if there is any improvement.

1 island eight pen theme theory cornfield chapel big

2 authentic forms their amend panels ancient bushels

3 body blame usual field turkey paid social chairman

. . . . 1 . . . . 2 . . . . 3 . . . . 4 . . . . 5 . . . . 6 . . . . 7 . . . . 8 . . . . 9 10

PART C

Numbers

Take out your decoding sheet. On the next page is another message to key and decode. Be sure you put five spaces between each word.

Look at your keyboard and locate the **Tab** key. It's on the left side of the keyboard close to the **Q** key, so you will use your **A** finger on it. Without striking the key, make the reach now—**A Tab, A Tab, A Tab.** All other fingers should stay in home position.

Now press the Tab key and watch what happens to your cursor. It immediately jumps to the right. Press the Tab key again and the cursor moves another five spaces. Keep doing this and your cursor is soon at the end of the line. That's the purpose of the Tab key. It quickly moves your cursor to a preset position on the screen. This is faster than hitting the Space Bar five times. Let's practice using the Tab key on the lines below. Key each paragraph **once**. If time permits, repeat.

```
[Tab]Use your Tab key to move the cursor quickly to any
position on the screen.
[Tab]The Tab key makes cursor movement so much quicker
than using the Space Bar.
[Tab]Once you learn how to use your Tab key, you will
not want to move the cursor any other way.
```

PART F

Drill Composition

Beginning with this lesson, your class is going to compose its own keyboarding drills. Your teacher will select the best ones for use later in the course. Your first job is to compose alphabetic sentences that could be used for accuracy practice. Each row (or each student) will be assigned a different letter of the alphabet by the teacher. You must then compose a sentence that is at least six words long in which every word, or almost every word, begins with your assigned letter. And your sentence must make sense. Suppose your assigned letter was **P.** You might compose a sentence like this one:

Pete practiced picking peppers and pickles.

When this exercise is finished, your class should have 26 good sentences starting with each letter of the alphabet. For now, concentrate on the letters **A** through **M.**

PART G

Language Arts Mystery

The paragraphs on the next page contain 12 capitalization errors. As you key, try to find all of these errors and correct them. Remember to use the Tab key to indent the first line of each paragraph.

My grandmother had some unusual uses for the herbs she grew in her garden. If you complained of a headache, she ~~instantly~~ made you some thyme tea. She always rinsed her hair with basil. In the fall she would pick sprigs of rosemary and spread them on her clothes to keep moths away during the winter. Grandmother always put a few sprigs by her bed, too. It was supposed to keep bad dreams away. I think it worked; she slept peacefully every night.

Composing and Formatting One-Page Compositions, Stories, and Book Reports

---

Application 68: Book Report

Directions:

Compose and format a one-page book report on a book you have recently read. Follow the same format given in the previous lesson. Name the file Ap68.

Application 69: Short Story

Directions:

Compose and format a one-page story. Follow the same format given in the previous lesson. Can you make your story have a surprise ending? Name the file Ap69.

Application 70: Composition

Directions:

Compose and format a one-page composition on *one* of these topics: (1) My Family Tree. Trace your relatives as far back as you can. Include any interesting points you may know about your family's history. (2) What My Mother [or another relative] Taught Me. Is there some advice you received that proved to be helpful in a particular situation? Describe the situation and the advice. Follow the same format given in the previous lesson. Name the file Ap70.

At the end of the nineteenth century, the frank h. fleer corporation began making Bubble Gum. For over thirty years it was the largest selling penny confectionary item in the world.

early bubble gum was called blibber blubber. It was very sticky and did not hold together well. It made a wet bubble that usually burst and stuck to the face so badly that only hard scrubbing would remove it.

It wasn't until much later that fleer introduced a strong bubble gum with good surface tension and the ability to snap back. It was called dubble bubble gum.

the new product had a dry bubble and was very elastic because it was made of rubberlike tree sap. It made huge, perfect bubbles. Today it is the largest selling brand in the world.

Challenge

Get ready to play Link-up. Your teacher will assign you to a team because this is a relay race. When the game starts, your teacher will write a girl's or boy's name on the chalkboard. You will each key that word on your screen. The next name you key must link up vertically with the last letter of the first name, as shown on the next page. You can use your Space Bar to line up the second word. After you key the second word, you must move to a new computer. Your teacher will tell you in what direction to move—left, right, forward, or back. When you get to your new computer, you must think of the third word, which must link up horizontally (see the next page) with the first letter of the last name, and so on. Keep

Accuracy Building

Below are more alphabetic sentences. Do not move on to the next line until you can key each one **three times** in succession with perfect accuracy.

1 An avid reader develops a vast vocabulary in time.

2 Jobs which are open--writer, power worker, lawyer.

3 Alexa expects extra boxes when she moves to Texas.

4 Peggy yearns to study about the pyramids in Egypt.

5 Liz dazzled us by zapping a pizza pie in the oven.

Numbers

Take out your decoding sheet. Here's another message to key and decode. Be sure you put five spaces between each word.

```
23-8-25        9-19        1        8-5-14
19-9-20-20-9-14-7      15-14        1        6-5-14-3-5
12-9-11-5        1      3-15-9-14?      2-5-3-1-21-19-5
19-8-5        8-1-19        1        8-5-1-4        15-14
15-14-5        19-9-4-5        1-14-4        1        20-1-9-12
15-14        20-8-5        15-20-8-5-18
```

Keying from Script

Key the lines below **once.** Then go back and do all the lines again.

1 Betty writes her thoughts down daily in her diary.

2 They were puzzled about the zebra seen in the zoo.

3 Chicago is known by many people as the Windy City.

Keying with Proofreader's Marks

Key the paragraph on the next page **once,** using wordwrap. Make all the corrections indicated.

linking and moving until you are back to your own computer. The first row to return to their own computers wins. Signify you are finished by raising your hand. When all members on your team have their hands up, your teacher will know your team is done.

Example:

```
              Martha
                   l
                   i
                   c
              eleanor
                       i
                       t
                       a
```

Introducing Caps Lock

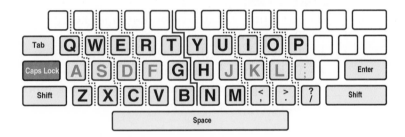

Objectives:

- To develop keyboarding speed and accuracy
- To compose at the computer
- To learn the location of the **Caps Lock** key
- To review language arts principles

PART A

Warmup

Key each paragraph on the next page **twice**. Use your Tab key to indent the first line of each paragraph.

the right kind of puppies. My dad made a phone call.
This was it!

   We piled into the car and drove off. My dad had
to backtrack a few times because we got lost on the
country roads. Finally we arrived at the house. In
the kitchen was the mother Lab with her squiggly
little pups. My dad looked them over and told me to
pick one. I didn't know which one to take. But then
my problem was solved. I bent down and one pup
crawled up into my arms and licked my face. He picked
me!

LESSON 63

Composing One-Page Reports

Objectives:
- To improve accuracy on alphabet keys
- To improve accuracy of numbers
- To key copy with proofreader's marks
- To key copy from script
- To compose and format one-page book reports, compositions, and
  stories with a by-line

Warmup

Key each line **twice.**

1 They are now planting tulip bulbs for next spring.
2 Ned made a touchdown at yesterday's football game.
3 Ann is heir to her aunt's fortune; she is wealthy.
4 Multiply 672 times 3; then subtract 48 and add 19.

. . . . 1 . . . . 2 . . . . 3 . . . . 4 . . . . 5 . . . . 6 . . . . 7 . . . . 8 . . . . 9 10

When we learn to keyboard, we will be able to use that skill in all computer applications.

People who can key with accuracy have learned to stroke the keys at the right speed.

`....1....2....3....4....5....6....7....8....9....10`

Speed Building

Here is another speed pyramid. Your goal is to begin at the top and work your way down, as you did in Lesson 21. Your teacher will decide which guide call to use, either 30 seconds or 20 seconds. If 30 seconds is used, your goal is to complete each line **twice** in a minute. If 20 seconds is used, your goal is to complete each line **three times** in a minute. After 20 or 30 seconds have gone by, your teacher will say "Return" to indicate that you should be returning and starting a new line. If you are ahead of your teacher's call, that's fine. But if you are not yet ready to return and start a new line when your teacher says "Return," you are falling behind and need to speed up your keying. The numbers in each column show your keyboarding speed if you finished the line the required number of times. Since this is a speed drill, do not be concerned about how many errors you make.

		30 sec	20 sec
1	The signs by Rich Lake irk my neighbors.	16	24
2	When she works right, they make a big profit.	18	27
3	The tutor works with Jay so he may pass auto shop.	20	30
4	This new year his goal is to visit the chapel six days.	22	33
5	That panel may halt their work if the city pays for the corn.	24	36

Composing at the Computer

Your teacher will read a list of ten words. Your job is to compose the word that has the opposite meaning. You will want to listen very carefully because your teacher will only read the word **once**. When finished, your teacher will read the word again and the entire class will read its list from the screen.

brought our world back to normal again.

     I'll never forget that weekend. It was one of the _____ weekends I've ever had. Now if they would just cancel school on Monday so I can rest up from my adventure!

Application 67: Picking a Puppy

Directions:
- 1-inch side and bottom margins
- 1.5-inch top margin
- Wordwrap
- Center the title and by-line; two double spaces after by-line
- Double space
- File name: Ap67

PICKING OUT A PUPPY

By [Your Name]

     I was very excited when my parents said I could have a puppy. I have been asking them for a dog since kindergarten and now they have finally given in.

     My parents said they did not want just _any_ dog. It had to be a good dog, one with papers and a fine upbringing. My friend down the street, Leon, had a dog who just had a litter. He offered me one of his puppies free, but my parents turned it down. I couldn't understand that because Leon's dog came with papers--all the newspapers you would ever want. (Leon's dad is in the newspaper business.)

     My folks started looking in the paper under "Animals for Sale." My dad would read the ad to my mother and she would analyze it to see if it was worth making a trip. Finally, they found a breeder who had

(continued on next page)

Accuracy Building

Below are four sentences that contain almost all the letters of the alphabet. Try to key each one with perfect accuracy. If you make a mistake, stop and begin again. When you have finished the first line with 100% accuracy, raise your right hand and then go on to the second line. Raising your hand is a signal to your teacher about the progress you are making. When you have done the second line with 100% accuracy, raise your left hand and go on to the third line. When you have completed the third line, raise both hands. When you have finished the final line, stand up and remain standing until your teacher tells you to sit down. Let's see who can be the first person to complete all lines accurately.

1 Our expert quartet sang very well but failed to win a prize.

2 Jackie expects to give Luke a quartz watch for his birthday.

3 Zachary must excel on the job to get a high raise in salary.

4 Zippy Waltman is afraid his boxed quaint jug may be cracked.

Drill Composition

Continue working on composing your own alphabetic sentences, as you did in Lesson 21. Your teacher will select the best ones for use later in the course. This time concentrate on sentences containing the letters **N** through **Z**.

Caps Lock Key

If you want to key several words in a row in capital letters, there's an easy way to do it. Simply press the **Caps Lock** key. Find it now on your keyboard. When you want to stop keying upper-case letters, just press the same key again and the letters return to lower case. Let's practice that key now. Key the lines below, **twice** each, using the **Caps Lock** key as needed. Stay alert and be sure to make the correct letters in all caps.

1 I tune to news on ABC but Carl and Pearl like CBS.

2 Rudolph reported on SIX YEARS IN THE MALAY JUNGLE.

3 They paid HOW MUCH? Who is going to pay for THAT?

4 When I say NO, I mean it. Was that a NO or a YES?

Application 66: What a Weekend!

Directions:

- 1-inch side and bottom margins
- 2-inch top margin
- Wordwrap
- Center the title and by-line; two double spaces after by-line
- Double space
- Fill in the blanks with your own words
- File name: Ap66

```
WHAT A WEEKEND!
By [Your Name]
     It was the beginning of a long weekend.  No
school for three days.  Great!  I had plans to
_____.  But then something happened
totally unexpectedly.
     My friend _____ came over and asked
me to _____.  I had never done that
before but I am always willing to try new things.  So
my friend and I started _____. Little
did we suspect that _____.
     Next thing I knew the police were there asking
_____.  How was I to know that
_____ was dangerous?  My friend pleaded
innocence from the start.  He _____
but I really didn't believe him and neither did the
police.  They _____.
     Then something strange happened.  We
_____ and then we _____.  Of
course, we tried to _____ but that
didn't work.  So we decided to _____
and that worked just fine.  But something we had not
figured on happened.  It was wild because
_____.  Only _____
```

(continued on next page)

Language Arts Mystery

The paragraphs below contain eight errors in homonyms (words that sound alike but are spelled differently). Read the paragraphs and try to find all of these errors; then as you key, correct the errors. Remember to use the Tab key to indent the first line of each paragraph.

Clarence Birdseye is known as the Father of Frozen Food, but he believed the credit for quick freezing should go two the Eskimos, who had been using it four centuries. Scientists no that as early as the seventeenth century Francis Bacon had the idea of preserving meet by freezing.

Won snowy day he decided too test his theory. He stopped at a house, purchased a foul, killed it, dug a whole, and stuffed the body with snow. The experiment was a success, but Mr. Bacon died shortly after that from a cold he caught while doing the experiment.

Challenge

Key the paragraphs below, placing all rhyming words in capital letters. Use your Shift Lock to accomplish this.

There once was a man, who had a great tan. He sat in the sun, just for the fun. When it got hot, a cold drink he got. Out on the beach he would sit for days trying to catch the rays.

If it rained, he ran into a shack and waited until the sun came back. Then out to the beach he would trek to see how much more tan he could get.

The last time I saw him he looked sad. His skin was red; he looked bad. He had to stay in the sun, but now living with sunburn is no fun.

Application 65: Dr. Wildlife

Directions:

- 1-inch side and bottom margins
- 2-inch top margin
- Wordwrap
- Center the title and by-line; two double spaces after by-line
- Double space
- File name: Ap65

BOOK REPORT

By [Your Name]

The Book

DR. WILDLIFE: THE CRUSADE OF A NORTHWOODS VETERINARIAN by Rory C. Foster, Watts Publishing Company, 1985.

The Author

Dr. Foster is a vet who writes about his real-life adventures in northern Wisconsin. He was forced to retire when he came down with Lou Gehrig's disease, but in retirement wrote another book, I Never Met an Animal I Didn't Like.

The Story

There are really two stories in this book. One tells of Dr. Foster's attempts to set up a wildlife hospital in Wisconsin; the other tells about the many animals he treated.

Their first wildlife patient is a two-day-old fawn who was hit by a car. The doctor puts steel pins in the fawn's broken leg and the animal is kept in the house while the doctor and his wife nurse it back to health. Then the sad day comes when the deer must be returned back to the wild.

Comments

I liked this book very much, though at times it was sad. I cried when Orville, the seagull, had to be put to sleep. I would recommend it to anyone who likes to read about animals.

LESSON 23

Introducing -

Objectives:
- To develop keyboarding speed and accuracy
- To compose at the computer
- To learn the location of the **hyphen (-)** key
- To review language arts principles

Warmup

As you key the paragraphs below, **twice** each, be sure to use the Tab key to indent the first line. At the end of each paragraph press Return/Enter **once.** Try to reach for the Tab key without looking for it.

    When you go fishing at Quail Lake, be sure to
take Pat with you. He wants to learn how to fish.
    If Jammie practices long and hard, she may be
able to get the lead part in the fall school play.
    Be careful when you go into the forest today.
There are some trails on which you could get lost.
. . . . 1 . . . . 2 . . . 3 . . . . 4 . . . . 5 . . . . 6 . . . . 7 . . . . 8 . . . . 9 10

PART B

Speed Building

The sentences on the next page contain short words. Key each line **several times.** Each time you repeat the line, try to stroke faster.

```
23-8-1-20        20-9-13-5        9-19        9-20
23-8-5-14        20-8-5        3-12-15-3-11
19-20-18-9-11-5-19        20-8-9-18-20-5-5-14?
20-9-13-5        20-8-5        3-12-15-3-11        23-1-19
18-5-16-1-9-18-5-4
```

PART D

Keying from Script

Key the lines below **once.** Then go back and do all the lines again.

1 *Rob paid Glen for taking his sister, Lu, with him.*
2 *Daniel can play the oboe and violin and the piano.*
3 *They all eat corn-on-the-cob dripping with butter.*
4 *Stop fooling around with that; start back to work!*

PART E

Keying with Proofreader's Marks

Key the paragraph below **once,** using wordwrap. Make all the corrections indicated as you key.

```
    If you lived before the American revolution, you
would have found some things very different from how
they are now.  There were no shopping centers, no
television sets, no free ways, and no super markets.
Clothing was made at home.  For those who could
afford it, dress makers and tailors were hired.  Most
families grew their own food and traded that food for
other items they needed.
```

PART F

Formatting a One-Page Report

A report that will be read by another person is usually double spaced. Double spacing makes the text easier to read and it allows space for a critical reader, such as your teacher, to make comments. The title is usually placed 1.5 or 2 inches from the top. The side and bottom margins are generally 1 inch. If side headings are included, they may be placed in bold type or underlined. A by-line can be included two spaces below the title. The by-line indicates who wrote the report.

1 If she can cut the big oak tree, I will cheer her.

2 Ship it by air or by bus; they want the boxes now.

3 The bank sold the bonds for cash; they made money.

4 I will pay for the red rug if you can make it fit.

5 Try very hard if you do not want to lose your job.

. . . .1. . . .2. . . .3. . . .4. . . .5. . . .6. . . .7. . . .8. . . .9. . . .10

PART C

Composing at the Computer

How many words can you think of in one minute that have the same endings or beginnings? Let's find out. Your teacher will select from the list below. Compose at the screen all the words you can think of that start or end with those letters.

Word Endings:	ing
	ly
	ed
	tion *or* sion
	ward
	hood

Word Beginnings:	be, for, *or* fore
	in
	ex
	self
	de
	dis *or* des
	re

PART D

Accuracy Building

Below are words beginning with opposite-hand letters. As you key each line **twice,** concentrate on striking the keys with the proper fingers.

1 ru rub rubble rubdown ruby rude rulers ruff rumble

2 ur urn urban urchins uranium Uranus urgent urgency

3 al also almost almond almanac alike alphabet altar

4 la lamp lament lantern lark lard latch laundry lap

5 directly display diamonds ditches dice discord die

6 idols ideal ideas ideally idolizes idle identifies

. . . .1. . . .2. . . .3. . . .4. . . .5. . . .6. . . .7. . . .8. . . .9. . . .10

Formatting One-Page Reports

Objectives:

- To improve speed on alphabet keys
- To improve accuracy of numbers
- To key copy with proofreader's marks
- To key copy from script
- To learn how to format one-page reports with a by-line

PART A

Warmup

Key each line **twice.**

1 The hot children decided to make a lemonade stand.

2 Bob and Joe are planning to join the bowling team.

3 Do not blame her if this operation gets backed up.

4 (1) Eat your food (2) Sleep 8-9 hours every night.

`. . . .1. . . .2. . . .3. . . .4. . . .5. . . .6. . . .7. . . .8. . . .9. . . .10`

PART B

Speed Building

Below are alternate-hand words. Your teacher will time you on each line to determine your speed. After practicing the lines, **three times** each, your teacher will time you again to see if there is any improvement.

1 chap town duck sign amend their lamb soap roam own

2 firm girl kept rich busy then eight when firms wit

3 fork city also lake lend melt nape title key bowls

4 ambush handle island profit enrich signals formals

`. . . .1. . . .2. . . .3. . . .4. . . .5. . . .6. . . .7. . . .8. . . .9. . . .10`

PART C

Numbers

Take out your decoding sheet. On the next page is another message to key and decode. Be sure you put five spaces between each word.

Drill Composition

In the time allotted by your teacher, compose as many words as you can think of that contain double letters.
Example:

```
letter, better, common, session, committee
```

Key

The hyphen key is used to hyphenate words and to make a dash. It is an important key, so let's learn it right now. Look at your keyboard and locate the **hyphen.** It's on the top row and you will use your sem finger to operate it. Place your hands in home position. Try it now. Key **;-** several times as you watch your finger make the reach. Be sure to keep your **J, K,** and **L** fingers at home. Now try the lines below, **twice** each. See if you can key them without looking at your hands.

```
1 ;-; -;; ;-; -;; ;-; -;; ;-; -;; ;-; -;;
2 ;;; --- ;;; --- ;;; --- ;;; --- ;;; ---
```

Here is a rule to learn and remember: When a word is hyphenated, one hyphen [-] is used without any spaces.
Example:

```
first-class mail
```

When a dash is used, two hyphens [--] are used without any spaces.
Example:

```
She stopped--knowing he was following her--and
crossed the street.
```

Now key the lines below, **twice** each.

```
3 self-paced home-made first-class one-hand two-tone
4 I joined the anti-cruelty society--free of charge.
5 Joe is a self-made man.  Ship by first-class mail.
6 You may take the sofa--not the table--when you go.
```

Priority Mail

Priority mail is zone rated first-class mail weighing more than 12 ounces. It is used when fast transportation and handling are desired. The maximum weight for priority mail is 70 pounds and the maximum size is 108 inches in length and width combined. When using this service, be sure to mark the package **Priority Mail** in large letters on all sides to ensure proper handling.

E-COM Service

E-COM stands for Electronic Computer Originated Mail. This service offers nationwide delivery within two days or less of messages composed on a computer. Messages are sent via telephone lines. There is a minimum of 200 messages per transmission.

Second-Class Mail

This service is used by newspaper and magazine publishers who mail large quantities. Second-class material must be published regularly at least four times a year. It must be reproduced by a printing process, and cannot be designed mainly for advertising purposes. Also, second-class material must have a list of paid subscribers.

Third-Class Mail

This service is used most often for large mailings of printed materials and merchandise parcels that weigh less than one pound. There are two rate structures for this class—single piece and bulk rate. Many organizations and businesses find it economical to use this service. Also, individuals may use third-class mail for sending parcels weighing under one pound.

Fourth-Class Mail

This service is also called *parcel post*. It is for packages weighing one pound or more that do not require priority treatment. The maximum weight for parcel post is 70 pounds, and the maximum size is 108 inches in length and width combined.

The paragraphs below contain four errors in verbs. Read the paragraphs and try to find all of these errors; then as you key, correct the errors. Remember to use the Tab key to indent the first line of each paragraph.

Pretzel bakers has their own coat of arms. To find out how this came about, one must look back in history. In the sixteenth century the Turks begun invading Europe but they was stopped at the wall of Vienna and could not break through. When their attacks failed, they decided to dig tunnels under the wall. To escape detection, they would do all digging at night.

The pretzel bakers also worked at night. From their basement bakeries they heard the digging and spread the word that the enemy was underground. Pretzel bakers were honored for their discovery with a coat of arms displaying a pretzel, which are still the emblem of pretzel bakers today.

Composing and Formatting Outlines

Application 62: Holiday Celebrations

Directions:

Compose and arrange an outline titled "Holiday Celebrations." Include in your outline the major holidays your family celebrates, how your family celebrates them, and what special traditions or customs are observed. Name the file Ap62.

Application 63: Word Processing Functions

Directions:

Compose and arrange an outline titled "Word Processing Functions." You may want to print out your Journal file, if you have not already done so, and use it as a reference for constructing this outline. Name the file Ap63.

Application 64: Mail Services

Directions:

Read the following information about the U.S. Postal Service. Then compose and arrange an outline titled "Mail Services." Name the file Ap64.

Express Mail Service

This is our fastest service for customers who want overnight delivery of letters or packages. To use this service, take your shipment to any Express Mail center by 5:00 p.m. Your mail will be delivered by 3:00 p.m. the next day or it can be picked up at a post office as early as 10:00 a.m. the next business day. Shipments are insured against loss or damage at no additional cost.

First-Class Mail

This service is used for such things as postal cards, greeting cards, personal notes, letters, and for sending checks and money orders. First-class mail may not be opened for postal inspection. First-class mail over 12 ounces is called Priority Mail. All first-class mail is given fast transportation. If your first-class mail is not letter size, make sure it is marked **First Class.**

(continued on next page)

Challenge

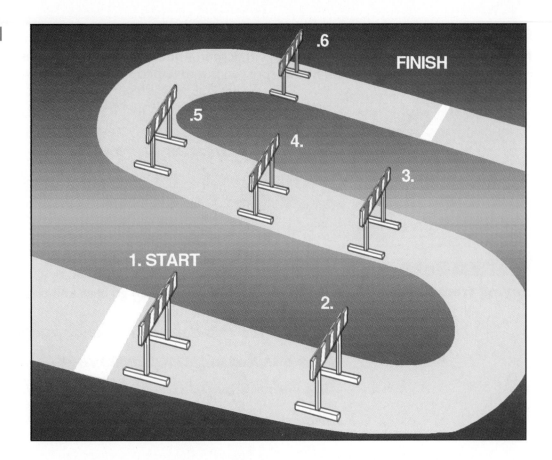

Find a partner. You and your partner are going to race each other in an obstacle race. Look at the track shown above. Your goal is to jump the hurdles by keying each line below accurately. When your teacher tells you to begin, start with line one. If you make a mistake when keying, press the Return/Enter key and begin that line again. You may only advance on the track if the line corresponding to the hurdle is keyed with 100% accuracy.

Hurdle One

Balanced-hand words are easier to key than others.

Hurdle Two

One-digit numbers are quicker than two-digit ones.

Hurdle Three

Their show--not hers--received a four-star rating.

Numbers

Take out your decoding sheet. Here's another message to key and decode. Be sure you put five spaces between each word.

23-8-1-20   9-19   20-8-5

4-9-6-6-5-18-5-14-3-5   2-5-20-23-5-5-14   1-14

15-12-4   4-9-13-5   1-14-4   1   14-5-23

16-5-14-14-25?   14-9-14-5   3-5-14-20-19

Keying from Script

Key the lines below **once.** Then go back and do all the lines again.

1 *Dixie works her dog in the field; Jackie does not.*

2 *Wayne threw his dirty socks into the wash machine.*

3 *This color is an unusual blend of violet and blue.*

4 *What a shame that she spilled red ink on the gown.*

Keying with Proofreader's Marks

Key the paragraph below **once,** using wordwrap. Make all the corrections indicated.

Herbs have a long histoy of use. Doctors brewed them to cure their patients. Ladies of the Court bathed in them and perfumed their spaniels with them. The Queen of sheba made a gift of herbs to king Solomon. The Red emperor of China ate them daily because he believed herbs helped one live longer. Perhaps there is some truth to that. He lived to be 123.

Hurdle Four

The first-class rate is expensive--but why ask me?

Hurdle Five

Her self-evaluation matches yours--can you fix it?

Hurdle Six

Buy a two-unit town house and SAVE start-up costs.

Introducing '

Objectives:

- To develop keyboarding speed and accuracy
- To compose at the computer
- To learn the location of the **apostrophe (')** key
- To review language arts principles

PART A

Warmup

Key each line **twice.** Try to key the lines without pausing between words.

1 self-made; self-defense; hand-made; self-propelled

2 Walt did a self-evaluation; he is a self-made man.

3 Barb shops at end-of-the-year sales for her goods.

4 Act today--do not wait--or you may be out of luck.

. . . . 1 . . . . 2 . . . . 3 . . . . 4 . . . . 5 . . . . 6 . . . . 7 . . . . 8 . . . . 9 10

Composing Outlines

Objectives:
- To improve accuracy on alphabet keys
- To improve accuracy of numbers
- To key copy with proofreader's marks
- To key copy from script
- To compose and format outlines

Warmup

Key each line **twice.**

1 Do not risk signing the contract without a lawyer.
2 Be sure to put a cork and label on the tomato jar.
3 Alan is handy at fixing things, but Nathan is not.
4 This panel has 7 members; but the committee has 8.

....1....2....3....4....5....6....7....8....9....10

Accuracy Building

Below are more alphabetic sentences. Do not move on to the next line until you can key each one **three times** in succession with perfect accuracy.

1 Without question the earthquake came very quickly.
2 School reforms require reading, writing, and math.
3 Seth succeeds by studying a subject outside class.
4 Take time to tell the terrible, true facts to him.
5 The use of unusual words is undoubtedly overrated.

Speed Building

Here are some more lines containing short words. Key each line **several times.** Each time you repeat the line, try to stroke faster.

1 I should be able to come to your new house by six.
2 They have many folks to thank for their rich life.
3 My very best book is lost; I hope to find it soon.
4 Do take a copy with you so all may see what it is.
5 Her much used desk must go, for his room is small.

. . . .1. . . .2. . . .3. . . .4. . . .5. . . .6. . . .7. . . .8. . . .9. . . .10

Composing at the Computer

Can you think alphabetically? Let's find out. Your job is to compose, within three minutes' time, an alphabetical list. Your teacher will tell you which of the items listed below will be your first list. You cannot skip any letter of the alphabet. Be sure to type accurately, because your teacher may ask you to read your list to the class. Of course, you will want to capitalize the first letter of each name.

Alphabetical list of
(a) girls' names (Alice, Betty, Carol, etc.)
(b) boys' names (Alan, Bob, Carl, etc.)
(c) grocery store shopping list (apples, bananas, catsup, etc.)
(d) cities of the world (Alexandria, Berlin, Chicago, etc.)

Accuracy Building

Here are some more lines containing one-hand words. Your goal is to key each line **three times** in succession with 100% accuracy. If you make a mistake, you must start all over from the beginning on that particular line. Can you do it? Let's find out.

1 saw lull pop him rare red gate sat bad bed art was
2 case pin extra were rare street brew cave vast red
3 bazaar knoll pink jump junk seats tests bare draft
4 John Jim Lynn Rex Polly Molly Lilly Lyon Milo July
5 minimum pumpkin decreased savages desserts gazette

. . . .1. . . .2. . . .3. . . .4. . . .5. . . .6. . . .7. . . .8. . . .9. . . .10

Application 61: Reading Skills

Directions:

- 2-inch top margin
- 1-inch side margins
- Center the title; return four times after it
- Single space; double space before and after each Roman numeral heading
- File name: Ap61

READING SKILLS

I. Reading for Speed

A. Pass eyes rapidly over line

B. Look for groups of words rather than single words

C. Do not use pencil to lead your eyes

D. Do not vocalize the words

II. Reading for Meaning

A. Concentrate

B. Look at chapter titles, headlines, subheadings for clues about subject matter

C. Find topic sentences in each paragraph

    1. Look for what is significant in paragraph

    2. Topic sentence can appear anywhere in paragraph

D. Question what you read

III.Reading to Remember

A. Look for the theme or main idea

B. Read the summary or conclusion first to get idea of how the parts fit into the theme

Drill Composition

How many words can you think of that contain letters struck by your "weak" fingers—**P** on the right hand and **A, Q,** and **Z** on the left hand? Practicing these words will help strengthen those weak fingers. Let's see who can come up with the longest list on your screen in the time allowed by your teacher.

' Key

Look at your keyboard and locate the **apostrophe** key. It is right next to the semicolon key, so you will use your sem finger to operate it. Try it now. Place your hands in home position and key ;' several times. Easy, isn't it? Now key the lines below, **twice** each. Try to make the reach without looking at the new key.

```
1 ;'; ';; ;'; ';; ;'; ';; ;'; ';; ;'; ';;
2 ;;; ''' ;;; ''' ;;; ''' ;;; ''' ;;; '''
```

Now key the lines below, **twice** each. Note there is no space before or after the apostrophe. Remember, keep your eyes on the book.

```
3 men's women's city's state's newspaper's
4 Al's Minnie's Grace's Rick's Lee's Joe's
5 I'll bring Sue's box if he'll just wait.
```

Language Arts Mystery

The paragraphs below contain three run-on sentences. Read the paragraphs and try to find all of these errors; then as you key, correct the errors. Remember to use the Tab key to indent the first line of each paragraph.

```
      Have you ever been to a button museum?  There
actually is such a place in Connecticut, people who
collect buttons do so for a number of reasons.  Some
are attracted to buttons for their variety, others
just want to build the biggest collection they can.
      Still others specialize in a period of button
history.  During the Civil War soldiers would have a
```

(continued on next page)

Application 60: History of Computers

Directions:

- 2-inch top margin
- 1-inch side margins
- Center the title; return four times after it
- Single space; double space where indicated
- Align Roman numerals
- File name: Ap60

HISTORY OF FIRST-GENERATION COMPUTERS

I.   Charles Babbage

    A.   Father of Computing

    B.   Designed Analytical Engine

    C.   1834

        1.   Never completed

        2.   Incorporated ideas behind modern computers

II. Herman Hollerith

    A.   Designed sorting and tabulating machine that processed data from punched cards

    B.   Machine used to process data for 1890 census

    C.   Formed his own company--IBM

III. ENIAC

    A.   First electronic digital computer

    B.   1940

    C.   Weighed 30 tons and took up whole room

    D.   Programmed by setting 6,000 switches

IV. UNIVAC

    A.   Program stored inside computer

    B.   1951

loved one sit for a photographer. Then the print was made into a button that was sewed onto the soldier's uniform.

If you are serious about collecting buttons, be ready to spend some money. A tiny button showing a Currier and Ives drawing known as Skating in Central Park sells for five hundred dollars today, a button known to have been made especially for guests at George Washington's inaugural sells for over a thousand. Trading in tiny objects requires big money.

Challenge

How good is your endurance? We can find out by going back to Part D, Accuracy Building. Your teacher will time you for 30 seconds on each line. Figure your speed by using the scale and multiplying the number of words by two. Then take a 60-second timing on the same line and compute your speed. Your goal is to type at the same speed for 60 seconds as you did for 30 seconds. Can you do this on each of the lines?

LESSON
25

Introducing /

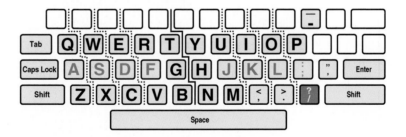

Objectives:
- To develop keyboarding speed and accuracy
- To compose at the computer
- To learn the location of the **diagonal (/)** key
- To review language arts principles

Application 59: Outlining

Directions:
- 1-inch side margins
- 2-inch top margin
- Double space
- Center the title; double space twice after the title
- File name: Ap59

```
                              TITLE

        I.    Tab to Get to Here

              A.    Indent at this point

              B.    Indent at this point

       II.    Use Margin Release to Line up Roman Numerals

              A.    Indent at this point

              B.    Indent at this point

                    1.    Tab twice and then indent at this point

                    2.    Tab twice and then indent at this point

      III.    Use Margin Release to Line up Roman Numerals

              A.    Indent at this point

              B.    Indent at this point
```

Warmup

Key each line **twice.** Try to key the lines without pausing between words.

1 Lu's old clothes were donated to the Women's Club.
2 Children's toys may be bought from Johnson's, Inc.
3 They're going to buy the boy's camping gear today.
4 I'll go--if you want me to--but not in John's car.
....1....2....3....4....5....6....7....8....9....10

Speed Building

Below are a number of speed paragraphs. Begin with the first paragraph and key for one minute. If you finish the paragraph within that time, move on to the next one. If you do not finish the paragraph, stay on that one until you can complete it within one minute. Your goal is to keep moving on to a different paragraph each minute.

20 words

Karen will try to get tickets for the game on Wednesday. If she is free, we will ride with her.

21 words

Joseph may buy a new desk for his den. He is shopping for antique oak desks which he could then redo.

22 words

The store where Kay works may have to cut her pay soon. If that happens, she might have to move away soon.

23 words

Dan plans to take the train on his next trip. Molly wants to fly but is afraid to go by airplane all by herself.

Keying from Script

Key the lines below **once.** Then go back and do all the lines again.

1 My friends and I plan to travel seven miles a day.
2 She finds it difficult to function when it is hot.
3 What we need is a soothing walk through the pines.
4 Her bubble gum may stick to the roof of her mouth.

Keying with Proofreader's Marks

Key the paragraph below **once,** using wordwrap. Make all the changes indicated as you key.

Today computers are replacing time-consuming tasks that once were performed by people. However, people are still needed to program the computers, for a computer is only as good as the information that is feed into it. Computers are also very useful for teaching. Unlike a teacher, they never get tired of repeating the same thing, and they have tremendous patience!

Formatting an Outline

Outlines are one way of organizing information. When doing an outline, consistency is important. Spacing between outline parts may be single or double, but should be consistent throughout. If you begin with complete sentences, then you must use complete sentences throughout. Or, if you begin with phrases, you must continue using phrases throughout. Also, each part of an outline must have at least two sections; thus if you have a Roman numeral I you must have a II, and if you have an *A,* you must have a *B,* etc.

When keying outlines, begin the Roman numerals at the left margin. Tab once to get to the position for A and B. Then use the left indent command and wordwrap. To line up the Roman numeral II under I, you must use the margin release command for your software. Your teacher will explain how to do this.

24 words

Next time you go down to the lake, please get a few greens from the market. Jill and Megan want greens to make soup.

25 words

The meeting for our church club is to be held at my house. Alice and Kevin will need to prepare snacks and bring them in.

26 words

I will check my mail to see if your check has arrived. If it has not, you must write me another check before I ship the goods.

27 words

Mary has been asked to do a report for school on the topic of tornados. Where do you think Mary can find information on this topic?

28 words

It is a good idea to read something every day to stay informed about what is happening. Mallory reads a news magazine almost every week.

29 words

Plan to meet at the mall tomorrow to shop for a new dress for the spring dance. After shopping, come to Al's house to listen to the new band.

30 words

The storm we had last week caused much damage to our house. Dad is going to try to fix it if he can do it, but mom says he should not do it today.

Formatting Outlines

Objectives:
- To improve speed on alphabet keys
- To improve accuracy of numbers
- To key copy with proofreader's marks
- To key copy from script
- To learn how to format outlines

LESSON 60

PART A
Warmup

Key each line **twice.**

1 I sent that letter certified mail but it was lost.
2 His favorite vegetables are spinach and wax beans.
3 If the plans do not work out, call us immediately.
4 Be sure to come by 6:00 p.m.; the play is at 7:30.
    . . . . 1 . . . . 2 . . . . 3 . . . . 4 . . . . 5 . . . . 6 . . . . 7 . . . . 8 . . . . 9 10

PART B
Speed Building

Below are alternate-hand names. Key each line **three times** in succession. As you repeat the line, try to stroke faster.

1 Jay Rob Gil Duke Nan Pam Rod Diane Mel Hal Viv Pat
2 Henry Bob Vivian Helen Rodney Blanche Nancie Duane
3 Sidney Burlan Glen Kay Pamela Rickey Tod Dick Jane
    . . . . 1 . . . . 2 . . . . 3 . . . . 4 . . . . 5 . . . . 6 . . . . 7 . . . . 8 . . . . 9 10

PART C
Numbers

Take out your decoding sheet. Here's another message to key and decode. Be sure you put five spaces between each word.

23-8-1-20   8-1-19   14-5-9-20-8-5-18
6-12-5-19-8   14-15-18   2-15-14-5   1-14-4
8-1-19   6-15-21-18   6-9-14-7-5-18-19
1-14-4   1   20-8-21-13-2?   1   7-12-15-22-5

Composing at the Computer

Below are some words for you to rhyme with other words. Your teacher will pick a word from this list. Then you will have one minute to key as many words as you can that rhyme with that particular word. Key carefully, for your teacher may ask you to read your answers to the class.

glad	gear
late	jam
bee	sing
night	hat
say	man

Accuracy Building

Below are four sentences that contain most letters of the alphabet. Try to key each one with perfect accuracy. If you make a mistake, stop and begin again. When you have finished the first line with 100% accuracy, raise your right hand and then go on to the second line. Raising your hand is a signal to your teacher about the progress you are making. When you have done the second line with 100% accuracy, raise your left hand and go on to the third line. When you have completed the third line, raise both hands. When you have finished the final line, stand up and remain standing until your teacher tells you to sit down. Let's see who will be the first person to stand.

1 The prized quick hog owned by Melvin was judged at the fair.

2 Quint was vexed when his lazy cat Bufkim perched on his car.

3 A quiet trapeze show viewed by large crowds jammed the road.

4 Vinton Prime analyzed taxes to justify his loss of benefits.

Drill Composition

How many good sentences can you compose that contain hyphenated words? Remember, hyphenated words are usually used as an adjective that comes before a noun.
    Example: first-class mail (first-class is the adjective; mail is the noun)
    Be sure your sentences use the hyphenated words correctly.

/ Key

Locate the **diagonal** key on your keyboard. There it is, down at the bottom right-hand corner. Because it's just below the semicolon key, you will use your sem finger on it. Try it now. Place your hands on home row

Composing and Formatting on Your Own

Application 56: Recycling Center Letter

Directions:

Compose and format a personal letter to The County Recycling Center, 129 N. Hammond Avenue, [Your City, State, Zip Code]. Use *Ladies and Gentlemen* for the salutation. Explain you are working on a report on recycling and ask them to send you any free materials they have on the topic. You specifically need to know what can be recycled in your area and what cannot. Be sure you sign the letter. Name the file Ap56.

Application 57: Candy Company Letter

Directions:

Compose and format a personal letter to the Crowcroft Candy Company, 459 W. Madison Street, Chicago, IL 60641. Use *Ladies and Gentlemen* as the salutation. Explain you purchased a chocolate Crow Bar from a vending machine and upon biting into it you found a worm. You were so disgusted you threw the whole thing in the garbage can so you do not have a wrapper to send them as proof of purchase. Ask for a refund. Name the file Ap57.

Application 58: "Dear Abby" Letter

Directions:

Compose and format a personal letter to an advice columnist such as "Dear Abby." Address the letter to a local newspaper. Ask for help or advice on a real or imaginary problem. Sign the letter with a pen name such as "Lonely," "Unhappy," "Upset," etc., and your real address. Your teacher may collect your letter and give it to another student to answer. Name the file Ap58.

and key **;/** several times. Now try the lines below. Be sure to keep your **J, K,** and **L** fingers at home when reaching for the diagonal.

1 ;/; /;; ;/; /;; ;/; /;; ;/; /;; ;/; /;;
2 ;;; /// ;;; /// ;;; /// ;;; /// ;;; ///

Now try these lines, **twice** each. As you key, keep your eyes on the copy. Note there is no space before or after the diagonal.

3 The on/off switch on the television set is broken.
4 It was stop/go traffic all the way to the airport.
5 Answer forms with N/A if something does not apply.

Language Arts Mystery

The paragraphs below contain five parenthetical expressions that are incorrectly punctuated. Read the paragraphs and try to find all of these errors; then as you key, correct the errors. Remember to use the Tab key to indent the first line of each paragraph.

Perhaps you have been to a circus and watched someone swallow a sword, and you may have wondered how it was done. Actually there are three different ways this feat can be accomplished. Two methods however are fake; only one is real.

For example one fake method is to insert a tube along the neck and chest under the performer's clothes with an opening near the mouth usually concealed by a fake beard.

Another fake method is to use a sword that retracts when pressure is put on the tip. On the other hand the real sword swallowers actually do swallow the sword, which is carefully measured to extend to the base of the stomach but no farther. Of course the sword swallower must not eat anything before the performance.

Numbers

Take out your decoding sheet. Here's another message to key and decode. Be sure you put five spaces between each word.

20-15   23-8-1-20   13-1-14   4-15   13-5-14

1-12-23-1-25-19   20-1-11-5   20-8-5-9-18

8-1-20-19   15-6-6?   20-8-5   2-1-18-2-5-18

Keying from Script

Sometimes you may not have a computer available for your composing and you may have to compose in handwriting and later key it on the computer. Let's practice that now. Key the lines below **once.** Then go back and do all the lines again.

1 *Di is moving across the country; we will miss her.*
2 *The severe summer storm was indeed a big surprise.*
3 *Act now, and you can get a free copy of this book.*
4 *My dog, Bingo, is going to have puppies very soon.*

Keying with Proofreader's Marks

Key the paragraph below **once,** using wordwrap. Make all the changes indicated.

Sally went to see Dr. Clark about the pain in her leg. He sent her to the Bayside medical clinic. They took x-rays but could find nothing wrong with her leg and so they sent her back home. Sally plans to see 2 more doctors to make sure her leg is okay.

Challenge

Remember the hurdles you tried to jump in Lesson 23? You are going to try that again but with a slightly different twist. Turn to Lesson 23, Part H, page 99. This time you are to work alone, not with a partner. Your goal is to jump the hurdles by keying each line accurately. However, if you make a mistake, you must press the Return/Enter key and start all over again with hurdle number one. To win this race you must have keyed all six lines accurately in succession.

LESSON 26

Introducing :

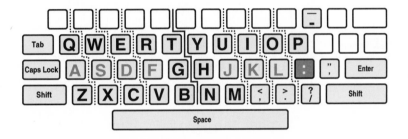

Objectives:
- To develop keyboarding speed and accuracy
- To compose at the computer
- To learn the location of the **colon (:)** key
- To review language arts principles

Warmup

Key each line **twice.** Try to key the lines without pausing between words.

1 Answer all my questions wisely with yes/no or N/A.

2 Make sure you use only he/she in your composition.

3 Take the finished project and material to him/her.

4 Is the current a/c or d/c? I may need an adaptor.

. . . . 1 . . . . 2 . . . . 3 . . . . 4 . . . . 5 . . . . 6 . . . . 7 . . . . 8 . . . . 9 10

Composing Personal Business Letters

Objectives:

- To improve accuracy on alphabet keys
- To improve accuracy of numbers
- To key copy with proofreader's marks
- To key copy from script
- To compose and format personal business letters

PART A

Warmup

Key each line **twice.**

1 Marcella needs to find some references on climate.
2 Check the Table of Contents and Index for a topic.
3 On vacation their family rents a large yellow van.
4 Lu's zip code is 60341; her phone No. is 788-0901.

. . . . 1 . . . . 2 . . . . 3 . . . . 4 . . . . 5 . . . . 6 . . . . 7 . . . . 8 . . . . 9 10

PART B

Accuracy Building

Below are more alphabetic sentences. Do not move on to the next line until you can key each one three times in succession with perfect accuracy.

1 Ms. Mary Mertz maintains monthly marketing charts.
2 No nanny caring for children can be too demanding.
3 Owning one's own business is an option open to me.
4 All products that appeal are priced appropriately.

Speed Building

Here are more speed paragraphs to key within one minute. If you did not finish the 30-word paragraph in Lesson 25, turn to page 105 and start from where you left off. If you did finish the 30-word paragraph, begin with the first paragraph below. Your goal is to complete the paragraph in one minute, as your teacher times you, and progress to the next one.

31 words

Tom has worked many different jobs during the summer vacation. This year he hopes to make a lot of money so he can travel to Montana. This is his goal.

32 words

Mary is a good leader. She knows how to meet the needs of the people who work under her. It is important to have everyone feel they are part of a good team.

33 words

Alfred is scared of high buildings. Whenever he goes to New York, he avoids looking at the tall buildings because it makes him dizzy. Alfred just takes medicine.

34 words

Patricia will try out for the foot races that will be held during the town picnic. She hopes to win a medal or at least a prize for her endeavors. Go, team; yeah team.

35 words

Carl wants to be a doctor or a lawyer when he grows up. Sue thinks it would be fun to be a meat cutter. Willy wants to become a forest ranger and put out big forest fires.

Application 55: Veterinarian Letter

Directions:

- 1-inch side margin
- Use the current date
- Begin the date 1.5 inches from the top
- Wordwrap
- See Appendix D for a list of two-letter state abbreviations
- Single space; double space between paragraphs
- Sign the letter in the appropriate space
- File name: Ap55

Mr. Robert Cortez, D.V.M.

2239 W. Ogden Avenue

[Your City, State, Zip Code]

Dear Dr. Cortez My school has a Career Day on the last Friday of every month. On that day we invite people with different careers to come and talk about their jobs. Could you come some Friday afternoon? Any time between 1:00 and 3:00 p.m. would be fine.

[New paragraph] Students who bring in a career speaker get extra credit, so I hope you will be able to come and talk about what it's like to be a vet. Please call me at 355-8921 if you can make it. By the way, my dog, Buster, is doing just fine after that shot you gave him. Cordially [Your Name] [Your Street] [Your City, State, Zip Code]

36 words

Karen does not like to take tests. They make her nervous. Her brother, Joe, does well on tests but he has trouble with book reports. He does not have time for writing reports.

37 words

Some students have trouble listening. Others find it a problem to write. Still others may have a problem with reading for meaning. Only practice will help to improve needed skills.

38 words

Lulu is planning to give a speech in her next class; her topic is about cake making. Lulu plans to demonstrate how to frost fancy cakes. She will bring a cake and frosting to class Tues.

39 words

John likes to play video games. Sometimes he wins and other times he does not. Mattie likes to listen to music. Marty is studying the violin and Jose likes to play the piano. All play well.

40 words

If you want to be a success, there are traits you should acquire. The first is loyalty; another is to become organized. A third is have a will to keep learning; attitude is a fourth consideration.

Application 54: Park District Letter

Directions:

- 1-inch side margins
- Use the current date
- Begin the date 1.5 inches from the top
- Wordwrap
- Single space; double space between paragraphs
- Sign the letter in the appropriate space
- See Appendix D for a list of two-letter state abbreviations
- File name: Ap54

Centerville Park District

567 W. Jefferson St.

[Your City, State, Zip]

Ladies and Gentlemen

My friends and I often play basketball on the court at Burr Oak Park, but lately it is becoming very difficult to play there because of all the broken glass on the court.

[New paragraph] Playing with broken glass beneath your feet is dangerous. Yesterday I fell and cut myself. A few times my friends and I brought brooms from home and swept up the glass, but it seems to keep coming back.

[New paragraph] My friends and I would appreciate anything you can do to clean it up. The rest of the park seems to be okay. Since this is the park closest to my house, I think of it as my own and would like to make it a safe place to play.

Sincerely

[Your Name]

[Your Street]

[Your City, State, Zip Code]

Composing at the Computer

Perhaps you have played the game Categories while riding in the car during a long trip or while waiting at the airport for a plane to depart. You are going to play it now using your computer. Below are some possible categories. Your teacher will select one of them, or add others, for you to work on. You have three minutes to compose as many words as you can think of that fit in that particular category. For example, if the category is "insects," you might key such words as spider, ant, butterfly, and so on. In this game, the person with the longest list wins.

Categories: names of cars, articles of furniture, names of rivers, colors, animals, girls or boys' names, pets, cities, states, countries, names of athletic teams, sporting events, careers or occupations

PART D

Accuracy Building

Below are words beginning with opposite-hand letters. As you key each line **twice,** concentrate on striking the keys with the proper fingers.

1 or order origins oriented oranges ornate
2 ro rock rocket rodent road roller robust
3 orders ordeals orbits ordained or oracle
4 row robots rotten rods rodent robust rob
5 payable paid paces patches patty partial
6 apply apples application aptly apartment

PART E

Drill Composition

Compose as many sentences as you can think of that have apostrophes used in contractions or to show possession. Can you get at least ten good sentences?

PART F

 Key

Can you locate the **colon** key? Yes, it's the shift of the semicolon. Place your hands on home position and try it now. Key ;: several times. Easy, isn't it? Let's try the lines below.

1 ;:; :;; ;:; :;; ;:; :;; ;:; :;; ;:; :;;
2 ;;; ::: ;;; ::: ;;; ::: ;;; ::: ;;; :::

Directions:
- 1-inch side margins
- Use the current date
- Begin the date 1.5 inches from the top
- Wordwrap
- Single space; double space between paragraphs
- Sign the letter in the appropriate space
- File name: Ap53
- Space parts as indicated

Current Date
↓4   *[date line]*

Public Affairs Office
State of Illinois   *[inside address]*
Capital Building
Springfield, IL 62703
↓2
Ladies and Gentlemen   *[salutation]*
↓2
I am doing a report on the history of Illinois. Please send me
any brochures or pamphlets you have available that would help me
with this report. ↓2

Also, do you have any maps showing the places that have   *[body]*
historical significance? I am particularly interested in "Abe
Lincoln country."
↓2
Any information you can send me will be very much appreciated.
↓2
Sincerely

Your Name ↓4

Your Name   *[complimentary closing]*
Your Street Address
Your City, State, Zip Code   *[sender's name and address]*

Now key these lines, **twice** each. After you reach for the shift key, be sure to bring that finger back home. Note that two spaces follow a colon.

3 You are asked to bring: pies and cakes.

4 For example: Use s to indicate plurals.

5 The question is: Is that proper for us?

Language Arts Mystery

The paragraphs below contain three errors in the use of who's/whose and it's/its. Read the paragraphs and try to find all of these errors; then as you key, correct the errors. Remember to use the Tab key to indent the first line of each paragraph.

The next time you eat in a restaurant, take a good look at the menu. Today's restaurant offers more items than the best of restaurants did just a few centuries ago.

The first restaurants were taverns who's menu consisted of just one dish and whose customers were men looking for a place to meet. In England coffee houses replaced the taverns. The coffee house served coffee, tea, and chocolate but also provided hot meals. Another attraction was it's supply of magazines kept on hand for its customers.

Credit for the first real restaurant goes to a Frenchman named Boulanger who's shop offered diners a choice of dishes rather than one meal of the day. He put a sign above his door that read "restaurants," meaning restoratives. Its restoratives were the soup and hot broth available inside.

PART C

Numbers

Take out your decoding sheet. Here's another message to key and decode. Be sure you put five spaces between each word.

23-8-5-18-5   1-18-5   8-1-16-16-9-14-5-19-19

1-14-4   10-15-25   1-12-23-1-25-19

6-15-21-14-4?   9-14   1

4-9-3-20-9-15-14-1-18-25

PART D

Reviewing Proofreader's Marks

Retrieve your Journal file. Add to your journal what you learned in previous lessons about each of these marks:

≡   ∧   #   ∽   /   ¶   .... (stet)   ⤴   ◠   ◡

PART E

Keying with Proofreader's Marks

Key the paragraph below **once**, using wordwrap. Make all the changes indicated as you key.

> Sneakers, the rubber-bottomed shoe, got that name because of the silent footsteps of whoever wore them. At the turn of the century rubber soles were glued to canvas tops to produce the first athletic (stet) shoe. The first sneakers were introduced in 1917 and were called keds. ¶In the 1960s a college runner and his coach developed a waffle-soled shoe for traction. The coach got the idea one morning while making waffles in his kitchen!

PART F

Personal Letters

A letter is a more formal type of written communication between two people. It has many parts that are the same as a personal note: the date, the salutation, the message or body, the complimentary close, and the sender's name. The new parts are the inside address—the address of the person you are writing to—and your address. In both of these addresses, be sure to use the two-letter abbreviation for your state. (See Appendix D for a complete list of these abbreviations. Note, all state abbreviations are keyed in capital letters with no spaces or periods in between.) All parts of the letter begin at the left margin and there is no indenting.

Challenge

How creative are you? Can you key the entire alphabet in capital letters using just one letter? Of course you can. Here are the first five letters to help you get started.

AAA	BBB	CCCC	DDDD	EEEEE	FFFFF
A A	B B	C	D D	E	F
AAAAA	BBB	C	D D	EEEEE	FFF
A A	B B	C	D D	E	F
A A	BBBBB	CCCC	DDDD	EEEEE	F

LESSON 27

Introducing "

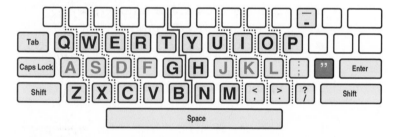

Objectives:
- To develop keyboarding speed and accuracy
- To compose at the computer
- To learn the location of the **quotation mark (")** key
- To review language arts principles

Warmup

Key each line **twice.** Try to key the lines without pausing between words.

```
1 Take these with you:  umbrella, blanket, and food.
2 Remember this rule:  What you see is what you get.
3 Here is one example:  Keep your arms by your side.
4 Stop--do not go further--unless you have approval.
  . . . .1. . . .2. . . .3. . . .4. . . .5. . . .6. . . .7. . . .8. . . .9. . . .10
```

Application 52: Pet Parade Note

Directions:

Compose and arrange a personal note to one of your friends, inviting him or her to participate in your city's Pet Parade next Saturday morning at ten o'clock at City Hall. All your friend has to do is march in the parade with a pet. Explain that there is a contest for the best-dressed pet, so your friend might want to consider some kind of costume for the pet. Ask your friend to call you if he or she is coming. Name the file Ap52.

LESSON 58

Formatting Personal Letters

Objectives:
- To improve speed on alphabet keys
- To improve accuracy of numbers
- To review proofreader marks
- To learn to format personal business letters

PART A

Warmup

Key the lines below, **twice** each.

```
1 It's not my fault that the new panel is too rigid.
2 The correspondence showed considerable difficulty.
3 Duane received an authentic autograph of the star.
4 I got 75% on the 1st test and 89% on the 2nd test.
....1....2....3....4....5....6....7....8....9....10
```

PART B

Building Speed

Below are alternate-hand phrases. Key each line **twice.** Then find a partner and take turns dictating the lines to each other.

```
1 and them|and they|for they|for them|for the|of the
2 to do|to us|to do it|it is|is it|when to|did their
3 they make|to their|the big|is he|is she|go by them
4 with them|and their|when to|did they work|they got
....1....2....3....4....5....6....7....8....9....10
```

Speed Building

All the words in the sentences below alternate striking a letter with one hand followed by striking a letter with the other hand. This type of copy is good for speed building because alternating between hands is faster than keying one-hand words. Take a one-minute timing on each line. Then repeat the line and try to add one more word. Repeat the same line a third time and try to add even one more word to your score.

```
1 Dixie may rush to town with the visitor for worms.
2 Doris may fix the fuchsia oak mantle for Rod Hale.
3 The panel paid a penalty to the towns for the sod.
4 The city paid Sofia to rush city maps to Gus Lake.
....1....2....3....4....5....6....7....8....9....10
```

Composing at the Computer

How many words can you make out of a certain group of letters? Let's find out. Your teacher will select one of the words or phrases listed below. Your job is to switch the letters around and compose as many words as you can think of that use those letters, and only those letters. You can arrange the letters in any order you wish, but you can't add other letters that are not in the original word or phrase.

Phrases: CONCENTRATION

HALLOWEEN

HAPPY THANKSGIVING

COLUMBUS DAY

SEASON'S GREETINGS

MARTIN LUTHER KING'S BIRTHDAY

WASHINGTON'S BIRTHDAY

LINCOLN'S BIRTHDAY

THREE DAY WEEKEND

Proofreader's Mark Explained

Sometimes proofreaders cross out a word and then change their minds and decide to put that word back in. To indicate this, they place a series of dots under the word crossed out and write *stet* in the margin. (The word *stet* is Latin for "let it stand.")

Example: She had ~~almost~~ perfect technique.

She had almost perfect technique.

Practice with Proofreader's Mark

Key the paragraph **once,** using wordwrap and making the changes indicated as you key.

```
     I want to thank you for inviting me to tour your
office yesterday.  I tried to make every possible
effort to be on time, but due to circumstances beyond
my control, I was not able to arrive on time.  It was
a wonderfully pleasant tour and I thoroughly enjoyed
myself.
```

Composing and Formatting on Your Own

Application 50: Carnival Night Note

Directions:

Compose and arrange a personal note to a friend of your choice asking him or her to work with you in a booth at your school's Carnival Night next Friday evening. You and your friend will be in charge of the cotton candy machine. You will make the candy and sell it. There is no pay but you can eat all the candy you want. Proceeds from the booth go toward buying more computers for your school. Name the file Ap50.

Application 51: Note to Teacher

Directions:

Compose and arrange a personal note to one of your teachers explaining you will be gone four days next week because you are going on vacation with your family, and you would like your assignments ahead of time so you can keep up with the work. Name the file Ap51.

Accuracy Building

The lines below contain long words. Big words can sometimes "throw" you just by their sheer length. Don't let these big words interfere with your concentration. As you key each line **twice**, concentrate on maintaining your control of the keyboard. A good way to get through long words is to break them up into syllables and key them syllable by syllable. Try that technique now.

1 immediately considerable governments comprehensive
2 representative headquarters individual responsible
3 organizing management qualifications conscientious
4 administrator supervisor cooperation dependability
5 extraordinary merchandise requirements publication

Drill Composition

Can you compose at least ten good sentences containing colons? Sure you can; give it a try right now.

Key

Locate the **quotation mark** key on your keyboard. It is the shift of the apostrophe key, so you will use your sem finger on it. Try it now. Place your hands on the home row keys and key ;" several times.

Now try these lines below, **two times** each. As you key, remember to bring your **A** finger back to home row after shifting.

1 ;"; ";; ;"; ";; ;"; ";; ;"; ";; ;"; ";;
2 ;;; """ ;;; """ ;;; """ ;;; """ ;;; """

Now key these lines, **twice** each. Note, there are no spaces between the quotation marks and the word they surround.

3 Mark keyed "bale" for "bail," but he knows better.
4 Sometimes I use "too" incorrectly as well as "to."
5 Jan said, "I think I will bake a cake for Thomas."

Composing Personal Notes

Objectives:
- To improve accuracy on alphabet keys
- To improve accuracy of numbers
- To learn the proofreader's mark for "let it stand"
- To compose and format personal notes

PART A

Warmup

Key the lines below, **twice** each.

```
1 No greater opportunity exists other than this one.
2 The key goal of that firm is to make a big profit.
3 Duke will play the bugle at the civic center gala.
4 My hotel lost 56 blankets and 36 towels in 9 days.
  . . . . 1 . . . . 2 . . . . 3 . . . . 4 . . . . 5 . . . . 6 . . . . 7 . . . . 8 . . . . 9 . . . .10
```

PART B

Accuracy Building

Below are more alphabetic sentences. Do not move on to the next line until you can key each one **three times** in succession with perfect accuracy.

```
1 Their information will be vital at the right time.
2 Jill is judging a jogging jamboree at Jeronimo St.
3 Kathryn's kittens in the kitchen keep her company.
4 A million folks work and play in a big metropolis.
```

PART C

Numbers

Get ready to decode another message. Key the numbers with five spaces between each word. Then turn to your decoding sheet and decode the message.

23-8-1-20	9-19	20-8-5	16-1-9-14	23-5
13-1-11-5	12-9-7-8-20	15-6?	1	
23-9-14-4-15-23	16-1-14-5			

The paragraphs below contain five sentence fragments. Read the paragraphs and try to find all of these errors; then as you key, correct the errors. Remember to use the Tab key to indent the first line of each paragraph.

The legend of Johnny Appleseed is based on fact. It tells of a fellow named John Chapman. A deeply religious man who walked the frontier planting apple trees wherever he went. He liked the name Johnny Appleseed and referred to himself that way.

He was born in 1774. At an early age he displayed a love for flowering apple trees. For almost fifty years he moved around the frontier. With a sack of seeds slung over his shoulder.

He wore a tin pan on his head, which served two purposes. As a cooking pot when he set up a campsite and as protection from rain.

He was barefoot and dressed in rags; yet this bearded hermit walked the earth with just one goal in mind. Plant apple trees. He also sold apple seeds and saplings to pioneers heading west. To areas he could not cover by foot.

PART H

Challenge

Do you like to pass notes to other students? Now you will have a chance to do just that. Remember those "alphabet" letters you created in Lesson 26? Use that same technique to send a short message to another person in the class. When you are finished, print out your message and deliver it to your classmate.

Application 48: Note to Aunt

Directions:
- Use the current date
- 1-inch side and top margins
- Wordwrap
- Single space; double space between paragraphs
- File name: Ap48

Dear Aunt Agnes

I want to thank you for the computer games you sent me for my birthday.

The whole family is really enjoying playing them. I especially like the chess game. Mom thinks the math and geography games will help me in school. Even Dad is starting to get hooked on chess.

Thanks again for making this birthday a great one.

Sincerely

[Your Name]

Application 49

Directions:
- Use the current date
- 1-inch side and top margins
- Wordwrap
- Single space; double space between paragraphs
- File name: Ap49

Dear Kevin As you know, Mrs. Macintyre is retiring after 30 years of teaching. Mrs. Macintyre's class is planning a retirement tea from 3:30 to 4:30 p.m. next Friday afternoon in the library.

As one of her former students, we would like to invite you to attend.

I hope you can join us in honoring Mrs. Macintyre. I am sure she would enjoy having her former students help her celebrate. Sincerely [Your Name]

Introducing + and =

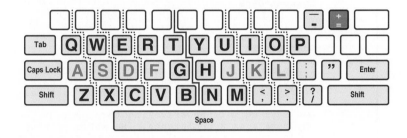

Objectives:

- To develop keyboarding speed and accuracy
- To compose at the computer
- To learn the location of the **plus (+)** and **equals (=)** key
- To review language arts principles

Warmup

Key each line twice. Try to key the lines without pausing between words.

1 Mary said, "I need to study for the history exam."

2 Karen Dodd confuses the word "their" with "there."

3 Look for the sign that says "domestic passengers."

4 Duke says, "If it's yours, then take it back now."

   . . . .1. . . .2. . . .3. . . .4. . . .5. . . .6. . . .7. . . .8. . . .9. . . .10

Speed Building

Here are some more sentences that alternate stroking between hands. Take a one-minute timing on each line. Then repeat the line and try to increase your speed by one word. Repeat the line a third time and try to improve one more word on that line.

1 Nema may go to the Orient to fight for the whales.

2 Mr. Dib is sickened by the sight of the lame buck.

3 Make the right quantity of cubic soap for Guthrie.

4 Dirk and Rodney got the box of corn curls for Mel.

   . . . .1. . . .2. . . .3. . . .4. . . .5. . . .6. . . .7. . . .8. . . .9. . . .10

Application 47: Note to Cousin

Directions:

- Use the current date
- 1-inch side and top margins
- Wordwrap
- Single space; double space between paragraphs
- File name: Ap47

Current Date

Dear Cousin

I'm planning to have a costume party on this coming Saturday and I would like you to come. If you don't have a costume, don't worry. I have plenty left over from past Halloweens.

Dad says he will be traveling through your town on Friday on his way home from a conference. He would be happy to give you a ride to our house. You could sleep over Friday and Saturday nights and then take the bus home Sunday afternoon.

What do you say? I hope you can come and stay the whole weekend. I can't wait for you to meet my friends from school.

Sincerely

Your Name

Your Name

Composing at the Computer

You are going on a treasure hunt. In three minutes, key the names of as many objects as you can find in your classroom. Remember, just names of objects, not people.

Accuracy Building

Here are some more lines containing long words. Remember the technique for keying long words—key by syllables—and the length of the words should not be a problem.

1 utilization agreements accomplishment professional

2 ornamentation mountainous monopolizes embarrassing

3 misapprehension hypercritical distributive customs

4 rambunctious picturesque enthusiastically vagabond

Drill Composition

Can you compose at least ten good sentences containing quotation marks? Let's find out. Your sentences may contain quotations from famous people or from your parents or teachers. Next to the quotation, write who said it. If you can't remember quotes from other people, make up some of your own.

 and **Key**

Look at your keyboard and locate the **equals** key. It's on the top row, up in the right-hand corner. You will use your "sem" finger on it. Try it now. Key ;= several times. Then key the lines below. As you key, be sure to keep your **J** and **K** fingers at home.

1 ;=; =;; ;=; =;; =;= =;; ;=; =;; ;=; =;;

2 ;;; === ;;; === ;;; === ;;; === ;;; ===

Now key the lines below, **twice** each.

3 A good rest and good nutrition = one healthy body.

4 Good study and mathematics skills = better grades.

Now try operating the shift of the equals key to get the **plus sign.** Try it now. Key ;=+ several times. Then key the lines on the next page.

Numbers

Get ready to decode another message. Key the numbers with five spaces between each word. Then turn to your decoding sheet and decode the message.

```
23-8-25       9-19      1      14-5-23-12-25
2-15-18-14     2-1-2-25     12-9-11-5      1
7-1-12-5     15-6     23-9-14-4?     2-5-3-1-21-19-5
9-20     2-5-7-9-14-19     23-9-20-8      1
19-17-21-1-12-12.
```

Proofreader's Mark Explained

The symbol for starting a new paragraph is $\mathcal{H}$. Whenever you see this mark, you should indent to indicate a new paragraph.

Example: $\mathcal{H}$It was dark when we got there. There were no cars. All was still. $\mathcal{H}$Suddenly a shot rang out.

It was dark when we got there. There were no cars. All was still.

Suddenly a shot rang out.

Practice with Proofreader's Mark

Key each line **once,** making the changes indicated.

```
$\mathcal{H}$He lay down on the cot completely exhausted. The run
through the park had been a good one, but now he just
wanted to sleep.$\mathcal{H}$Then he remembered that tomorrow was
his friend's birthday and he needed to go shopping
for a present.
```

Personal Notes

A personal note is a short message between two people. It consists of a date line, a salutation [Dear So and So], the body or message, a complimentary close, and the sender's name. The easiest way to format a personal note is to begin every part at the left margin; do not indent any of the parts.

```
5 ;+; +;; ;+; +;; ;+; +;; ;+; +;; ;+; +;;
6 ;;; +++ ;;; +++ ;;; +++ ;;; +++ ;;; +++
```

Now key these lines, **two times** each.

```
Formula for improving grades:  read + listen well.
To Ann's recipe you must add salt + pepper + mace.
```

PART G
Language Arts Mystery

The paragraphs below contain two errors in punctuating appositives. Read the paragraphs and try to find all of these errors; then as you key, correct the errors. Remember to use the Tab key to indent the first line of each paragraph.

```
    A young man worked at a soda fountain in a drug
store.  This young man had a special affection for
the owner's daughter.  To impress his lady, he spent
many hours mixing special fountain drinks for the
young lady to sample.  The owner a doctor named
Pepper did not like the attention his daughter was
getting and fired the young man.
    The young man left town and traveled to Texas
where he got a job at another soda fountain.  He
continued to dream of the girl he left behind.  One
day he came up with a soft drink that everyone seemed
to like.  He named it Dr. Pepper in honor of his lost
romance.
    A customer at the drug store a chemist named
Lazenby became interested in the beverage.  After two
years of testing, he put Dr. Pepper on sale at soda
fountains in Texas.  The drink became popular and
spread to other areas.  But the story has another
happy ending too.  The two lovers were eventually
reunited and married.
```

Formatting Personal Notes

Objectives:

- To improve speed
- To improve accuracy of numbers
- To learn the proofreader's mark for new paragraph
- To format personal notes

Warmup

Key the lines below, **twice** each.

1 Arlene likes to travel by train; she fears flying.

2 All railroad tickets must be purchased in advance.

3 Talk to my travel agent about new tours and rates.

4 Send us 12 hammers, 18 screwdrivers, and 9 pliers.

. . . . 1 . . . . 2 . . . . 3 . . . . 4 . . . . 5 . . . . 6 . . . . 7 . . . . 8 . . . . 9 10

Building Speed

Below are alternate-hand sentences. Your teacher will time you for 30 seconds on each line. Compute your speed by multiplying the number of words by two. Then take a 60-second timing on the same line and use the scale to figure speed. Your goal is to build endurance—get the same speed for 30 seconds and 60 seconds.

1 The girl by the antique auto may make it downtown.

2 Mr. Rich R. Turke may lend a hand to fix the sign.

3 Dirk got a dog and a fox and a duck and a big ape.

4 They blame the neighbor for the town duck problem.

. . . . 1 . . . . 2 . . . . 3 . . . . 4 . . . . 5 . . . . 6 . . . . 7 . . . . 8 . . . . 9 10

Perhaps you have heard of the Indianapolis 500 car race. Now you are going to play your own version, the Keyboarding 500. You will be competing with your classmates. Your teacher will time you for five minutes. Each time you complete one of the sentences below with 100% accuracy, you travel one lap around the track. If you make an error, start the line over again. If you finish all the lines, begin again from the beginning. At the end of five minutes your teacher will ask you to total up the number of laps you did. The winner is the person who travels the most laps within the time period.

1 Mr. Dodds emphasizes managerial agreements in his contracts.

2 Approximately fifty-six endorsements were recommended today.

3 My article is an exemplary representation of the principles.

4 Four administrators have many professional responsibilities.

5 Employment agencies require really professional cooperation.

6 Considerable outstanding merchandise was visible on display.

7 Recommended requirements for managerial jobs were discussed.

8 Outstanding shrubbery clearly revealed conscientious effort.

9 Personal commitments to extraordinary devotion are required.

10 Dependability is necessary for your professional counselors.

Proofreader's Mark Explained

A circle around a figure or abbreviation means it should be spelled out.

Example: Derek was their number ①player.

Derek was their number one player.

Practice with Proofreader's Mark

Key each line **once,** making the changes indicated as you key.

1 (Dr.) Spock has given advice on rearing children.
2 Marilyn was elected (Pres.) of the Booster Club.
3 Joe takes ②tablets before eating his breakfast.

Composing and Formatting on Your Own

Application 44: Lost Pet Flyer

Directions:

Compose and arrange a flyer advertising a lost pet. Include the pet's name, description, and a phone number where you can be reached. You may want to offer a reward for the pet's return. Name the file Ap44.

Application 45: Bike for Sale Flyer

Directions:

Compose and arrange a flyer advertising a bike for sale. Include the make of bike, its age, and a description of special features. State a price or say "Best offer." Also give your name, address, and phone number. Name the file Ap45.

Application 46: Family Reunion Flyer

Directions:

Compose and arrange a flyer that could be mailed to all your relatives announcing a family reunion to be held at your house on July 4. Everyone should bring a dish to pass. The time is 10:00 a.m. to 4:00 p.m. Explain that your family will be happy to arrange motel accommodations for those who wish to stay overnight. Ask your relatives to RSVP and state your phone number. Name the file Ap46.

SECTION 3

Computer Features and Word Processing Functions

Composing Flyers

Objectives:
- To improve speed
- To improve accuracy of numbers
- To learn the proofreader's mark for spell out
- To compose and format flyers

Warmup

Key the lines below, **twice** each.

1 Ned needs to purchase pencils and pens for school.

2 Find it in the atlas, dictionary and encyclopedia.

3 My library reference and pamphlet files have data.

4 This school has 1135 boys, 850 girls, 23 teachers.

....1....2....3....4....5....6....7....8....9....10

Accuracy Building

Below are more alphabetic sentences. Do not move on to the next line until you can key each one perfectly **three times** in succession.

1 Ethyl and Edy enjoy eating Em's eggs and eggrolls.

2 Finding fifty fried foods on the menu, Frank fled.

3 George's gloomy girlfriends gave him a gaudy gift.

4 Human hesitation hampers hours and hours of labor.

Numbers

Get ready to decode another message. Key the numbers with five spaces between each word. Then turn to your decoding sheet and decode the message by keying the words.

23-8-25   4-15-5-19   1   6-9-18-5-13-1-14

23-5-1-18   18-5-4   19-21-19-16-5-14-4-5-18-19?

20-15   11-5-5-16   8-9-19   16-1-14-20-19

21-16

LESSON 29

Changing Margins and Line Spacing

Objectives:
- To learn the cursor movement keys
- To learn how to change side margins
- To use wordwrap
- To learn how to change spacing between lines
- To use the Delete and Backspace keys to correct errors
- To practice composing at the computer

PART A

Warmup

Key the lines below, **twice** each. As you key, try to keep your cursor moving and eliminate all pauses between words.

1 Stop! I have you covered. The police are nearby.

2 We sell hand-made toys and custom-built doghouses.

3 Be sure you bring the following: paper, ink, pen.

4 My father's famous saying is, "No work, no money."

. . . . 1 . . . . 2 . . . . 3 . . . . 4 . . . . 5 . . . . 6 . . . . 7 . . . . 8 . . . . 9 10

PART B

Composing at the Computer

Here's an exercise that will tickle your imagination. Your teacher will read a list of phrases and your job is to compose an answer. But don't think too hard or long on this one; key the first thing that comes into your mind. Listen carefully because your teacher may not read the words in the exact order in which they are given below. Remember, key only your answer to the phrase.

If I were a[n] ... [teacher reads phrase], I would be ... [student supplies response].

piece of furniture	famous person	dessert
animal	sports star	automobile
color	movie star	state
book	country	river or lake
flower	bird	store at the mall
president of the United States	musical instrument	flavor of ice cream
	sandwich	breed of dog

Application 42: Lawn Mowing Flyer

Directions:
- Center top to bottom
- Center each line
- Boldface and underline where indicated

- Arrange spacing between lines attractively (use your own judgment)
- File name: Ap42

[Insert Your Last Name and 's here] Lawn Mowing Service

We do any size yard.

We provide our own equipment.

We aim to please. No job is too little or too big.

CALL US NOW!

[Insert Your phone number here]

<u>Low</u> <u>Hourly</u> <u>Rates</u>

We will gladly furnish references if requested.

Your satisfaction guaranteed or your money back.

Application 43: Garage Sale Flyer

Directions:

- Center top to bottom
- Center each line
- Underline where indicated
- You decide how much information to place on each line

- Arrange spacing between lines attractively (use your own judgment)
- File name: Ap43

<u>GARAGE</u> <u>SALE</u> at [insert your street address] Date: Saturday, June 5. Time: 8:00 to 3:00. Antiques, toys, baby furniture, computers, dishes, and glassware.

Cursor Movement Keys

As you know by now, the cursor is the dot or line of light that shows the point on the screen where the letter will be entered. If you want to move the cursor to another part of the screen, you must use the arrow keys. Look at your keyboard now and find where these are located. If you are having trouble finding them, ask your teacher. Moving the cursor quickly around the screen is a big help when it comes to correcting or changing the copy. Let's practice moving the cursor. Follow the steps below:

IBM PS/2

1. Quickly move the cursor to the beginning of your document.

2. Quickly move the cursor to the end of your document.

3. Quickly move the cursor to the top of your screen.

4. Quickly move the cursor to the bottom of your screen.

5. Place your cursor in the middle of a line and quickly move it to the end of the line.

6. Place your cursor in the middle of a line and quickly move it to the beginning of the line.

7. Repeat the first six items again.

Apple IIe

Using Wordwrap

Wordwrap is a feature of some software programs that eliminates the need for the operator to decide where to end a line; the computer determines this for you. Your teacher will tell you if your software has this feature. If it does, try using it on the paragraphs below. Remember, do not press Return/Enter until you finish the last line of the first paragraph. Then press Return/Enter twice to leave a blank line between the paragraphs. Let the computer decide where to end the lines. Your lines on the screen will not look like the lines in the book.

```
    Remember your first day of school?  You were
just a little nervous and excited, all at the same
time.  You probably wondered what your new teacher
would be like?  Would you like that teacher?  Would
you have homework on the first day?  Would the
teacher like you?
```

(continued on next page)

Application 41: Car Wash Flyer

Directions:

- 1-inch side, top, and bottom margins
- Begin first line of message two inches from top
- Center each line; to spread out "Free Car Wash" put one space between letters and three spaces between words
- Double space as indicated
- Use the word "Free" as a border across the top and bottom of the page (The copy command will make this easy to do.)
- File name: Ap41

```
Free Free Free Free Free Free Free Free Free Free Free Free Free
Free Free Free Free Free Free Free Free Free Free Free Free Free


              F R E E   C A R   W A S H




              Bartlet's Service Station
               2967 W. Cermak Road




                Saturday, April 21
                 10:00 to 4:00




                (Donations Accepted)



Free Free Free Free Free Free Free Free Free Free Free Free Free
Free Free Free Free Free Free Free Free Free Free Free Free Free
```

Then when your first break in classes came you
got over your nervousness. You started sharing
thoughts with your friends. You just couldn't wait
to tell them about all the exciting things you did
during the summer. And all too soon, the bell to
start class rang and you were back in the classroom
again.

Setting the Side Margins

The margin is the white space that appears at the top, bottom, and sides of your document (also called a printout). Most software programs have a preset margin, called the **default margin**, which is usually set in a particular number of inches or lines. For most of your keying, the default margin will probably be adequate, but sometimes you may want to change it to make your words fit better on the page. Your teacher will explain how to change the margin settings for the software you are using. When you understand how to do this, try keying the paragraph below **four times**, using the different side margin settings indicated for each step listed below:

1. Use default side margins and wordwrap.

2. Use 1.5-inch side margins and wordwrap.

3. Use 2-inch side margins and wordwrap.

4. Use a 1.5-inch margin on the left and a 1-inch margin on the right and wordwrap.

Caring for the aged has become a problem of
national importance. Modern medicine has helped
older people live longer, but there is still the
problem of locating good housing and the funding
to pay for medical assistance. Congress is just
beginning to look into the problems of the aged.

Numbers

Get ready to decode another message. Key the numbers with five spaces between each word. Then turn to your decoding sheet and decode the message.

23-8-1-20	8-1-19	5-9-7-8-20-5-5-14
12-5-7-19	1-14-4	3-1-20-3-8-5-19
6-12-9-5-19?	1	2-1-19-5-2-1-12-12
20-5-1-13		

Proofreader's Mark Explained

The mark ╱ is used to change a capital letter to a lower-case letter.

Example: This Ẉinter we will chop our own firewood.

This winter we will chop our own firewood.

Practice with Proofreader's Mark

Key each line **once,** making the changes indicated as you key.

1 You should turn Ṣouth when you reach Augusta Blvd.
2 In Ṣpring all William can think about is baseball.
3 Elizabeth Brown was elected Ṭreasurer of our Ċlub.

Flyers

A flyer is similar to an announcement. Flyers contain information in a form designed to attract the reader's eye. Artwork, wide margins, borders, and different kinds of type are used to create interest. Underlining, boldfacing, and putting words in all caps are other ways to attract attention and get the reader to notice the flyer.

Changing Spacing

Most software programs permit the user to change the default spacing, which is single spacing, to double spacing. When you key using single spacing, there are no blank lines between lines of type. When you use double spacing, there is one blank line after each line of type. Keying a document in single spacing allows you to put more lines on a page. Although keying in double spacing means you will have less lines per page, the lines of print are more readable because of the blank lines between each line of type. Most teachers prefer double-spaced papers because it allows room for their comments.

Your teacher will show you how to change the spacing. When you feel comfortable with this, key the first paragraph below in **single** spacing, the second paragraph in **double** spacing, the third in **single,** and the fourth in **double.** Use wordwrap. Then change back to single spacing for the rest of this lesson.

```
     Katie and Ellie went to the park to fly their
new kite.  It was a beautiful kite--big and sleek--
with a long tail covered with different colored
ribbons.

     Both girls made it from a kit, and they were
anxious to see if their creation would fly.  The wind
was just right.

     Slowly Ellie let out the string and both girls
watched it soar higher and higher toward the sun.
And then the kite disappeared.  Where could it have
gone?

     Both girls followed the string up into the sky.
And there it was--perched on top of the tallest oak
tree in the neighborhood.  They took turns tugging at
the string trying to dislodge the kite, but it would
not budge.  Finally, they gave up and went home.
```

Formatting Flyers

Objectives:

- To improve accuracy on alphabet keys
- To improve accuracy of numbers
- To learn the proofreader's mark for lower case
- To learn how to format flyers

PART A

Warmup

Key the lines below, **twice** each.

1 If you are late, you will miss the plane Saturday.
2 Mail the attached card and receive your free gift.
3 Double chocolate cake is the reason for Al's diet.
4 Add 76 and 89 and 34; then subtract 2 and 7 and 9.

`....1....2....3....4....5....6....7....8....9....10`

PART B

Accuracy Building

Below are some alphabetic sentences. Do not move on to the next line until you can key each one **three times** in succession with perfect accuracy.

1 All artists have a great deal of skill and talent.
2 Baking batches of bread and biscuits is a big job.
3 Cleo got a curt card from Mac in charge of claims.
4 Deal with this board directly on their daily data.

Using the Delete and Backspace Keys to Correct Errors

The Backspace and Delete keys are used to correct errors. The Backspace key removes the character to the left of the cursor. The Delete key removes the character where the cursor is located. Some computers have both keys; others have just one. Let's practice using each of these. Key the line below exactly as it appears, including the errors.

Mrs. Grimes asked Sanyd to travle with her tomorow.

Using either the Backspace or Delete key, make the following changes:

1. Change Mrs. to Mr.

2. Change Sanyd to Sandy

3. Change travle to travel

4. Add the missing "r" in the last word

The paragraph below contains nine keyboarding errors. Key it exactly as it appears. Then use your Backspace or Delete key to correct the errors.

IBM PS/2

Apple IIe

Imagine a computor that fits on your lap being as powerfull as the one that sits on a desk. If you decide to travel on a plane or train, you can take your computer with you because it operates on a batery. No, this is not the world of make-beleive. It is the real world. Experts predict even more changes in the futrue. Comptuers will recognise handwriting; a pen and pad may replase the keyboard. There is one drawback, howevre, which is that most people can keyboard faster than they can write.

Application 39: Limerick

Directions:

Compose a limerick—a humorous five-line poem in which the first, second, and fifth lines rhyme and the third and fourth lines rhyme. Arrange it attractively on the page. Be sure to title the limerick. Name the file Ap39.

Application 40: "Take-Off" Poem

Directions:

Write a humorous "take-off" on a famous poem. Here are some lines to get you started or you may choose another poem if you wish. Arrange your poem attractively on the page. Title it, "An Adaption of _____." Name the file Ap40.

```
It was the night before Christmas
      and all through the class,
Not a keyboard was stirring,
      not even a cap.


                or


I think that I shall never see,

      a _____ as lovely as _____.


                or


Listen my children and you shall hear

      of the _____ ride of _____.
```

Production

In the next lessons you will have an opportunity to apply what you have learned by keying different documents. Each document should be started on a blank screen and saved as a separate file. A suggested file name is given in the directions, or your teacher may instruct you to name the documents in a different way. After keying the document, you will want to proofread carefully to correct all errors before printing it. If your teacher permits, you may also wish to use a spell check program to help find all your errors.

Application 1: Backpacking

Directions:
- Default top and bottom margins
- 1.5-inch left margin; 1-inch right margin
- Double spacing
- Wordwrap
- File name: Backpack

One of the best ways to observe nature is to hike with a backpack. Many different kinds of packs are available, but the ones with a frame and bag offer the most advantages. The frame allows weight to be concentrated higher on the back so the person can walk more comfortably.

For the most comfort, the bag must be packed in a certain way. Light items, such as clothing and food, go at the bottom, and heavier items, such as cooking utensils and tent, go on top. This concentrates the weight on the shoulders, not the lower back.

Weight of the pack is important. For a man the suggested weight is thirty-five pounds; for a woman, twenty-five pounds. To keep weight down, be sure you take only those items that are absolutely necessary for your trip.

Numbers

Here is another message in number code. Key the numbers with five spaces between each word. Then turn to your decoding sheet and decode the message by keying the words.

23-8-1-20   9-19   23-15-18-19-5   20-8-1-14

6-9-14-4-9-14-7   1   23-15-18-13   9-14

1-14   1-16-16-12-5?   6-9-14-4-9-14-7

8-1-12-6   1   23-15-18-13

Proofreader's Mark Explained

The mark **#** is used to add a space between words. When a + or − sign is used with this symbol, it indicates the number of spaces to leave between lines of type.

Example: Try to^# leave before noon. ₊#

I cannot make that flight.

Try to leave before noon.

I cannot make that flight.

Practice with Proofreader's Mark

Key each line **once,** making the changes indicated as you key.

1 Al's favorite is cherry#cobbler topped with cream.

2 Just#follow directions, and you will avoid errors.

3 Please mail these two#packages via certified mail.

Composing and Formatting on Your Own

Application 38: Short Poem

Directions:

Compose a short poem of at least eight lines. Arrange it attractively on the page. Be sure to give it a title. Name the file Ap38.

Application 2: Sleeping Bags

Directions:
- Default top and bottom margins
- 2-inch left- and right-side margins
- Single spacing
- Wordwrap
- File name: Sleepbag

Sleeping bags are an important part of camping. Without a good night's sleep, your trip could be ruined. Buying the right kind of bag depends on the type of camping you will be doing and the time of year.

One thing to look for is warmth. Will the filling keep you warm at night? Another thing to consider is the weight of the bag. Also, does it compress for packing? Does it fluff out when unpacked?

For comfortable sleeping, experts recommend that you not get into your sleeping bag wearing your hiking clothes. Clothes worn during the day may have moisture in them. You are better off to put on dry clothes or long underwear before going to sleep.

Composing Poems

Objectives:
- To improve accuracy on alphabet keys
- To improve accuracy of numbers
- To learn the proofreader's mark for inserting a space
- To compose and format poems

PART A

Warmup

Key the lines below, **twice** each.

```
1 We were addressed by the chief of the Sioux tribe.
2 My qualifications are not appropriate for the job.
3 The interviewer asked humorous questions about me.
4 Beth and Di baked 14 pies, 15 cakes, and 16 tarts.
  . . . .1. . . .2. . . .3. . . .4. . . .5. . . .6. . . .7. . . .8. . . .9. . . .10
```

PART B

Accuracy Building

The lines below are designed to force you to concentrate. Your job is to decode as you key. Do the paragraph **once.**

```
    Please do not B L8 for our dinner meeting next

week.  The D8 is July 23.  We R all looking 4ward to

hearing the guest speaker.  Someone will have 2 B at

the airport to greet him and drive him to the hotel.

It should be EZ 4 U 2 do that.  Let me know if U can

take care of that job.  I can hardly wait 2 B with U 4

that meeting.
```

Centering Horizontally

Objectives:

■ To learn automatic horizontal centering
■ To learn how to change top and bottom margins
■ To learn the hard space
■ To learn the hard hyphen
■ To practice composing at the computer
■ To practice proofreading

PART A

Warmup

Beginning with this lesson, your warmup routine will sometimes change. Instead of keying a group of lines, you will use the time your teacher gives you for warmup to work on journal notes. What are journal notes? They are brief statements about what happened during the last class. For example, in the previous lesson you learned:

■ what the default side margin is
■ how to change the side margins
■ what wordwrap is
■ how to change spacing between lines
■ how to use the Delete and/or Backspace keys to correct errors

Key your thoughts about these now on your computer screen. Explain what each item is or how each one is done. Then save your notes. Unless your teacher gives you a special name for that file, use the name Journal. You will be adding entries to your journal as time goes on, and your teacher may ask you to print out the journal at some point in time. So do your best work. Use complete sentences and correct your errors.

PART B

Composing at the Computer

Do you have a favorite book? A favorite television show? Here's a chance to list your favorites. As your teacher reads the word, quickly compose your answer. Do not think about it too long, or you may be at a loss for words. Listen carefully; your teacher may skip around. And remember to capitalize all names.

Application 37: A Day at Lorado

Directions:

- Center top to bottom
- Center the title and author's name; double space once after title, twice after author's name
- Center the key line and set left margin accordingly
- Single space; double space between stanzas
- File name: Ap37

```
A DAY AT LORADO

By Richard Nelson

As I walked out on the paths of Lorado,
Out on the paths of Lorado at night,
I tripped on the tree roots, the rocks, and bushes,
Trapped in the darkness, the stars for my light.

Sturdy companions, shouting encouragement,
Lending a warning, a warning so true,
"The step is a mean one, the bush is thorny,
Watch for the gulley or we'll lose you too."

Borealis Aurora aglow in its splendor
Provided us beauty so wondrously bright,
From north sky to south sky with stars by the millions,
Breaking the darkness, the darkness of night.

Then back in the cabin made warm by the fire,
Made warmer still by our new friends and old,
Stunts, skits, and stories to add to the evening,
Popcorn, guitar strings, still more tales unfold.

Our campout together amid common efforts
Gave chance for a banquet with sky as our dome,
The learning came easy--rocks, soils, trees, and water,
All memories to savor as we returned home.
```

My favorite...	book	time of day
	television show	holiday
	day of the week	sandwich
	teacher	dessert
	relative	breakfast cereal
	sports team	magazine
	color	movie
	song	drink
	meat	vacation spot

Automatic Horizontal Centering

When a line of type has equal white space to the left and right of it, the line is said to be centered horizontally. Most word processing software centers lines across the page automatically. This is a command you will use often when doing reports for other classes because you will always center the title. Your teacher will explain what the center command is for your software. Use this command to practice centering the lines below. Remember to use your Shift Lock key where appropriate.

BABYSITTING ARTS AND CRAFTS

Scribble Pictures

Button Hide-and-Seek Game

Brown Bag Masks

Balloon Faces

Popsicle Stick People

Changing the Top and Bottom Margin

In the previous lesson you learned about default side margins. Now you will learn how to change the default top and bottom margin. Your teacher will explain the command(s) to use. When you understand how to do this, try keying the paragraph on the next page, **three times**, using the three different top and bottom margin settings indicated for each step:

1. Set the top and bottom margins for 2 inches.

2. Set the top and bottom margins for ½ inch.

3. Set the top margin for one and ½ inch and the bottom for 1 inch.

Application 36: December Holiday

Directions:

- Center top to bottom
- Center the title and author's name; double space once after title, twice after author's name
- Center the key line and set left margin accordingly
- Single space; double space between stanzas
- File name: Ap36

```
DECEMBER HOLIDAY, 1990

By Richard Nelson

Over Chicago we flew at night
And beheld in amazement the wonderful sight.
Look on the left, and look to the right!
There were miles and miles of glorious light.

Thousands of lights illuminated the dark.
What beautiful trees over there in the park.
Look at the roads with street lights at attention.
Rectangles and squares, too many to mention.

As the plane landed, our flight at an end,
It rolled down the runway, made its left bend;
Then turned right, into gate one-four.
We're happy to be at home once more.
```

Today malls have replaced movies, football
games, and eating places as the favorite place for
teenagers to gather. In some cities malls are
underground shopping centers served by subway lines.
Some are connected by miles of underground walkways.
Because these buried malls are weatherproof, they are
active day and night.

Hard Space

Sometimes the wordwrap feature will split a title, initials, or dates between two lines. A **hard space** makes the printer keep titles, dates, and initials together for ease of reading. Your teacher will explain the hard space command for your software. Then practice using that command when keying the lines below. Be sure you have your side margins set for 1 inch.

Both Michael and Marietta are planning to ask their
parents, Mr. and Mrs. Thomas.
You must first see the person in charge of
complaints, Mr. L. Markham.

Hard Hyphen

The **hard hyphen** is similar to the hard space. A hard hyphen prevents the printer from separating a dash between lines. Your teacher will explain the command(s) your software uses to accomplish this. Then practice using that command as you key the lines below. Be sure you have your side margins set for 1 inch.

The chorus and band have practiced thirty hours for
this program--Flag Day.
Eduardo's parents volunteered to bring food for the
special date--Friday Fling.

Application 35: Mr. Quadratic

Directions:

- Center top to bottom
- Center the title and author's name; double space once after title, twice after author's name
- Center the key line and set left margin accordingly
- Single space; double space between stanzas
- File name: Ap35

Note: The longest line in the poem is underlined. Do not key the underline.

```
                    MR. QUADRATIC

                  By Richard Nelson

           My name is Quadratic.
           My power is two.
           In many equations
           I'll stand before you.

           Sometimes I'll be factored.
           Sometimes it's not so.
           But I'll always be useful
           Wherever I go.

           When you get to know me,
           I'll then be your friend.
           Not just for today
           but down to the end.
```

Proofreading Practice

The paragraph below contains seven errors. Use wordwrap as you key it. Your job is to find and correct all errors. If it is available, you might wish to use a spell check program. However, a word of caution. There are three words spell check will not find.

```
        Dieting has become on of America's health

conserns.  Experts agree that many people overeat

because of emotional rather than physicle reasons.

Some people find it easier to tackle a hot-fugde

sundae rather than face up to the problem fasing

them.  If we can learn and under stand the forces

that control our eating habits, we can maintain our

     weight
⋀wait.
```

Production

Application 3: Recycling

Directions:
- Default top, bottom, and side margins
- Automatic horizontal centering
- Double spacing
- File name: Recycle

```
       ITEMS THAT ARE ACCEPTED FOR RECYCLING
            PLASTIC SODA POP BOTTLES
           PLASTIC DETERGENT BOTTLES
              PLASTIC MILK BOTTLES
                  NEWSPAPERS
                COMPUTER PAPER
               TIN (STEEL) CANS
           GLASS BOTTLES OF ANY COLOR
```

Speed Building

Below are alternate-hand sentences. Pick a partner, and as your teacher times you for one minute, race with your partner on each line. Then repeat the race by doing the set of lines one more time.

```
1 Henry may fix the pens for the turkeys by the lake.
2 Dirk's neighbor kept the dog downtown by the autos.
3 The rich widow also laughs when they blame Blanche.
4 Duane and Sydney may work on the antique oak shelf.
  . . . .1. . . .2. . . .3. . . .4. . . .5. . . .6. . . .7. . . .8. . . .9. . . .10
```

Numbers

Here is another message in number code. Key the numbers with five spaces between each word. Then turn to your decoding sheet and decode the message by keying the words.

```
1      4-15-12-12-1-18      7-15-5-19       22-5-18-25
6-1-19-20      14-15-23-1-4-1-25-19      2-21-20
14-15-20      22-5-18-25      6-1-18
```

Proofreader's Mark Explained

The mark ℘ is used to delete or take out a word.

Example: They will ~~not~~ be able to attend.

They will be able to attend.

Practice with Proofreader's Mark

Key each line **once,** making the changes indicated as you key.

```
1 Her speech should not be ready early Monday morning.
2 The lavish gala was held at the Mill Country Club.
3 Cal expertly illustrated his position on the deal.
```

Poems

Poetry is usually centered top to bottom on the page as well as horizontally. To determine where to set the left margin, find the key line—the longest line in any of the stanzas. Then center that line electronically. Use your arrow keys to determine where the margin should be set, just as you did with tables. See page 202. Set your right margin at zero.

Application 4: Eco-Awareness

Directions:

- 1-inch side margins
- 2-inch top margin; 1-inch bottom margin
- Center title horizontally; Return/ Enter twice after the title
- Double spacing
- Use hard space and hard hyphen where appropriate
- File name: Ecology

ECO-AWARENESS

What is ecology? The dictionary defines it as our relationship to our environment. Many of us give lip service to improving our environment, but we may not always practice what we preach.

However, families who care about the environment give their garbage a second thought before throwing it out. My neighbors, Mr. and Mrs. Weatherbee, are eco-conscious. They put their organic waste-- leftover food, peelings, and rinds--into a compost heap. Garbage that will not decompose is sent to a recycling center.

The Weatherbees also try to conserve energy. In the winter the thermostat is turned down, windows are insulated, and shades adjusted to use the sun's heat. Their children, Clyde and Beth, ride their bicycles to school. Mr. Weatherbee uses only public transportation--bus or train--to go to work. My neighbors, the Weatherbees, believe that eco- awareness needs to become a way of life if our environment is to improve.

Application 33: Game Rules

Directions:

Compose and print a list of six rules for a game that involves a ball, such as basketball, softball, soccer, etc. If the game has lots of rules, include the six most important ones. Write an introductory paragraph before starting the list. Give the paper an appropriate title and name the file Ap33.

Application 34: Things That Drive Teachers Crazy

Directions:

Compose and print a humorous list of ten things that you believe drive teachers crazy. An example might be, "Get up and sharpen your pencil while the teacher is giving directions." Write an introductory paragraph before starting the list. Be sure to give your list an appropriate title and name the file Ap34.

LESSON 52

Formatting Poems

Objectives:

- To improve speed on alphabet keys
- To improve accuracy of numbers
- To learn the proofreader's mark for delete
- To format poems

PART A

Warmup

Key each line **twice.**

1 Pam works for them but may want to change careers.

2 Be sure not to blame the boys for the new problem.

3 Accomplish what we want, and we will have success.

4 (1) Eat breakfast; (2) Exercise; (3) See a doctor.

. . . .1. . . .2. . . .3. . . .4. . . .5. . . .6. . . .7. . . .8. . . .9. . . .10

Underlining and Boldfacing

Objectives:

- To learn soft and hard page breaks
- To learn how to use strikeover to insert words
- To learn how to underline as you key
- To learn how to boldface as you key
- To practice proofreading
- To practice composing at the computer

Warmup

Retrieve your Journal file. Add to your journal what you learned in the previous lesson about these topics:

- horizontal centering
- changing top and bottom margins
- hard space
- hard hyphen

Composing at the Computer

Listed below are the beginning parts of some adages—wise, old sayings. Key each statement on a separate line and complete it.

```
a. A picture is worth...

b. Absence makes the heart...

c. Two heads are better...

d. If you can't say something good, don't...

e. Children should be seen...

f. Time heals...

g. If you can't beat 'em...

h. Every cloud has...

i. Rome wasn't built...

j. The grass is always greener...

k. Early to bed and early to rise...

l. A dog is man's...
```

Now key the following numbers. Each group of numbers is a code for a word. Put five spaces between each word for ease of reading. Then decode and key the message.

23-8-1-20   9-19   6-21-12-12   15-6

8-15-12-5-19   1-14-4   25-5-20   8-15-12-4-19

23-1-20-5-18?   1   19-16-15-14-7-5

PART D

Proofreader's Mark Explained

The mark $\wedge$ is used to insert a letter, letters, words, or punctuation.

Example: When we receive your payment, we will send the box.

When we receive your payment, we will send the box.

Do not try to get the book.

Do not try to get the book.

PART E

Practice with Proofreader's Mark

Key each line **once,** making the changes indicated as you key.

1 They plan to board all their dogs at Hal's kennel.
2 Computers are only as good as the data entered in.
3 You will enjoy the features of this unique camera.

PART F

Composing and Formatting on Your Own

Use the software commands for indenting from the left and right margins.

Application 32: Directions to Your House

Directions:

Compose a list of directions for someone walking or riding from school to your house. Be sure to include landmarks, such as a gas station, stop sign, mail box, bank, etc. Write an introductory paragraph before starting the list. Give the paper an appropriate title and name the file Ap32.

Soft and Hard Page Breaks

A page break is the point where the printer automatically advances to a new page. A soft page break is inserted automatically by the software, usually when 54 lines of type have been used. A hard page break is inserted by the user. Your teacher will show you the command(s) your software uses to insert a hard page and how to remove it. Let's practice putting in hard page commands. Key the lines below, in horizontal center, one line to a page. When you are done, you should have six pages on your screen.

Page 1: `Bananas`
Page 2: `Apples`
Page 3: `Oranges`
Page 4: `Strawberries`
Page 5: `Pears`
Page 6: `Grapefruit`

Now delete the hard pages you put in so all six lines appear on the same page on your screen.

Using Strikeover and Insert to Insert Words

Strikeover, sometimes also called **typeover**, allows you to key over characters. As you key, existing text is replaced with the new text. Most software does not include typeover as a default setting. If your software has this feature, your teacher will explain the command(s) for using it.

Some software has an **insert** feature, which allows you to add new text without replacing the old text. In the insert mode, the program simply moves the existing text to make room for the new word(s). Most software does include insert as a default setting.

Now let's practice using both of these editing methods. We will start with the insert method. Key the paragraph below exactly as it is given, using wordwrap. Then make the changes given in the steps that follow.

```
     A number of reasons have been given for some
biting their nails.  One theory is they like to feel
pain.  Another theory is that nail biters were not
allowed to suck their thumb when they were children.
Nail biting is just a bad habit and, like all habits,
can be changed with will power.  If you have trouble
stopping, try wearing a bad-tasting nail polish.
Soon your nails will start to look better.
```

Composing Enumerations

Objectives:

- To improve accuracy on alphabet keys
- To improve accuracy of numbers
- To learn the proofreader's mark for inserting a letter
- To compose and format enumerations

PART A

Warmup

Key the lines below, **twice** each.

```
1 Marion is so busy that she cannot audit the books.
2 Dana plans to get a new gown for the winter dance.
3 Rex and Al will cook all the food at the rib fest.
4 Shelly got a 97% on the test but Rob only got 65%.
. . . . 1 . . . . 2 . . . . 3 . . . . 4 . . . . 5 . . . . 6 . . . . 7 . . . . 8 . . . . 9 . . . .10
```

PART B

Accuracy Building

Below are sentences containing one-hand words. Key each line **once** without correcting errors. Then go back and rekey those lines on which you made errors. Keep working on the line(s) until you achieve 100% accuracy.

```
1 In July we were aware Lil regretted my union case.
2 I saw Bart create a stage act after I treated him.
3 Milo was awarded a great tax rebate after Phillip.
4 Johnny Bretz treats water in my pink pool at noon.
```

PART C

Numbers

You are going to decode a message where numbers stand for letters of the alphabet. To do this, you must first prepare a decoding sheet. Key one letter and number to a line as follows: 1 = A, 2 = B, 3 = C, etc. Print a copy of the code or save it as a separate file called *code* for future lessons.

Using Insert Mode

1. Insert *people* before the word *biting* in the first sentence.

2. Insert *of course* after *Nail biting* in the fourth sentence.

3. Insert *much* before the last word in the paragraph.

    Using Strikeover (Typeover) Mode

4. Insert *like a picture in a magazine.* after the word *look* in the last sentence.

PART E

Automatic Underline (As You Key)

Underlining words is done for emphasis and to indicate book titles. Your teacher will show you how to operate the automatic underline feature for your software. With most software, you must turn this feature on before keying the words that are to be underlined. When you want underlining to stop, simply turn the feature off. Try it now on the lines below. Key each line **once.**

1 Sue reads the book, <u>Weeping Willow</u>, to her sister.

2 <u>Do</u> <u>not</u> leave disks in the sunlight or in the cold.

3 Your coach says <u>teamwork</u> scores points, not stars.

4 To do well you need <u>talent</u>, <u>ability</u> and <u>some</u> <u>luck</u>.

PART F

Automatic Boldface (As You Key)

Boldface type is printed darker than other type for emphasis. The printer does this by double striking the letters. Your teacher will explain the command your software program uses to achieve this. To turn off bold, simply strike the same key(s) again. Practice using this feature by keying the lines below **one time.**

1 To avert any hurt feelings **think** before you speak.

2 Stand up and battle for what you believe is **right**.

3 The **best exercise is walking;** do it **every** morning.

4 **Think positive.** Negative thoughts weigh you down.

PART G

Proofreading Practice

The paragraph on the next page has six errors. Use wordwrap as you key it. Your job is to find and correct all errors as you key. If it is available, you might wish to use a spell check program. However, a word of caution. There is one word spell check will not find.

Application 31: Great Lakes Trivia

Directions:

- 1-inch side and bottom margins
- 2-inch top margin
- Center the title; double space twice after the title
- Double space throughout
- Indent enumerated items five spaces from left and right margins
- File name: Ap31

GREAT LAKES TRIVIA

The area surrounding the Great Lakes is a contrast of wilderness and activity. Travel around the Great Lakes and you will find international port cities, quaint fishing villages, historic logging camps, and rich farmland. Here are some little known facts about the Great Lakes area.

1. Minnesota is called the "land of 10,000 lakes" but there really are thousands more.

2. Wisconsin's Door County, the thumb on the state map that juts out into Lake Michigan, is known as the "Cape Cod of the Midwest."

3. Mackinac Island, located in the Upper Peninsula of Michigan, was once a key fur trading post.

4. Traverse City, located in the Lower Peninsula of Michigan, is the "Cherry Capital of the World."

5. The "City of Big Shoulders" is a nickname for Chicago.

6. Minnesota is also known as Paul Bunyon Territory and the "Land of Hiawatha." The Chippewa tribe once hunted along the shores of the "Shining Big-Sea-Water."

Some people skip the most important meal of the day--breakfast. Most experts beleive a good breakfast is essential to sensable eating. It restores the body's energy, which was used during the nite. Those who skip breakfast becuase they don't have time, need to change their habits. Wake up a half-hour earlier and their will be time for that all-improtant meal.

Production

Application 5: An Eye for Fashion

Directions:

- Default side margins
- 2-inch top margin; default bottom margin
- Center title; Return/Enter twice after title
- Double spacing
- Underline and boldface where indicated
- File name: Fashion

AN EYE FOR FASHION

Quality is the **key** to good fashion buying, but that doesn't mean that the most expensive item is the best quality. Here are some clues to quality:

Read labels carefully. Labels should tell you washing instructions, how much the fabric will shrink, and what finishes have been applied--waterproofing, mothproofing, or wrinkle resistant. If a label says nothing but fabric content, you can assume none of these special finishes has been applied.

Check construction. Stitching should be small and straight. Hems should be flat and even. Hooks, snaps, and buttons should be securely attached. Buttonholes should fit snugly over buttons. Points of strain should be reinforced with extra stitching, metal rivets, or patches.

Application 30: Preparing for Recycling

Directions:

- 1-inch side and bottom margins
- 2-inch top margin
- Center the title; double space twice after the title
- Double space throughout
- Indent enumerated items five spaces from left and right margins
- File name: Ap30

PREPARING PLASTIC FOR RECYCLING

In order to make recycling easier, manufacturers of plastic are starting to use a standardized coding system on the bottom of the container. The code consists of a number surrounded by the arrows and letters underneath that tell recyclers at a glance what kind of plastic was used to make the container. Presently, only the numbers 1, 2, and 6 can be recycled at the county recycling center.

Here are some things to keep in mind when preparing your plastics for recycling.

1. Make your materials as flat as possible. Get the air out by crushing the plastic container.

2. Keep the materials clean. Be sure to rinse out the container.

3. Separate your materials. Put plastics in a separate container from your other recyclables.

4. Precycle. If you can't recycle it, avoid buying it in the first place. That sends a loud and clear message to the manufacturer to get on the recycle bandwagon.

Application 6: Shape-Up Exercises

Directions:
- 2-inch side margins
- 2-inch top margin; default bottom margin
- Center title; Return/Enter twice after title
- Double spacing
- Underline and boldface where indicated
- File name: Exercise

EXERCISES TO SHAPE UP

Most people do not understand that it is not **how much** you exercise but **how you exercise**. Slow movements help firm muscles. Fast movements are tiring and decrease the desire to keep going. As with any exercise, see your doctor before you begin.

The <u>Stretch.</u> Use this exercise to warm up. Lie on your back with your arms over your head. Extend your left arm and hold it for five seconds. Do the same with the right arm. Do a total of ten stretches.

The <u>Bend.</u> Sit on a chair and spread your legs wide. Bend over and touch the floor between your feet. Sit up and throw your arms sideways. Do this exercise ten times.

The <u>Slow Rock.</u> Lie on your stomach with your legs together and palms down under your shoulders. Push your body up and back until you are sitting on your heels with your head between your arms. Do this modified pushup ten times.

Application 29: Packing Your Luggage

Directions:

- 1-inch side and bottom margins
- 2-inch top margin
- Center the title; double space twice after the title
- Single space; double space between paragraphs and between enumerated items
- Indent enumerated items five spaces from left and right margins
- File name: Ap29

PACKING YOUR LUGGAGE

How you pack your suitcase and what you take with you can make the difference between an enjoyable vacation and a terrible one. Here are some tips by the experts.

1. Pack only clothes that can be washed and hung to dry. Leave clothes that require dry cleaning at home. No-iron synthetics are the most practical; they are light and require little care.

2. Pack two or three basic colors and build your wardrobe around them. You will have a variety of outfits with a minimum of items.

3. Always put your name on both the inside and outside of the case. There are lots of bags that look exactly like yours. Having your name inside is insurance in case your outside tag gets lost.

4. Pack tightly but do not over pack. Fill in gaps and corners with small items like socks, underwear, and scarves.

5. Avoid wasting space. Shoes can hold socks, underwear, and even small plastic bottles of cosmetics and shampoo.

6. Remember to take along plastic bags for carrying home your dirty laundry.

Indenting Text

Objectives:

- To learn how to underline existing text
- To learn how to boldface existing text
- To learn how to indent text from the left margin
- To learn how to indent text from both left and right margins
- To practice composing at the computer
- To practice proofreading

PART A

Warmup

Retrieve your Journal file. Add to your journal what you learned in the previous lesson about these topics:

- soft page break
- hard page break
- strikeover (typeover) to insert words
- underlining text as you key
- boldfacing text as you key
- insert mode

PART B

Composing at the Computer

Here are some more adages for you to complete. Key each beginning on a separate line and complete the rest of it.

```
a. The early bird...

b. Time flies when...

c. April showers bring...

d. Don't cry over...

e. If at first you don't succeed...

f. Better to have loved and lost than...

g. All that glitters...

h. Finders keepers...

i. Don't put the cart...

j. Look before...

k. Where there's smoke...

l. Don't count your chickens...

m. Strike while the iron...
```

Numbers

Your teacher will dictate the numbers below. Close your eyes and see if you can key them without looking at your fingers. Be prepared to read back the numbers line by line.

1 45 89 34 01 29 67 48 39 65 23 90 21 44 96 38 72 18
2 234 895 673 901 738 284 39 576 482 385 495 192 406
3 386 754 592 304 781 65 485 329 574 092 784 388 296

Proofreader's Mark Explained

The symbol ∿ means to transpose or switch the letters around.

Example: Plant the aok tree.

Plant the oak tree.

Practice with Proofreader's Mark

Key each line **once,** making the changes indicated.

1 The catlaog will be ready for distributino Friday.
2 Our group spent the nihgt cheernig for their team.
3 Please mend the brokne window panes before winter.

Enumerations

Enumerations are lists of things. They are easy to key if you use the commands for your software that indent text from the left and right margins. To begin the list below, tab to the paragraph indention point. Key the number 1 followed by a period. Then use the software command that indents text from the left and right margin and wordwrap the paragraph. Your copy will look like this:

1.   Always pronounce your words so other people can
      understand what you are saying.

When you use the indent command, there will be 3 spaces after the period. Note in the example above that the first letter of the second line aligns under the first letter in the first line.

Underlining Existing Text

Sometimes you may decide to underline text after you have keyed it. Your teacher will show you how to do this with your software. Then practice by underlining only *your responses* to the phrases in Part B on the previous page.

Boldfacing Existing Text

Sometimes you may decide to boldface text after you have keyed it. Your teacher will show you how to do this with your software. Then practice by boldfacing the *entire phrase* given in Part B on the previous page.

Indenting from the Left Margin

You already know that pressing the Tab key indents the first line on the left. If you want all lines to be indented, use the Indent command. Your teacher will explain how your software accomplishes this. Then key each paragraph below so all lines are indented from the left margin. Use wordwrap.

```
The pitch of your voice is important.  A high
pitch means you are tense or fearful.  Too low a
pitch means you are tense or unsure of what you
are saying.


The rate at which you speak is another part of
your voice.  When you talk fast, people think
you are nervous.  On the other hand, if you talk
very slowly, people may think that you think
slowly too.


Voice volume is the third part of your voice.  A
loud volume tells others how you feel.  A soft
volume makes people think you are not sure of
what you are saying.
```

Application 28: Music Audition Announcement

Directions:

Compose and print an announcement for auditions for the school band or orchestra. Be sure to state the time and place. Remind students not to be tardy!

LESSON 50

Formatting Enumerations

Objectives:

- To improve speed
- To improve accuracy of numbers
- To learn the proofreader's mark for transpose
- To learn how to format invitations and announcements

PART A

Warmup

Key the lines below, **twice** each.

1 Please fix the gas burners so the flames are high.

2 The ivory panel is the focus of the new city hall.

3 Kent works down by the dock but dislikes the odor.

4 Use a No. 2 pencil for the test, not a No. 1 or 3.

. . . . 1 . . . . 2 . . . . 3 . . . . 4 . . . . 5 . . . . 6 . . . . 7 . . . . 8 . . . . 9 10

PART B

Speed Building

Below are more lines containing alternate-hand phrases. Practice them in this manner: The first time you do each line, key at a moderate speed. The second time you do the same line, increase your speed. The third and final time you do the same line, key just as fast as you possibly can.

1 paid me│pay us│fix the bus│fix the cot│fix the rut

2 then do│then bid│then rush│then make│then do it by

3 mend the panel│mend the dial│do mend the clay bowl

4 pale dish│pale clay│pale born│to chant│tow the tub

. . . . 1 . . . . 2 . . . . 3 . . . . 4 . . . . 5 . . . . 6 . . . . 7 . . . . 8 . . . . 9 10

Indenting from Both Left and Right Margins

One way to make text stand out on the page is to indent it from both the left and right margins. Your teacher will show you the commands to accomplish this. Then rekey the three paragraphs in Part E so all paragraphs are indented from both the left and right margins.

Proofreading Practice

The paragraph below contains seven errors. Use wordwrap as you key it. Your job is to find and correct all errors as you key. If it is available, you might wish to use a spell check program. However, a word of caution. There is one word spell check will not find.

A kangaroo has just given birth to a baby that is only one-inch long. The elephant is acting panickey. A snake has refused its food; the snake has not eatten for all most eighteen months. The monkey is scraeming at the top of his lungs. The polar bear has a sick stomach from eating too many marshmellows. The penguin has a borken beak, and the wallrus keeps whistling at passers-by. These are some of the problems the zoo veterinarian faces every day.

Proofreader's Mark Explained

The symbol ⌒ means to close up or bring the letters together.

Example: Please turn (⌒)he dial.

Please turn the dial.

Practice with Proofreader's Mark

Key each line **once,** making the changes indicated.

1 Marilyn tries to avoid dark city parks a⌒fter dark.
2 It was dif⌒ficult to see the dock because of a fog.
3 Turn right here if you w⌒ant to see the new garden.

Composing and Formatting on Your Own

In this part of the lesson, you are on your own. Follow the directions given for each problem. You must decide on the content and how to arrange it attractively on the page. The word processing commands for your software will help you accomplish this. It is your decision whether to single or double space and where to set the margins. If in doubt about how to arrange the problem, look back at the sample in the previous lesson. Remember to spell check and proofread carefully before printing a copy of each job. Then decide on a file name and save it for future reference.

Application 26: Birthday Party Invitation

Directions:
Compose and print an invitation to a birthday party for yourself or a friend or relative. It should be at least six lines long. Be sure to include the time, date, and location. Ask those invited to RSVP to your phone number.

Application 27: Pet Birth Announcement

Directions:
Compose and print a humorous birth announcement for a dog who just gave birth to a litter of puppies. Use your imagination. What information should be included in such an announcement?

Production

Application 7: Handwriting Analysis

Directions:
- 1-inch side margins
- 2-inch top margin; default bottom margin
- Center title; Return/Enter twice after title
- Double spacing
- Wordwrap
- Indent second, third, and fourth paragraphs from both left and right margins
- File name: Writing

HANDWRITING ANALYSIS

Have you ever had your handwriting analyzed? To a trained eye, your handwriting is a map of your basic personality. Here are some basic rules about handwriting.

Writing Position on the Line. If your writing slants uphill, this means you are an optimist. You always look on the bright side of things. If your writing slants downhill, then you are pessimistic or skeptical. You tend to focus on the negative things. If your writing is straight across, then you are levelheaded.

Writing Slant. If your writing slants to the right, you prefer to work with people, not alone. If your writing slants to the left, you are a shy person. If your writing is vertical, your mind and heart are balanced.

Size of Writing. If your writing is very large, you like to surround yourself with people. If your writing is small, you are interested in facts, details, and figures rather than companionship.

Composing Invitations and Announcements

Objectives:
- To improve accuracy on alphabet keys
- To improve accuracy on numbers
- To learn the proofreader's mark for close up
- To compose and format invitations and announcements

PART A

Warmup

Key each line below **twice.**

1 John and Fred will play in the league game on Fri.
2 If you can work the dials, you are a smart person.
3 A rigid disk is needed for the old model computer.
4 Buy $5 worth of lottery tickets and $25 of tokens.
....1....2....3....4....5....6....7....8....9....10

PART B

Accuracy Building

Below are lines containing word patterns. Key each line **three times** in succession with 100% accuracy before you move on to the next line.

1 ern southern northern western eastern patterns ern
2 ble bubble tables stables able capable durable ble
3 der sender builder reader fender gender tender der
4 mp stamp ramp lamps camp damp tramp champs limp mp

PART C

Numbers

Your teacher will dictate the numbers below. Close your eyes and see if you can key them without looking at your fingers. Be prepared to read back the numbers, line by line.

1 13 89 61 90 38 46 28 89 45 20 06 48 71 82 94 34 51
2 125 783 90 020 893 175 187 298 382 964 010 458 217
3 238 493 766 190 500 365 671 843 982 674 239 132 85

Application 8: Wilderness Safety

Directions:

- 1-inch side margins
- 2-inch top margin; default bottom margin
- Center title; Return/Enter twice after title
- Double spacing
- Wordwrap
- Boldface where indicated
- Indent boldfaced paragraphs five spaces from the left margin
- File name: Safety

PLAYING IT SAFE IN THE WILDERNESS

Next time you vacation in the wilderness, play it safe. Here are some tips from the U.S. Department of Agriculture.

Bears. When in bear country, never camp or hike alone. Make your presence known; most bears will avoid hikers if they know where they are. The more noise you make, the better it is.

Poisonous Plants. Poison ivy and poison oak commonly grow as vines attached to trees. If the plant has leaves in sets of three, let it be. Don't touch it. Poison sumac is identified by its white berries.

Water. Always filter or boil your drinking water.

Campsites. The best places to camp are on ridges, hills, or near canyon walls. These sites have natural drainage and will not flood during a storm.

Fires. Do not place rocks around the fire. They will not keep fire from spreading and may explode from intense heat. Always be sure the fire is out before leaving and never leave a fire unattended.

Application 24: Computer Club Announcement

Directions:
- Center each line horizontally
- Center top to bottom
- Double space between lines
- File name: Ap24

<u>Calling</u> <u>All</u> <u>Hackers!</u>

Don't miss the next COMPUTER CLUB meeting

Guest Speaker: Barry Mickelson

Topic: Computer Viruses

Date: April 16

Time: 3:30 p.m.

Place: Room 47

Application 25: Candy Company Announcement

Directions:
- Center each line horizontally
- Center top to bottom
- Double space between lines
- File name: Ap25

LOFTON CANDY COMPANY NEEDS TASTERS

To Test New Products

<u>Must</u> <u>like</u> <u>chocolate</u> <u>and</u> <u>licorice</u>

<u>Must</u> <u>be</u> <u>between</u> <u>the</u> <u>ages</u> <u>of</u> <u>12</u> <u>and</u> <u>16</u>

Report to Company Headquarters

234 Maple Avenue

Saturday, February 17

9:00 to 12:00

First Fifty People Accepted

SECTION 4

Learning Number Keys and the Most Frequently Used Symbol Keys

Invitations and Anouncements

Application 23: Talent Show Invitation

Directions:
- Center each line horizontally
- Center top to bottom
- Double space twice between lines
- File name: Ap23

YOU ARE INVITED

TO THE DAWSON JUNIOR HIGH

TALENT SHOW

Monday, March 24

Gymnasium

7:30 p.m.

Introducing 1 and 9

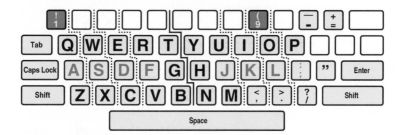

Objectives:

- To learn the number **1** and number **9** keys
- To compose at the computer
- To review language arts principles
- To work on building speed

PART A

Warmup

Retrieve your Journal file. Add to your journal what you learned in the previous lesson about these topics:

- underlining existing text
- boldfacing existing text
- indenting text from the left margin
- indenting text from both the left and right margins

PART B

1 Key

Some computer keyboards have two sets of numbers. One set is located on the top row above the alphabet keys. The other is located to the right of the alphabet keys and is called a number pad. The number pad is arranged similar to a calculator and is operated by only one hand. To activate the number pad, you must press certain keys to turn it on and off. The number pad is used if the operator is entering data that contains only numbers. If the operator is keying data that contains numbers mixed with alphabetic characters, it is easier to use the number keys located on the top row of the keyboard. In this book we will not use the number pad. You will be using the number keys above the alphabet keys.

The number **1** key is located on the top row of the keyboard, just above the **Q**, and you will use your **A** finger on it. Try it now. Key **aq1** several times. Now try the lines on the next page, **twice** each. As you key, try to keep your **F**, **D**, and **S** fingers at home.

Proofreader's Mark Explained

Anyone who reads a paper for errors is a proofreader. There is a set of standard marks used by proofreaders. One of them is this one: ≡ Whenever you see this mark, it means you must capitalize the letter or letters that are underlined.

Example: John miller is captain.

John Miller is captain.

Practice with Proofreader's Mark

Key each line **once,** making the changes indicated.

1 mr. aspen wants to buy a new car before next year.
2 Our new treasurer is derek; our new secretary, Jo.
3 Ann's report is on the book, History of Computers.

Now key the paragraphs below making the changes indicated.

You may be wondering how certain gestures got started. According to one legend a thumbs-up sign was first used by roman emperors and the audiences at coliseums where gladiators battled. The thumbs up meant the victors should spare the lives of the rivals; a thumbs-down sign meant death. Sometimes president bush would use two thumbs up when he got off air force one. That meant his travels had all gone well.

A different president, mr. nixon, used a sign when speaking to the american people. He used the victory sign. He spread his first two fingers far apart to form the letter "v" which meant he surely would win the election. Sir winston churchill is credited with inventing this sign during world war II.

```
1 a1a 1aa a1a 1aa a1a 1aa a1a 1aa a1a 1aa
2 aaa 111 aaa 111 aaa 111 aaa 111 aaa 111
```

Now try these lines, **twice** each.

```
3 11 apples; 11 oranges; 11 pears; 11 peas; 11 beans
4 Study page 1; it contains 11 things you will need.
5 Refer to pages 1 through 11 for the data you want.
```

Key

The number **9** key is located on the top row of the keyboard, just above the **O**, and you will use your **L** finger on it. Try it now. Key **lo9** several times. Now try the lines below, **twice** each. As you key, be sure to keep your **J** and **K** fingers at home.

```
1 191 911 191 911 191 911 191 911 191 911
2 111 999 111 999 111 999 111 999 111 999
```

Now key these lines, **twice** each. Try to key the number without looking at your hands.

```
3 9 students; 9 parents; 9 teachers; 9 teams; 9 dogs
4 Daniel took 9 picnic baskets and 9 folding chairs.
5 Only 9 of the boys did not take our test number 9.
```

PART D

1 and 9 Keys Combined

Key the lines below, **twice** each. Note when using numbers to indicate time, there is no space before or after the colon.

```
1 19 tables; 19 chairs; 11 sofas; 11 carts; 91 boxes
2 Take 11 players plus 9 of the alternates with you.
3 Remind Michael to be there at 11:19 sharp or else.
....1....2....3....4....5....6....7....8....9....10
```

LESSON 48

Formatting Invitations and Announcements

Objectives:
- To improve speed
- To improve accuracy of numbers
- To learn the proofreader's mark for capitalize
- To learn how to format invitations and announcements

Warmup

Retrieve your Journal file. Add to your journal what you learned in the previous lesson about this topic:
- center tables horizontally

Speed Building

Below are lines containing alternate-hand phrases. Practice them in this manner: The first time you do each line, key at a moderate speed. The second time you do the same line, increase your speed. The third and final time you do the same line, key just as fast as you possibly can.

```
1 she may│he may│dig sod│key the map│the icy bus may
2 they paid│she paid│he paid│the icy lane│make a bid
3 work the dials│both of them chant│sue both of them
4 fix the bus│fix the dock│fix the dish│fix the cork
  . . . .1. . . .2. . . .3. . . .4. . . .5. . . .6. . . .7. . . .8. . . .9. . . .10
```

Numbers

Key each line below **twice.** Try to be as accurate as you possibly can.

```
1 we 23 jk 78 fg 45 hj 67 as 12 l; 90 fj 47 a; 10 we
2 dk 38 sl 29 a; 10 jf 74 kd 83 ls 92 ;a 01 gh 57 dk
3 asd 123 sdf 234 dfg 345 hjk 678 jkl 789 kl; 890 as
```

Composing at the Computer

Complete the sentences below as you key them. Fill in the blanks with your own personal thoughts and feelings.

a. Getting a good education is important because...

b. If I could do something over again, it would be _____ because...

c. If I could talk with any famous person in history, it would be _____ because...

d. I think one of the best careers is _____ because...

e. My favorite subject at school is _____ because...

f. One of my most successful experiences was _____ because...

g. A place I enjoyed visiting on vacation was _____ because...

h. A specific age that I would like to be again is _____ because...

i. If I could change one thing about my school it would be _____ because...

j. For one day I wish I could switch places with _____ because...

k. For my birthday I would like _____.

l. One thing I enjoy doing with my time is...

m. If I could change one thing in the world today it would be _____ because...

SECTION 6

Producing Different Documents

Speed Building

The lines below contain common phrases. Key them **twice** each. After you have had a chance to practice them, your teacher will time you for one minute on each line. Try to add an extra word to your speed score on the second timing on the same line.

```
1 may go│may have│may be│may want│may need│may leave
2 for the│for it│for him│for her│for our│for if they
3 and the│and will│and may│and get│and send│and come
4 to sing│to think│to bake│to plant│to pick│to speak
 . . . .1. . . .2. . . .3. . . .4. . . .5. . . .6. . . .7. . . .8. . . .9. . . .10
```

Language Arts Mystery

The paragraph below has three sets of series commas omitted. Read the paragraph and try to find all of these errors; then as you key, correct the errors.

Next time you eat some popcorn, think about how it was made in the old days. Native Americans had three methods for popping corn. One way was to skewer an ear of corn on a stick roast it over a fire and gather the kernels as they fell free of the flames. The second method was to scrape the cob throw the kernels directly into a low fire and catch the popped corn as it jumped out of the fire. The third method used a shallow clay cooking pot containing sand. First the sand was heated until it reached a high temperature. Then the kernels were stirred in. As the kernels popped, they came to the surface of the sand. Today the average American consumes two pounds of popcorn a year and pops it in a microwave oven electric corn popper fireplace or on top of the stove.

COMMON METRIC EQUIVALENTS

inch	centimeters
foot	meters
yard	meters
mile	kilometers
ounce	grams
pound	kilograms
pint	liters
quart	liters
gallon	liters

Application 22: Newberry Award Winners

Directions:

- Determine left margin and two tab settings using key line; leave five spaces between columns
- Center the title; double space twice after the title
- Center top to bottom
- Double space the body of the table
- File name: Books

TEN YEARS OF NEWBERRY AWARD WINNERS

1981	JACOB HAVE I LOVED	Paterson
1982	A VISIT TO WILLIAM BLAKE'S INN	Willard
1983	DICEY'S SONG	Voight
1984	DEAR MR. HENSHAW	Cleary
1985	THE HERO AND THE CROWN	McKinley
1986	SARAH, PLAIN AND TALL	MacLachlan
1987	THE WHIPPING BOY	Fleischman
1988	LINCOLN: A PHOTOBIOGRAPHY	Freedman
1989	JOYFUL NOISE: POEMS FOR TWO VOICES	Fleischman
1990	NUMBER THE STARS	Lowry
1991	MANIAC MAGEE	Spinelli

Challenge

In the next five lessons, you are going to play a board game called Number Challenge. Your teacher will give you a copy of the game, which appears below. You must keep this paper for the next five lessons so you can keep track of your progress and your teacher can determine who is the winner.

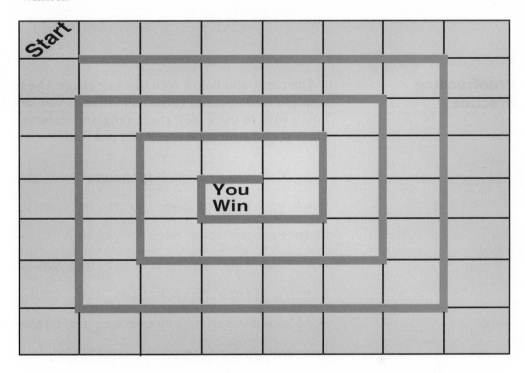

To play the game, you will need a partner, someone who is sitting near you. Find one now. Everyone begins on the "start" square. To move on the board you must key with 100% accuracy the lines that appear below. Your teacher will time you for two minutes on each line. Both you and your partner are to key at the same time. At the end of the timing, your partner will verify how many lines you completed with 100% accuracy and mark your progress on the game board. You will do the same for your partner. Remember, to move one square on the game board, you must have completed the line once with 100% accuracy. Partial lines do not count. Ready to play?

1 Mike bought 19 books, 91 pencils, 11 clips, and 19 staplers.

2 Sue needs 191 reams of paper, 911 ribbons, and 919 red pens.

3 That book was written in 1991 not 1911; Al checked the date.

```
1 first-rate deal; low-cost printing; self-confident
2 foreign-born actor; out-of-date book; out-of-doors
3 bigger-than-life; lean-tos; fourth-class packages;
4 out-of-the-way places; self-inflicted; co-signers;
```

PART G

Proofreading Practice

The paragraph below contains five errors. Use wordwrap as you key it. Your job is to find and correct all errors as you key. If it is available, you might wish to use a spell check program. However, a word of caution. There is one error spell check will not find.

```
You were probably taught to cover your mouth
when you yawned because it is considred good maners.
This custom goes back to ancent times when doctors
observed that new-born infants yawned shortly after
birth.  Since many babies died young, the doctors
concluded that the yawn was to blame for there death
and advised mothers to cover the baby's mouth to
prevent the breath of life from sliping away.
```

PART H

Production

Application 21: Metric Equivalents

Directions:

- Determine left margin and one tab setting using key line; leave 20 spaces between columns
- Center the title; double space twice after the title
- Center top to bottom
- Double space the body of the table
- File name: Metric

(continued on next page)

Introducing 2 and 0

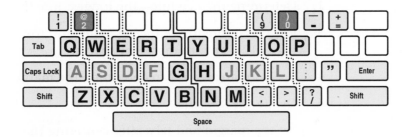

Objectives:

- To learn the number **2** and the zero (**0**) keys
- To compose at the computer
- To review language arts principles
- To work on building accuracy

PART A

Warmup

Key the lines below, **twice** each. As you key the numbers, try to avoid looking at your fingers.

```
1 9 trumpets, 1 drum, 9 violins, 1 piccolo, 9 organs
2 11 days, 19 months, 9 years, 11 minutes, 1 century
3 Please buy 19 dozen cinnamon buns and 1 gal. milk.
4 For breakfast Ed had 91 donuts and 19 cups of tea.
  . . . .1. . . .2. . . .3. . . .4. . . .5. . . .6. . . .7. . . .8. . . .9. . . .10
```

PART B

2 Key

The number **2** key is located just above **W**, and you will use your **S** finger on it. Try it now. Key **sw2** several times. Then try the lines below, **twice** each. As you key, keep your **F** and **D** fingers at home.

```
1 s2s 2ss s2s 2ss s2s 2ss s2s 2ss s2s 2ss
2 sss 222 sss 222 sss 222 sss 222 sss 222
```

Now key the lines on the next page, **twice** each. Try to avoid looking at your fingers when you key the numbers.

Horizontally Centering a Short Table

Horizontally center the table below, leaving six spaces between columns. Follow these steps:

1. Use the automatic centering command to center the title.

2. Determine the key line—the longest line in each column.

3. Use the automatic centering command to key the key line, using the digits 123, etc., to represent spaces.

4. Use your arrow keys to determine the margin and tab settings.

5. Delete the key line.

6. Set the margin and tabs after centering the title.

```
                    VACATION SITES

Everglades                      Florida

Washington Monument             Washington, D.C.

Glacier National Park           Montana
```

Speed Practice

The lines below are designed for skill comparison. The first line uses primarily home-row keys. The second line uses third row keys. The third line uses bottom row keys. The fourth line uses top row keys. Practice the lines for a few minutes. Your teacher will time you for one minute on each line. Compute your speed on each line and then compare the lines to see on which keys you need further practice.

```
1 Dad or Sal had a half a salad; Sasha added a flag.
2 A witty quarterly report was written on Wednesday.
3 Vincento can fix six or seven boxes for Benny Cox.
4 Key 1 or 2 or 8 or 9; then add 56 and 438 and 710.
  . . . .1. . . .2. . . .3. . . .4. . . .5. . . .6. . . .7. . . .8. . . .9. . . .10
```

Accuracy Practice

The lines on the next page contain more hyphenated words. Practice them for a few minutes. Then find a partner. As one person dictates the line, the other keys. Then switch roles. If you wish, you may turn back to other pages containing hyphenated words and include these in your dictation to your partner. Try to beat your partner by getting more phrases correct.

3 2 cups flour, 2 spoons of sugar, 2 pats of butter.

4 Her report is 22 pages and must be done by May 22.

5 Take 22 disks for Thomas; he also needs 22 labels.

PART C

Key

Look at your keyboard and locate the **0** key. It's just above P, and you will use your sem finger on it. Try it now. Key **;p0** several times. Keep your **J** and **K** fingers at home when striking **0**. Now try the lines below, **twice** each.

1 ;0; 0;; ;0; 0;; ;0; 0;; ;0; 0;; ;0; 0;;

2 ;;; 000 ;;; 000 ;;; 000 ;;; 000 ;;; 000

Now try these lines **twice**.

3 0 pears; 0 oranges; 0 apples; 0 bananas; 0 mangoes

4 If you multiply 0 times 0, your answer is still 0.

5 At the Paris airport we saw 0 planes and 0 people.

PART D

2 and **0** Keys Combined

Key the lines below **twice** each. As you key the numbers, try to avoid looking at your fingers.

1 20 boxes, 22 cartons, 20 trucks, 22 cars, 20 trees

2 Jake needs 22 parts to fix 20 pieces of equipment.

3 Is it check number 200 or number 02 that you want?

. . . . 1 . . . . 2 . . . . 3 . . . . 4 . . . . 5 . . . . 6 . . . . 7 . . . . 8 . . . . 9 10

PART E

Composing at the Computer

Can you coin a phrase? Let's find out. Listed on the next page are some letters of the alphabet. Your job is to make up a phrase where each word begins with one of the letters given. For example, suppose you were given the letters E, Y, K, and C. You might come up with the phrase, *Keep Your Eyes Closed*, or *You Can Eat Ketchup*.

Composing at the Computer

Compose a short story in which the first sentence begins with the letter *a*, the second with the letter *b*, and so forth. The last sentence of the story should begin with the letter *z*.

Centering Tables Horizontally

You already know how to center a line horizontally. Centering a table horizontally involves using the same command. However, first you must look at the entire table and pick the "key line." The key line contains the longest words in each column plus the number of spaces left between columns. For example, suppose you wanted to horizontally center the short table below and leave eight spaces between the columns.

Statue of Liberty	New York
Mt. Rushmore	South Dakota

The longest line in the first column is Statue of Liberty. The longest line in the second column is South Dakota. Using the automatic horizontal center command for your software you would key the following line:

Statue of Liberty12345678South Dakota

Then you would move your cursor to the beginning of the first column and note the position of the "S" in Statue. That would become your left margin setting. Then you would move your cursor along the key line and note the position of the "S" in South Dakota. That would be your first tab setting. Since you do not need a right margin, you would set it for 0, or as close to 0 as your software will permit. *If the table has a title, you must horizontally center that before making margin and tab changes.* After you have set the margin and tab, then delete the key line before starting the body of the table.

Incidentally, if you are wondering how many spaces to leave between columns, there is no magic number. If directions do not state this information, it is left to your judgment. Generally, the space between columns should not be so great that the reader has trouble following the line of type across the page. Nor should the space be so small that the reader has difficulty distinguishing where one column ends and another begins.

a. A, W, T, R
b. M, P, D, Y
c. W, B, L, F
d. O, H, N, G
e. C, P, J, K

PART F
Accuracy Building

The lines below contain the same letter combinations. You will have to concentrate to key them accurately. Do each line three times in succession. Try for three perfect lines.

1 ail fail bail mail jail pail ail fail bail pail ail

2 ire dire fire mire tire wire ire dire fire mire ire

3 ill bill mill will sill dill ill bill mill will ill

4 ate gate hate date mate late ate hate date mate ate

PART G
Language Arts Mystery

The paragraph below needs three commas before conjunctions to join compound sentences. Can you find them and make the corrections as you key?

A sandwich is food eaten between two slices of bread. It is a convenient way to eat lunch when a hot meal is not possible. We have John Montagu, the fourth Earl of Sandwich, to thank for this convenience. It seems that Mr. Montagu was a gambler and he enjoyed gambling so much that he refused to leave the gambling tables to eat a meal. Once he gambled for twenty-four hours straight. To avoid leaving, he ordered that sliced meats and cheese be served to him between pieces of bread. This food enabled him to eat with one hand for he could gamble with the other. Some time later the episode became known as the sandwich incident and the earl's trademark was born.

Application 20: State Nicknames and Capitals

Directions:

- 1-inch side, top, and bottom margins
- Clear out default tab settings
- Set two tabs: the first 25 spaces from the left margin; the second 27 spaces from the first tab
- (If your own state is not in the list, add the appropriate information as the last line.)
- Double space
- Center the title; double space twice after the title
- File name: Capitals

STATE NICKNAMES AND CAPITALS

Alabama	Cotton State	Montgomery
Delaware	Diamond State	Dover
Florida	Sunshine State	Tallahassee
Indiana	Hoosier State	Indianapolis
Kansas	Sunflower State	Topeka
Massachusetts	Bay State	Boston
Texas	Lone Star State	Austin
[Your State]	[Nickname]	[Capital]

LESSON
47

Centering Tables Horizontally

Objectives:

- To learn how to use a key line to center tables horizontally
- To practice composing at the computer
- To practice proofreading
- To improve speed
- To improve accuracy

PART A

Warmup

Retrieve your Journal file. Add to your journal what you learned in the previous lesson about this topic:

- how to clear out the preset tab settings
- how to set new tab settings

Challenge

Take out your Number Challenge gameboard, which you used in Lesson 33. You will continue playing, using the directions given in that lesson. Here are your lines for the game:

1 If you add 19 and 20, and then subtract 29, what do you get?

2 Check figure 209 on page 119; then review chart 210 and 211.

3 By the yr. 2019 there will be 9100 people in our small town.

LESSON 35

Introducing 3 and 7

Objectives:

- To learn the number **3** and number **7** keys
- To compose at the computer
- To review language arts principles
- To work on building speed

PART A

Warmup

Key the lines below, **twice** each. As you key the numbers, try to avoid looking at your fingers.

1 2 brothers, 0 sisters, 1 aunt, 9 uncles, 0 cousins

2 12 knives, 91 spoons, 10 forks, 19 plates, 21 cups

3 Order 10 pizzas, 19 bottles of pop, and 12 plates.

4 Bart will meet me at 11:19 instead of 11:20 today.

. . . . 1 . . . . 2 . . . . 3 . . . . 4 . . . . 5 . . . . 6 . . . . 7 . . . . 8 . . . . 9 10

Proofreading Practice

The paragraph below contains six errors. Use wordwrap as you key it. Your job is to find and correct all errors as you key. If it is available, you might wish to use a spell check program. However, a word of caution. There are two errors spell check will not find.

There really was a Mother Goose. Some historeans say she was a Boston widow who was born in 1665. When she maried Isaac Goose, she became the stepmother of ten children, and she had six more of her own. Her ryhmes were published in 1719 by one of her sons-in-law. Others say Mother Goose was really a man! In 1697 Charles Perrault published a book containing eight children's stories called "Tales of My Mother Gose." Perhaps we shall never no if Mother Goose was really a man or a women.

Production

Application 19: State Birds and Flowers

Directions:
- 1-inch top, bottom, and side margins
- Clear out default tab settings
- Set two tabs: the first 26 spaces from the left margin; the second 23 spaces from the first tab
- Double space
- Center the title; double space twice after the title
- File name: States

<u>State</u> <u>Birds</u> <u>and</u> <u>Flowers</u>

Yellowhammer	Alabama	Camellia
Brown Thrasher	Georgia	Cherokee Rose
Robin	Connecticut	Mountain Laurel
Brown Pelican	Louisiana	Magnolia
Cardinal	Kentucky	Goldenrod
Meadowlark	Oregon	Oregon Grape
Seagull	Utah	Sego Lily
Robin	Wisconsin	Wood Violet
Lark Bunting	Colorado	Columbine

3 Key

Look at your keyboard and locate the number **3** key. It's just above the **E** key, and you will use your **D** finger on it. Try it now. Key **de3** several times. Now try the lines below, **twice** each. Be sure to keep your **A** finger at home when keying these lines.

1 d3d 3dd d3d 3dd d3d 3dd d3d 3dd d3d 3dd
2 ddd 333 ddd 333 ddd 333 ddd 333 ddd 333

Now try the lines below, **twice** each. As you key, keep your eyes on the book and not on your fingers.

3 33 bats, 33 balls, 33 bases, 33 hats, 33 programs,
4 They traveled 33 long miles on 33 different roads.
5 She moved to 33 Park Place from 33 Berkley Street.

7 Key

Look at your keyboard and locate the number **7** key. It's just above the **U** key, and you will use your **J** finger on it. Try it now. Key **ju7** several times. Now try the lines below, **twice** each. Be sure to keep your sem finger at home when keying these lines.

1 j7j 7jj j7j 7jj j7j 7jj j7j 7jj j7j 7jj
2 jjj 777 jjj 777 jjj 777 jjj 777 jjj 777

Now key the lines below, **twice** each. Keep your eyes on the book.

3 77 oaks, 77 elms, 77 pines, 77 maples, 77 lindens,
4 Ted purchased 77 pairs of gloves and 77 ear muffs.
5 Please plan to meet in Room 77 at 77 E. Marvin Rd.

3 and 7 Keys Combined

Key the lines below, **twice** each. As you key the numbers, try to avoid looking at your fingers.

1 37 cartons, 73 boxes, 37 planes, 77 trucks, 33 ads
2 Stan waits at Pier 37, not Pier 73, for the cargo.
3 Their closet has 37 pairs of shoes and 73 dresses.
. . . . .1. . . . .2. . . . .3. . . . .4. . . . .5. . . . .6. . . . .7. . . . .8. . . . .9. . . .10

Changing the Default Tab Settings

Be sure you have a 1-inch left margin. Clear out preset tabs. Set a tab 15 spaces from the left margin. Set another tab 15 spaces from the first tab setting. Now key the columns of data below as follows: Key *Benjamin* at the margin. Press the Tab key so you are at your first tab stop and key *Sarah*. Then press Tab once again so you are at your second tab stop and key *Olivia*. Now press Return/Enter and do the next line in the same way. Note, columns of data are called tables, and tables are always keyed by going across the columns.

Benjamin	Sarah	Olivia
George	Patricia	Ruth
Arthur	Helene	Theresa
William	Kirk	Dorothy

Speed Practice

You are going to work again on building speed endurance. Below are sentences containing alternate-hand words. Take a 30-second timing on each line and compute your speed by multiplying the number of words keyed by two. Then repeat the same line for one minute and compute your one-minute speed by using the scale given. Your goal is to achieve the same speed for one minute as you did for half a minute.

1 To make a profit the girls sign half of the forms.
2 Sign the form for clay panels and rush them to us.
3 The man to blame for the big fight is Ken Guthrie.
4 Al may make six city signs for the downtown firms.
. . . . 1 . . . . 2 . . . . 3 . . . . 4 . . . . 5 . . . . 6 . . . . 7 . . . . 8 . . . . 9 10

Accuracy Practice

The lines below contain more hyphenated words that may slow you down. Key each line **twice.** Try to be as accurate as you can.

1 low-cost plan; camera-ready copy; self-evaluation;
2 personal-injury claim; five-year plan; self-denial
3 jam-packed days; moment-by-moment; off-color humor
4 back-breaking efforts; burnt-sugar cake; by-lines;

Composing at the Computer

Here are some cartoons without dialogue. Compose sentences to fill in the empty balloons for each picture. Be sure to identify the dialogue you compose as picture **a**, **b**, **c**, and **d**.

Speed Building

The lines below contain more common phrases. Key them **twice** each. After you have had a chance to practice them, your teacher will time you for one minute on each line. Try to add an extra word to your speed score on the second timing on the same line.

```
1 as you know|as you may know|as you will|as you can
2 be able|can be able|will be able|might not be able
3 if he|if she|if they|if my|if and when|if they can
....1....2....3....4....5....6....7....8....9....10
```

Print a copy before proceeding to the steps below.

1.   Search and replace one instance of *creative* with *imaginative*.

2.   Search and replace one instance of *creative* with *inventive*.

3.   Search and replace *rejected* with *refused*.

4.   Search and replace *trait* with *quality*.

5.   Underline the words replaced and print a copy.

LESSON 46

Changing Default Tab Settings

Objectives:
- To learn how to change the default tab settings
- To practice composing at the computer
- To practice proofreading
- To improve speed
- To improve accuracy

PART A

Warmup

Retrieve your Journal file. Add to your journal what you learned in the previous lesson about this topic:

- how to search for a word or phrase and replace it with another word or phrase

PART B

Composing at the Computer

Remember composing the "What am I?" riddle in Lesson 45? This time you are to think of a famous person, living or dead. Compose five clues. For example, suppose you selected Thomas Jefferson. One clue might be, "I was a signer of the Declaration of Independence." Another clue might be, "I lived in Virginia." When you have finished your clues, switch computers with another student and see if he or she can figure out the riddle.

PART C

Default Tab Settings

Most software programs have tabs preset at certain intervals, such as every five spaces. This is called the *default setting*. If you want to change the tabs and set them at different intervals, you must first clear out the default tabs. Your teacher will show you the commands to clear out preset tabs and set new tabs.

Language Arts Mystery

The paragraph below has four errors in possessive case apostrophes. Can you find all of them and make the corrections as you key?

Legend says that the American flag was designed by a seamstress, Betsy Ross, who was visited by General George Washington. They were supposed to have discussed various flag designs. Washington design was composed of seven red and six white stripes and thirteen six-pointed stars arranged in a circle. Betsy Ross convinced him it would be easier for her to cut out five-pointed stars and General Washington agreed. But Washington diary makes no mention of meeting a local seamstress. The tale was told by Betsy Ross grandson who claims to have heard it as a boy on his grandmothers deathbed. Whether history or legend, Betsy Ross is now part of American folklore.

Challenge

Take out your Number Challenge gameboard, which you used in Lesson 34. You will continue playing, using the directions given in Lesson 33. Here are the lines for the game:

1 By April 19 Mark must have finished 12 reports and 10 books.

2 She ordered 327 cases of No. 201 and 219 cartons of No. 731.

3 The most important day in 1937 is remembered by all in 1973.

Application 18: Creativity

Directions:

- 1-inch side and bottom margins
- Double space
- Center the title; double space twice after the title
- Wordwrap
- 2-inch top margin
- File name: Creative

BEING CREATIVE

If you think you have to be a genius to be creative, you're wrong. People who study creativity say that intelligence and creativity are two different things and are not related. People who are creative have more fantasies, more ability, and tend to think about ideas. When a problem arises, the creative person tends to look for a solution rather than get angry. Creative people also have a good sense of humor.

Walt Disney believed that everyone is creative in childhood, but as we get older, we tend to lose our powers of imagination. People only turn on their creative "motor" when motivated to do so. Creative people want and go after change. Creativity results when one looks for the answers to problems.

Creativity is not easy to recognize. When twenty well-known American companies were given Albert Einstein's job application with the name omitted, two-thirds rejected it because of poor education.

How can you tell if your creative efforts are coming through? One expert suggests that you look inside yourself. Produce what you feel. Creativity is a trait that we all possess to some degree.

(continued on next page)

Introducing 5 and 8

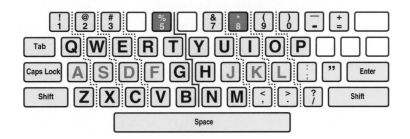

Objectives:
- To learn the number **5** and number **8** keys
- To compose at the computer
- To review language arts principles
- To work on building accuracy

PART A

Warmup

Key the lines below, **twice** each. As you key the numbers, try to avoid looking at your fingers.

1 3 blue, 7 pink, 3 slate gray, 9 purple, 0 rose red

2 19 tulips; 37 daisies; 21 daffodils; 10 marigolds;

3 Nick purchased 10 cones, 9 sundaes, and 12 floats.

4 Her goal is to sell 291 tickets by 10:00 Thursday.

. . . . 1 . . . . 2 . . . . 3 . . . . 4 . . . . 5 . . . . 6 . . . . 7 . . . . 8 . . . . 9 10

PART B

 Key

The number **5** key is located on the top row of the keyboard, just above the **T**, and you will use your **F** finger on it. Try it now. Key **ft5** several times. Now try the lines below, **twice** each. As you key, be sure to keep your **A** and **S** fingers at home.

1 f5f 5ff f5f 5ff f5f 5ff f5f 5ff f5f 5ff

2 fff 555 fff 555 fff 555 fff 555 fff 555

Use the lines on the next page to practice the reach to the number **5** key. Do them **twice** each. Try to keep your eyes on the book as you key.

Don't select a particular field because you like the job surroundings or you are impressed with a title. None of these are reasons for entering that career. You, and only you, must be interested in the job.

The second area to consider is your abilities. What are you good at? Most abilities fall into one of five categories--verbal, numerical, mechanical, spatial, and clerical. Verbal is the ability to express yourself in words and ideas. Numerical is the ability to solve problems with numbers. Mechanical is the ability to solve problems involving machines. Spatial is the ability to put parts together to form a whole. Clerical is the ability to handle details.

The third important area to consider is personality. Do you prefer to be alone or with people? Do you work well under pressure? Are you easily upset when things go wrong? Would you rather carry out other people's plans or make your own?

Now is the time to start thinking about your career. Planning is the first step to finding the right career.

Print a copy before proceeding to the steps below.

1. Search and replace one instance of *career* (not in the title) with the word *vocation.*

2. Search and replace another instance of *career* (not in the title) with the word *occupation.*

3. Search and replace one instance of *abilities* with the word *skills.*

4. Underline the words replaced and print a copy.

3 5 plans, 55 charts, 55 graphs, 55 diagrams, 5 maps

4 Only 55 of the members came; 55 folks were absent.

5 Joe's keyboarding speed is 55; I can also type 55.

8 Key

The number **8** key is located on the top row of the keyboard, just above the **I**, and you will use your **K** finger on it. Try it now. Key **ki8** several times. Now try the lines below, **twice** each. As you key, be sure to keep your **J** finger at home.

1 8k8 8kk 8k8 8kk k8k 8kk k8k 8kk k8k 8kk

2 kkk 888 kkk 888 kkk 888 kkk 888 kkk 888

Use the lines below to practice the reach to the number **8** key. Do them **twice** each. Try to keep your eyes on the book as you key.

3 8 blankets, 8 sheets, 88 beds, 88 pillows, 8 lamps

4 Of 88 students only 8 came late and 8 were absent.

5 Ted ate 8 chili dogs, 8 hotdogs, and 8 sandwiches.

5 and 8 Keys Combined

Key the lines below, **twice** each. Try to keep your eyes on the textbook as you key the numbers.

1 58 boards, 58 drills, 85 nails, 85 screws, 85 saws

2 For the answer to problem 85 see page 5, figure 8.

3 Their club sold 85 pies, 58 cakes, and 85 cookies.

. . . . 1 . . . . 2 . . . . 3 . . . . 4 . . . . 5 . . . . 6 . . . . 7 . . . . 8 . . . . 9 10

Composing at the Computer

Below are some letters of the alphabet. For each group, compose a sentence using a word that begins with each letter. Words must follow the order in which the letters are given.

1. p, i, d, u, t.
2. w, h, b, e, n.
3. a, k, c, j, m.
4. u, r, g, a, l.
5. s, j, o, h, b.

Proofreading Practice

The paragraph below contains six errors. Use wordwrap as you key it. Your job is to find and correct all errors as you key. If it is available, you might wish to use a spell check program. However, a word of caution. There are two errors spell check will not find.

Teen agers are the target of many advertising campains. Sometimes those adds make the teen buy something that realy is not wanted or needed. One thing some ads try to do is direct the teen toward a "fad" item. When it comes to clothes, fad clothnig costs up to 25% more than regular fashion items. Another item to keep in mind when buying clothes is where you buy them. If you by your clothes in stores that sell strictly by cash, you can save about 25%.

Production

Application 17: Choosing a Career

Directions:
- 1-inch side and bottom margins
- Double space
- Center the title; double space twice after the title
- Wordwrap
- 1.5-inch top margin
- File name: Career

CHOOSING A CAREER

The first step in planning a career is to look carefully at yourself. There are three areas that you should consider when deciding upon a career.

The first area, and most important, is your interests. Don't let people persuade you to enter a field just because they happen to like that career.

(continued on next page)

Accuracy Building

The lines below contain the same letter combinations. You will have to concentrate to key them accurately. Do each line **three times** in succession. Try for three perfect lines.

```
1 all ball falls tall hall ball tall fall halls tall
2 ing sing ring flings sting sings rings fling sting
3 er dealer sealer hunter power dealer hunters power
4 ay may say bay hay ray days may gay says bays gray
```

Language Arts Mystery

The paragraph below contains two rambling (run-on) sentences. Correct these as you key.

```
    Blue jeans were not always blue nor were they
made of denim.  Their invention is credited to a
young seventeen-year-old tailor named Levi Strauss
who immigrated to San Francisco during the gold rush
of the 1850s.  He sold canvas for tents and covered
wagons but realized that the miners could use
trousers made of the heavy material. He began stitching
canvas into overalls.  The stiff pants held up well
and made Strauss a popular tailor, he replaced canvas
with denim, a softer fabric.  He discovered that
dyeing the denim indigo blue helped to minimize stains
and this greatly increased its popularity.  When the
miners complained about their tools splitting the
pocket seams, Strauss applied copper rivets at each
pocket seam to solve the problem.  Although invented
to be work clothes, today blue jeans are play clothes.
```

Searching and Replacing

Key the explanation given in Part C on the previous page. Then follow the steps below.

1. Search for the word *many* and replace it with *several*.

2. Search for the word *replace* and replace it with *restore*.

3. Search for the word *teacher* and replace it with *instructor*.

4. Search for the word *helpful* and replace it with *useful*.

5. Search for the word *accomplish* and replace it with *achieve*.

PART E
Speed Practice

You are going to work on building speed endurance. Below are sentences containing alternate-hand words. Take a 30-second timing on each line and compute your speed by multiplying the number of words keyed by two. Then repeat the same line for one minute and compute your one-minute speed by using the scale given. Your goal is to achieve the same speed for one minute as you did for half a minute.

```
1 The busy social panel forms the focus of the work.
2 Their autos may jam by the rocks down by the lake.
3 Dirk is sick due to the odor of clams by the dock.
4 A man and a dog got a box of soap for Mr. Dirkens.
 . . . .1. . . .2. . . .3. . . .4. . . .5. . . .6. . . .7. . . .8. . . .9. . . .10
```

PART F
Accuracy Practice

The lines below contain more one-hand words that may slow you down. When you have one line keyed with perfect accuracy, raise your left hand. When you have two lines done with perfect accuracy, raise your right hand. When you have three lines done accurately, raise both hands, and when you finish the fourth line, stand up. When there are ten people standing, your teacher will stop the exercise.

```
1 are hip bet joy car kin ear oil set him web ply as
2 join bread milky aware phony grade kiln acre holly
3 draw lily exact plump water knoll deter upon edges
4 fades puny jump vast nylon wasted onion crafted no
```

Take out your Number Challenge gameboard, which you used in Lesson 35. You will continue playing, using the directions given in Lesson 33. Here are the lines for the game:

1 Rita took part in 59 races in which she got 12 first places.

2 Find page 831 and then look at page 952 to check the answer.

3 She has moved from 7931 N. Bower Road to 8510 W. Wenonah Dr.

LESSON 37

Introducing 4 and 6

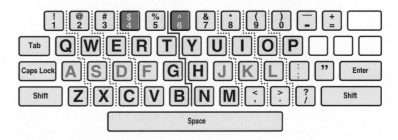

Objectives:

- To learn the number **4** and number **6** keys
- To compose at the computer
- To review language arts principles
- To work on building speed

PART A
Warmup

Key the lines below, **twice** each. As you key the numbers, try to avoid looking at your fingers.

1 5 goats, 8 sheep, 7 dogs, 2 pigs, 9 horses, 3 cows

2 12 tractors, 20 trucks, 18 farmers, 31 corn cribs,

3 The geography exam will cover pages 237 up to 391.

4 Jorge weighs only 117 pounds but Ramos weighs 180.

. . . . .1. . . . .2. . . . .3. . . . .4. . . . .5. . . . .6. . . . .7. . . . .8. . . . .9. . . .10

Searching and Replacing Text

Objectives:
- To learn how to search for a group of characters and replace it with different characters
- To practice composing at the computer
- To practice proofreading
- To improve speed
- To improve accuracy

PART A

Warmup

Retrieve your Journal file. Add to your journal what you learned in the previous lesson about this topic:
- how to search for a word
- the advantages of using search

PART B

Composing at the Computer

Can you write a good "What Am I?" riddle? Let's find out. Think of an inanimate object found in your classroom. Compose five clues. For example, suppose you selected the chalkboard. One clue might be, "I sometimes squeak." Another clue might be, "I am only one color." When you have finished your clues, switch computers with another student and see if he or she can solve the riddle.

PART C

The Search and Replace Function

You already know how to search, either forward or backward, to locate a particular group of characters. Many word processing programs have another feature, which not only allows you to search for a particular word or phrase but to replace it with another word or phrase. The search and replace feature can be helpful in editing your document. You can search for one word and replace it with another. Or you can perform a *global* search and replace, which means the program will automatically replace every instance of the word you are searching for with the replacement word. Your teacher will explain the command your software uses to accomplish this.

Key

The number **4** key is located on the top row of the keyboard, just above the **R**, and you will use your **F** finger on it. Yes, the **F** finger controls two number keys, the **4** and **5.** Try it now. Key **fr4** several times. Now try the lines below, **twice** each. As you key, be sure to keep **A** and **S** fingers at home.

1 f4f 4ff f4f 4ff f4f 4ff f4f 4ff f4f 4ff
2 fff 444 fff 444 fff 444 fff 444 fff 444

Now key these lines, **twice** each. Try to key the numbers without looking at the keyboard.

3 4 snakes, 44 turtles, 4 alligators, and 4 dolphins
4 Glen must fill out form 44 and take it to room 44.
5 I am stationed with unit 4 and must serve 44 days.

 Key

The number **6** key is located on the top row of the keyboard, just above the **U**, and you will use your **J** finger on it. Yes, the **J** finger controls two number keys, the **6** and **7.** Try it now. Key **ju6** several times. Now try the lines below, **twice** each. As you key, be sure to keep your **L** and sem fingers at home.

1 j6j 6jj j6j 6jj j6j 6jj j6j 6jj j6j 6jj
2 jjj 666 jjj 666 jjj 666 jjj 666 jjj 666

Now key these lines, **twice** each. Remember to keep your eyes on the textbook as you key.

3 66 books, 66 magazines, 66 bulletins, 6 references
4 Ned needs 66 volunteers for the 66th bicycle race.
5 Why is it that only 6 of the 66 hikers have packs?

4 and 6 Keys Combined

Key the lines on the next page, **twice** each. Try to key the numbers without looking at your hands.

are different varieties to choose from, but that was not the case in the beginning.

Back in 1920 the girl scouts gathered in their homes and baked the cookies in their mothers' kitchens. There was one basic recipe, and everyone followed it. As one story goes, some Girl Scouts were standing in the window of the Philadelphia Gas Works, where they were working on their cooking badges baking cookies and handing them out to passersby. Someone suggested the girls sell the cookies, and a new idea was born.

In 1934 the Keebler Baking Company was hired by the girl scouts to bake a shortbread cookie in the shape of the official symbol of the girl scouts. The cookies sold for 23 cents a box. Today each local Girl Scout Council makes an agreement with one of the bakeries licensed to produce the cookies. Nowadays you can sink your teeth into thin mints, shortbreads, peanut butter sandwiches, lemon pastry cremes, caramel and toasted coconut, or peanut butter and chocolate cookies.

Print a copy of the document. Position your cursor at the beginning of the text. Use the search command to answer the questions below. Write your answer on your printed copy. Some of these words may be followed by a comma or period, so you may need to search several times—once for the word followed by a space, the second time for the word followed by a comma, and the third time for the word followed by a period.

1. How many times was the word *cookies* used?

2. How many times was the word *shortbread* used?

3. Search for the phrase *Girl Scouts* to determine (a) how many times it was used, and (b) if it was capitalized each time. If you find it was not, make the correction.

```
1 46 coats, 64 hats, 64 sweaters, 46 jackets, 4 caps
2 What do you get when adding 66 and 46 and then 64?
3 Look at Case No. 46; it is similar to Case No. 64.
. . . .1. . . .2. . . .3. . . .4. . . .5. . . .6. . . .7. . . .8. . . .9. . . .10
```

PART E

Composing at the Computer

Find a partner. Each person should key a list of letters of the alphabet similar to the one that appears in Lesson 36, Part E. There should be at least six letters in each group. Now switch computers and compose a sentence using a word that begins with each letter. Words must follow the order in which the letters are given.

PART F

Speed Building

The lines below contain more common phrases. Key them **twice** each. After you have had a chance to practice them, your teacher will time you for one minute on each line. Try to add an extra word to your speed score on the second timing on the same line.

```
1 about it│about the│about when about│their│about us
2 if you│are if│they are│if we are│if she│is if I am
3 and when│and why│and what│and where│and how│and no
. . . .1. . . .2. . . .3. . . .4. . . .5. . . .6. . . .7. . . .8. . . .9. . . .10
```

PART G

Language Arts Mystery

The paragraph below contains two double negatives. Can you find and correct them as you key?

```
    Next time you throw a Frisbie, think of pie.
Yes, pie.  Were it not for the Frisbie Pie Company of
Bridgeport, Connecticut, and its pie tins, there
couldn't hardly be Frisbies thrown today.  William
Frisbie operated a bakery that delivered pies in tins
bearing his name.  Students at Yale University amused
themselves by tossing the pans through the air.  The
college fad might have died were it not for a
Californian, Walter Morrison, who had an interest in
```

(continued on next page)

teenager, you should see an oculist at least once
every two years.

An oculist is a doctor who specializes in
diseases of the eye. That person may be a medical
doctor who is qualified to treat diseases of the eye
or an optometrist, someone who examines eyes and
prescribes glasses but is not a medical doctor.
Opticians are people who make and sell glasses. When
you visit the eye-care professional or oculist, be
prepared to describe any vision problems you are
having.

Print a copy of the document. Position your cursor at the beginning of
the text. Then use the search command to answer the questions below.
Write your answer on your printed copy. Because some of these words may
be followed by a comma or period, you may need to search several times—
once for the word followed by a space, the second time for the word
followed by a comma, and the third time for the word followed by a
period.

1. How many times was the phrase *eye-care professional* used?

2. How many times was the word *oculist* used?

3. How many times was the word *doctor* used?

Application 16: Girl Scout Cookies

Directions:

- 2-inch top margin
- Double space
- Center the title; double space twice after the title
- Wordwrap
- 1-inch side and bottom margins
- File name: Cookies

GIRL SCOUT COOKIES

If you have not sold the cookies yourself,
perhaps you have had a sister or classmate invite you
to have one of these special cookies. Today there

(continued on next page)

flying saucers and hardly never missed the chance to read about aliens. He wanted to capitalize on this interest and invented a light metal toy disk, which he sold through the Whamo-O Company as a "Flying Saucer." Soon plastic replaced the metal, and saucers were flying on California beaches. By 1959 tossing pie tins on college lawns had been replaced by a national craze.

Challenge

Take out your Number Challenge gameboard, which you used in Lesson 36. This is the last opportunity you will have to make progress on the gameboard. Continue playing, using the directions given in Lesson 33. Here are the lines for the game:

1 Joleen picked out 46 cards to send but Stephen only sent 25.

2 Beginning Wednesday Catalog No. 690 will be replaced by 824.

3 Meet me at 12:00 sharp on Saturday, at 9273 N. Glidden Road.

LESSON 38

Introducing $ and %

Objectives:
- To learn the **dollar sign** (**$**) and the **percent sign** (%) keys
- To compose at the computer
- To review language arts principles
- To work on building accuracy

Proofreading Practice

The paragraph below contains eight errors. Use wordwrap as you key it. Your job is to find and correct all errors as you key. If it is available, you might wish to use a spell check program. However, a word of caution. There is one error spell check will not find.

What do you collect? Some people collect animal figureens. Others like anteek jewelery. Still others get satisfaction out of collecting baseball cards, or bottel caps, or marble eggs. When people travel, they usualy bring back some kind of souvanir. Some travelers collect plates or spoons that bare the name of the place visited. Others delight in taking photografs and pasting them in scrapbooks or collecting postcards or T-shirts or mugs showing their destination.

Production

Application 15: Eye Care

Directions:

- 2-inch top margin
- Double space
- Center the title; double space twice after the title
- Wordwrap
- 1-inch side and bottom margins
- File name: Eyes

EYE CARE

Eye fatigue can be a problem to students. When studying, take an occasional three-minute "eye break"--look straight ahead and far away. Then come back to what you were doing.

If your eyes feel tired or you are getting lots of headaches, you may need to see an eye-care professional. Even if you do not have symptoms, you should see an oculist. By the time you are a

(continued on next page)

Warmup

Key the lines below, **twice** each. As you key the numbers, try to avoid looking at your fingers.

1 9 birds, 8 fish, 7 kittens, 4 puppies, 3 hamsters,
2 12 sandals, 34 boots, 56 sneakers, and 78 slippers
3 Add 127 plus 789 plus 346 plus 201 plus 896 to 30.
4 A note written on May 26, 1988, is most important.

. . . . 1 . . . . 2 . . . . 3 . . . . 4 . . . . 5 . . . . 6 . . . . 7 . . . . 8 . . . . 9 10

 Key

The symbol for dollars is the shift of the number **4** key, so you will use your **F** finger on it. Try it now. Key **fr4$** several times. Then key the lines below, **twice** each. Be sure to bring your sem finger back home after shifting.

1 f$f $ff f$f $ff f$f $ff f$f $ff f$f $ff
2 fff $$$ fff $$$ fff $$$ fff $$$ fff $$$

Now try these lines, **twice** each. Try to keep your eyes on the book as you key. Note there is no space between the dollar sign and the number nor before or after the decimal.

3 $34 and $78 and $90 and $12 and $56 and $80 and $1
4 The blue coat costs $65 but the brown coat is $85.
5 The bill is for $36.95 but I paid $25.00 Saturday.

 Key

The symbol for percent is the shift of the number **5** key, so you will use your **F** finger on it. Try it now. Key **fr5%** several times. Then key the lines below, **twice** each. Be sure to bring your sem finger back home after shifting.

1 f%f %ff f%f %ff f%f %ff f%f %ff f%f %ff
2 fff %%% fff %%% fff %%% fff %%% fff %%%

Now key the lines on the next page, **twice** each. Try to avoid looking at your hands as you key. Note there is no space between the percent sign and the number that precedes it.

Searching

Use the search command to locate the following words in work you have keyed so far today:
the
and
I
center
centering top to bottom
the name of the job you wrote about in Part B

Speed Practice

Below are more lines containing common phrases. Take a one-minute timing on each line. Try to key each phrase as one complete thought. Then repeat the same line for another minute and try to increase your speed on the second try.

```
1 if the│if he│if they│if she│if we│if our│of course
2 for their│for our│for him│for her│for us│thank you
3 to make│to take│to sign│to give│to talk│because of
4 about our│about us│about them│all of the│all of us
  . . . .1. . . .2. . . .3. . . .4. . . .5. . . .6. . . .7. . . .8. . . .9. . . .10
```

Accuracy Practice

Below are lines that contain hyphenated words. Key each line **twice**. When you have finished practicing, your teacher will ask you to team up with a partner. You and your partner will take turns dictating, in any order, the words you have just practiced. The person keying must key that word accurately **three times** in succession. If you make a mistake, start counting from one again. Then switch roles. Continue until your teacher stops the activity.

```
1 two-inch strips; double-coated tape; self-defense;
2 right-hand corner; tricks-of-the-trade; short-cut;
3 double-wide load; mobile-home owner; home-made pie
4 circle-tour rates; round-trip fares; out-of-print;
```

3 14% and 39% and 17% and 86% and 90% and 52% and 6%
4 Wendy got 98% on her test, but Randy got only 87%.
5 Lionel got 40% and Marilyn got 30% of the profits.

PART D

$ and % Keys Combined

Key the lines below, **twice** each. Try to key the symbols without looking at your hands.

1 50% $23 89% $19 36% $60 14% $31 52% $29 $74 87% $1
2 They sold 85% of the tickets and obtained $246.68.
3 From your bill of $276.51, do take a 20% discount.
....1....2....3....4....5....6....7....8....9....10

PART E

Composing at the Computer

A humorist created a series of statements called Murphy's Laws. These statements are based on the idea that if anything can go wrong, it will. Here are some examples that apply to computers:

- A computer will do strange things when you are operating it, but when you call the teacher over to see what it is doing, the computer will work fine.
- When you get ready to print, the printer always runs out of paper.

Compose as many of these "laws" as you can that relate to school.

PART F

Accuracy Building

The lines below contain the same letter combinations. You will have to concentrate to key them accurately. Do each line **three times** in succession. Try for three perfect lines.

1 oss loss toss boss floss gloss toss boss loss toss
2 old gold told hold mold sold gold molds sold holds
3 aze daze mazes amaze blazes gaze daze blaze amazes
4 ent bent sent rent agent dent bent sent rent agent

Searching Text

Objectives:
- To learn how to search for a group of characters
- To practice composing at the computer
- To practice proofreading
- To improve speed
- To improve accuracy

Warmup

Retrieve your Journal file. Add to your journal what you learned in the previous lesson about this topic:

- how to center text vertically (from top to bottom)

Composing at the Computer

Compose a short paragraph answering the question, If I could have any job (occupation) in the world, it would be _____. In your paragraph explain why you would like this job.

The Search Function

A group of characters may be composed of alphabetic letters, numbers, or symbols, or any combination of the three. Many word processing programs have a command that allows you to search, either forward or backward, to locate a particular group of characters. Searching for a particular word or phrase can be helpful. You may want to search to verify that the word or phrase was capitalized each time it was used. Or you might search to make sure that you have not used the same word over and over in the text. In a long document you might use search to find the particular topic you want to read rather than cursor through page after page. Your teacher will explain the command your software uses to accomplish this.

Language Arts Mystery

The paragraph below contains several choppy sentences. See if you can redo them as you key.

```
     Some dogs go to school.  Schools are maintained
by the Army and Air Force.  These schools train dogs
to sniff out drugs or bombs.  This training takes
several months.  Dogs at these schools must be able
to sniff and retrieve.  Training begins by tossing a
plastic bag filled with drugs.  Praise is given if
the bag is retrieved.  Then the dog is told to stay.
The handler hides the bag.  Now the dog must depend
on his nose, not eyes, to find it.  Next, the handler
hides the bag in luggage or packages.  First there
are only a few packages.  Then more packages are
added.  If the dog succeeds at this, the bag is then
hidden in a car or building.  Next, the handler
disguises the scent with nearby articles smelling of
perfume.  Gradually the amount of perfume is
increased.  Eventually the dog is able to find the
bag when as much as 90% of the scent is perfume.
Dogs are taught to sit or lie down when discovering a
scent.  Pawing explosives could be dangerous.
```

Challenge

How high can you count on your keyboard? We're going to find out now. Your teacher will time you for one minute on each of the items listed below. Try to be as accurate as you can without looking at your hands.

1. Count by ones—example: 1 [space] 2 [space], etc.

2. Count by twos—example: 2 [space] 4 [space], etc.

3. Count by fives—example: 5 [space] 10 [space], etc.

4. Count by tens—example: 10 [space] 20 [space], etc.

Application 14: Dieter's Diet

Directions:

- Center top to bottom
- Boldface the three titles: Breakfast, Lunch, Dinner
- Double space
- Center all lines horizontally
- Double space twice between each segment (Breakfast, Lunch, Dinner)
- File name: Diet

<u>The</u> <u>Dieter's</u> <u>Recommended</u> <u>Diet</u>

BREAKFAST

4 oz. orange, grapefruit, or tomato juice

1 egg or 2 oz. cottage cheese or 2 oz. fish

1 slice whole grain bread or 2/3 oz. cold cereal

8 oz. skim or 2% milk

LUNCH

3 oz. cooked fish or chicken or 6 oz. cottage cheese

1 slice whole grain bread

Green or yellow vegetables of your choice

Fresh fruit or 1 c. sugarless canned fruit

8 oz. skim or 2% milk

DINNER

6 oz. cooked meat, fish, or chicken

Leafy green vegetable and root vegetable

Fresh fruit or 1 c. sugarless canned fruit

8 oz. skim or 2% milk

Introducing (and)

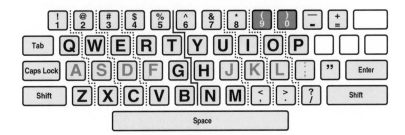

Objectives:
- To learn the **parentheses (and)** keys
- To compose at the computer
- To review language arts principles
- To work on building speed

PART A

Warmup

Key the lines below, **twice** each. Try to avoid looking at your hands when you key the numbers and symbols.

```
1 9% were approved; $3 are owed; 7% passed; $2 lost;
2 95% passed; 24 voted; $70 was discounted; 57 left;
3 This amendment vote was 781 in favor, 924 opposed.
4 Camille's proportions were 25% flour to 75% water.
....1....2....3....4....5....6....7....8....9....10
```

PART B

(Key

Look at the keyboard and locate the **left parenthesis** key. It's the shift of the number **9** key, so you will use your **L** finger on it. Try it now. Key **lo9(** several times. Then try the lines below. Be sure to keep **J** at home.

```
1 l(l (ll l(l (ll l(l (ll l(l (ll l(l (ll
2 lll ((( lll ((( lll ((( lll ((( lll (((
```

Now key the lines on the next page, **twice** each.

**Proofreading
Practice**

The paragraph below contains eight errors. Use wordwrap as you key it. Your job is to find and correct all errors as you key. If it is available, you might wish to use a spell check program. However, a word of caution. There are four errors spell check will not find. One of them is a spacing error.

How text is aranged on a page is very important. Weather the reader is attracted to the page depends on it. To make a page invitng to the reader, you must watch out for crowding. Narrow margins and too little space between headings and paragraphs require more effort to read; some people may opt not to try. When test is cramed together, it looks as if you were more interested in saving paper then getting your mesage across to the reader.

Production

Application 13: Alaska Time Zones

Directions:

- Center top to bottom
- Double space twice after the title and between the time zones

- Center all lines horizontally
- Double space
- File name: Zones

TIME ZONES IN ALASKA

Bering Sea Time

Nome

Alaska Standard Time

Anchorage

Fairbanks

Yukon Time

Dawson

Pacific Standard Time

Juneau

Ketchikan

3 (1 and (2 and (3 and (4 and (5 and (6 and (7 and (

4 Always use your "l" finger to hit the (or 9 keys.

5 The expert uses the shift key to strike the (key.

PART C
) Key

Look at the keyboard and locate the **right parenthesis** key. It's the shift of the zero key so you will use your sem finger on it. Try it now. Key **;p0)** several times. Then try the lines below. Be sure to keep **J** at home.

1 ;););; ;););; ;););; ;););; ;););;

2 ;;;))) ;;;))) ;;;))) ;;;))) ;;;)))

Now key these lines, **twice** each.

3 1) and 2) and 3) and 4) and 5) and 6) and 7) and)

4 Always use your ";" finger to hit the) or 0 keys.

5 The expert uses the shift key to strike the) key.

PART D

(and) Keys Combined

Key the lines below, **twice** each. Try to key the symbols without looking at your hands.

1 Steps to follow: (1) relax; (2) take deep breaths

2 Solutions to problems: (1) 67%; (2) $38.71; (3) 0

3 Ted Wilson's account (No. 481) has been cancelled.

. . . . 1 . . . . 2 . . . . 3 . . . . 4 . . . . 5 . . . . 6 . . . . 7 . . . . 8 . . . . 9 10

PART E
Composing at the Computer

Your teacher will call on every student to supply a word. Each word must be different. As each student calls out his or her word, key it on your screen. Your job is to use every word supplied by your classmates in as few sentences as possible.

PART F
Speed Building

The lines on the next page contain more common phrases. Key them **twice** each. After you have had a chance to practice them, your teacher will time you for one minute on each line. Try to add an extra word to your speed score on the second timing on the same line.

Center Top to Bottom

You already know the command for centering a line horizontally across the page. Now your teacher will explain how your software allows you to center all the lines on a page so there is equal white space at the top of the page and at the bottom. This is called centering top to bottom, or vertical centering.

Practicing Centering Top to Bottom

Starting with a blank screen, key the names of five teachers in your school, one name to a line. Then center the names top to bottom and print a copy for your teacher to check.

Speed Practice

Below are some common phrases. Take a one-minute timing on each line. Try to key each phrase as one complete thought. Then repeat the same line for another minute and try to increase your speed on the second try.

```
1 to a | have a | may be | to the | if we | for us | to be | may I
2 of our | to our | for our | that we | that they | is a | to be
3 for you | for your | for them | for him | for her | they can
4 we may | she may | he may | they may | be able to | could do
  . . . .1. . . .2. . . .3. . . .4. . . .5. . . .6. . . .7. . . .8. . . .9. . . .10
```

Accuracy Practice

Below are more lines that contain big words. Key each line **twice.** When you have finished practicing, your teacher will ask you to team up with a partner. You and your partner will take turns dictating, in any order, the words you have just practiced. The person keying must key that word accurately **three times** in succession. If you make a mistake, start counting from one again. Then switch roles. Continue until your teacher stops the activity.

```
1 erasure indicator experienced cylinder approximate
2 endorsement diagonally horizontally parallel paste
3 tendency dictation executive organization receipts
4 preliminary conveniences achievements accommodates
5 foundation virtually luxurious subdivision employs
```

```
1 he is able to|she is able to|we are able|to enable
2 of course it is|of course it will|of course I will
3 and so he|and so she|and so we|and so they|and so;
 ....1....2....3....4....5....6....7....8....9....10
```

PART G

Language Arts Mystery

The paragraph below has five places where quotation marks were omitted. Can you find them and make the correction as you key?

```
    If you are a typical American, you have probably
sung the song, Happy Birthday to You, many times.
Did you know you were singing a kindergarten song?
Written by two sisters, the tune was never intended
to be a birthday song; its original title was Good
Morning to All.  The Hill sisters copyrighted their
song in October of 1893, but it appeared in a songbook
published by Robert Coleman in 1924.  Mr. Coleman
changed the second stanza's opening to read Happy
birthday to you.  The original line, Good morning,
dear children, became Happy birthday, dear (name).
The tune became popular at birthdays.  Today the song
still is a birthday tradition.
```

PART H

Challenge

Remember the counting you did in the previous lesson? You are going to count again, but this time you must do it **with your eyes closed!** No peeking; your teacher will be watching. Ready? You will be timed for one minute on each of the items listed below. Try to be as accurate as you can.

1. Count by ones—example: 1 [space] 2 [space], etc.

2. Count by twos—example: 2 [space] 4 [space], etc.

3. Count by fives—example: 5 [space] 10 [space], etc.

4. Count by tens—example: 10 [space] 20 [space], etc.

Print a copy before proceeding further. To save paper, several permission slips can be printed on one sheet and cut into strips. Change the paragraph to single spacing. Use the copy command to copy the permission slip three more times on the same page. Put two double spaces between each permission slip. Then print a copy showing four slips on one sheet.

LESSON 43

Centering Vertically

Objectives:

- To learn how to center top to bottom
- To practice composing at the computer
- To practice proofreading
- To improve speed
- To improve accuracy

PART A

Warmup

Retrieve your Journal file. Add to your journal what you learned in the previous lesson about this topic:

- how to copy text from one place to another
- the advantages of copying text

PART B

Composing at the Computer

Listed below are some famous quotations. Your teacher may add others to this list. Your job is to expand on **one** of these quotations. Compose at least one paragraph explaining what this quotation means to you.

1. Education is a chest of tools.—Herbert Kaufman

2. Use the talents you possess, for the woods would be silent, indeed, if no birds sang except the best.—Henry VanDyke

3. Want is the mistress of invention.—Susanne Centlivre

4. The road to success is dotted with many tempting parking places.—Anon.

5. It is the person who knows everything that has the most to learn.—Anon.

6. The longest journey is the journey inward.—Dag Hammarskjold

7. The will to win is worthless if you do not have the will to prepare.—Thane Yost

Introducing * and !

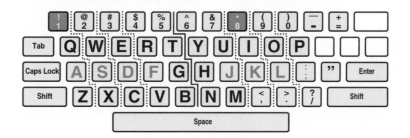

Objectives:

- To learn the **asterisk (*)** and **exclamation mark (!)** keys
- To compose at the computer
- To review language arts principles
- To work on building speed

Warmup

Key the lines below, **twice** each.

```
1 They tried (1) swimming; (2) aerobics; (3) soccer;
2 There will be a 20% increase starting February 15.
3 Plan to meet the group at 4:30 at 7641 W. Bayside.
4 Jeremy received $45, but he has already spent $35.

. . . . .1. . . . .2. . . . .3. . . . .4. . . . .5. . . . .6. . . . .7. . . . .8. . . . .9. . . .10
```

PART B

 Key

Look at your keyboard and locate the **asterisk** key. It's the shift of the number **8** key, so you will use your **K** finger on it. Try it now. Key **ki8***
several times. Now key the lines below, **twice** each.

```
1 k*k *kk k*k *kk k*k *kk k*k *kk k*k *kk
2 kkk *** kkk *** kkk *** kkk *** kkk ***
```

Print a copy of the menu before proceeding any further. Then follow the instructions below. You will use the copy command to eliminate rekeying the same information.

1. Center a new subtitle, <u>FOR</u> <u>THE</u> <u>HEALTH</u> <u>CONSCIOUS</u>, a double space below the last line.

2. Below this heading, copy the first part of the menu, starting with *MAIN DISHES,* and ending with *Frankfurters and Baked Beans.*

3. In the first item, change *Fried Shrimp* to *Broiled Shrimp.*

4. In the first item, delete *French Fried Potatoes.*

5. In the fourth item, change *with Gravy Sandwich, Mashed Potatoes, Vegetable* to *without Gravy, Two Vegetables.*

6. In the fifth item, change *with Gravy Sandwich, Fried Potatoes, Vegetable* to *without Gravy, Two Vegetables.*

7. In the sixth item, change *Breaded* to *Baked.*

8. In the last item, add *Low-Fat* in front of the word *Frankfurters.*

9. Print a copy showing these changes.

Application 12: Permission Slip

Directions:

- 1-inch top, bottom, and side margins
- Double space twice after the title and after the last line before "Parent Signature"
- Center the title
- Wordwrap
- Double space
- Estimate how long to make the line after "Parent Signature"
- File name: Slip

```
              FIELD TRIP PERMISSION SLIP
      I hereby give permission for my child to
accompany his/her class on the school field trip to
the zoo on Friday, October 15.  I understand my child
is expected to bring a sack lunch and his/her own
spending money.
      Parent Signature  _____
```

(continued on next page)

Now key these lines, **twice** each.

```
3 Some reference manuals use the * for one footnote.
4 You might also use the * to clarify word meanings.
5 The * is also used as sources of charts or tables.
```

 Key

Look at your keyboard and locate the **exclamation mark** key. It's the shift of the number **1** key, so you will use your **A** finger on it. Try it now. Key **aq1!** several times. Now key the lines below. As you key, be sure to keep your **F** and **D** fingers at home and keep your left elbow close to your body.

```
1 a!a !aa a!a !aa a!a !aa a!a !aa a!a !aa
2 aaa !!! aaa !!! aaa !!! aaa !!! aaa !!!
```

Now key the lines below, **twice** each. Note that the exclamation mark is similar to the period—there are two spaces following an exclamation mark unless it comes at the end of a line.

```
3 Stop, thief!  You cannot get away from the police.
4 Help!  Someone, please help me.  He is stuck here.
5 You expect me to change my plans.  Never!  No way!
```

 Combined

Key the lines below, **twice** each. As you key, try to reach for the symbol keys without looking at your hands.

```
1 Why did Jess put an * on this item?  Stop it, now!
2 Help!  My brother can't swim.  Hurry.  Save Frank!
3 *Note:  Mail left after 5:00 will go out tomorrow.
 . . . .1. . . .2. . . .3. . . .4. . . .5. . . .6. . . .7. . . .8. . . .9. . . .10
```

Composing at the Computer

Homonyms are words that sound alike but are spelled differently and have different meanings. Your job is to compose sentences that contain the homonyms on the next page—one homonym to a sentence. Count off by twos. If you are a No. 1, do the odd ones; if you are a No. 2, do the even. Be sure to compose good sentences because your teacher may call on you to read yours.

Headaches and tearing eyes can be caused by many things--air polution, sinus problems, or poor lighting. The lighting level should be even all over the room. Working under one brite lite in a dark room puts a lot of strain on your eyes. Glare can be a problem to; use draps and window shades to control sunlite. Avoid siting facing an unshaded window; the glare will cause eye strain. Also, paint walls and seilings with dull-finish paints to cut down on glare.

Production

Application 11. Menu

Directions:
- 1-inch top, bottom, and side margins
- Center the title and two subtitles
- Double space
- File name: Menu

<u>MENU</u>

MAIN DISHES

Jumbo Fried Shrimp with Cole Slaw, French Fried Potatoes ($6.99)

Broiled Filet of Sole, Cole Slaw, Baked Potato ($5.95)

Chopped Steak with Fried Onion Rings, Fried Potatoes ($4.95)

Hot Beef with Gravy Sandwich, Mashed Potatoes, Vegetable ($4.99)

Hot Turkey with Gravy Sandwich, Fried Potatoes, Vegetable ($4.50)

Breaded Veal Cutlet, Mashed Potatoes, Vegetable ($5.50)

Frankfurters and Baked Beans ($3.95)

DESSERTS

Small Scoop Ice Cream with your choice of syrup ($1.50)

Ice Cream Soda (all flavors) served with whipped cream ($2.50)

Ice Cream Sundae (all flavors) served with whipped cream ($2.50)

* Note: Non-Fat Yogurt may be substituted in any of the above.

(continued on next page)

1. principal, principle
2. gait, gate
3. weather, whether
4. who's, whose
5. bear, bare
6. its, it's
7. your, you're
8. hair, hare
9. deer, dear
10. wait, weight
11. site, sight
12. scene, seen
13. way, weigh
14. rite, right
15. there, their
16. too, two
17. real, reel
18. steel, steal
19. brake, break
20. for, four

Speed Building

The lines below contain alternate-hand words. Practice them for a few minutes. Your teacher will then time you for one minute on each line. Try to increase your speed by at least one word on the second timing on the same line. Then, on the third timing on that same line, try to increase your rate by even one more word.

```
1 of but for am is me to if us or by he she and with
2 jams keys land rich soap form glen halt clam docks
3 maid envy fuel goal worm busy dock them work forms
4 city paid hand wish odor chap airy held they field
  . . . .1. . . . .2. . . . .3. . . . .4. . . . .5. . . . .6. . . . .7. . . . .8. . . . .9. . . .10
```

Language Arts Mystery

The paragraph below is missing two colons. Can you put them in their proper places as you key?

```
    Tradition says that it would not be Thanksgiving
without turkey, cranberries, and pumpkin pie.  Yet
two of these were absent from the Pilgrims' meal.
Though wild turkeys roamed the woods of
Massachusetts, the bird did not grace the Pilgrims'
table.  In place of turkey the following meats were
present ducks, geese, lobsters, clams, venison, and
bass.  Since flour from the ship had been exhausted,
there was no flour to make a pie crust.  The Pilgrims
```

(continued on next page)

Practicing Copying Text

Select your two favorite horoscopes from those you composed in Part B. Copy and move them to another part of the screen.

Speed Practice

Below are more lines that contain alternate-hand words. Practice them for a few minutes. Your teacher will then time you for one minute on each line. Try to increase your speed by at least one word on the second timing on the same line. Then, on the third timing on that same line, try to increase your rate by even one more word.

```
1 panel auditor handle problems visible make signals
2 soap form goal wish lend firm island antique towns
3 social eighty half robot penalty blame claps visor
4 neighbor chair formal dismantle downtown usual six
  . . . .1. . . .2. . . .3. . . .4. . . .5. . . .6. . . .7. . . .8. . . .9. . . .10
```

Accuracy Practice

The lines below contain more one-hand words that may slow you down. When you have one line keyed with perfect accuracy, raise your left hand. When you have two lines done with perfect accuracy, raise your right hand. When you have three lines done accurately, raise both hands, and when you finish the fourth line, stand up. When there are ten people standing, your teacher will stop the exercise.

```
1 treat oily extra junk desserts union savages hilly
2 pupil exaggerates pop aged exact knoll water raced
3 tract moon rages million weeds terrace after water
4 garages vast served opinion referred cedar streets
```

Proofreading Practice

The paragraph on the next page contains nine errors. Use wordwrap as you key it. Your job is to find and correct all errors as you key. If it is available, you might wish to use a spell check program. However, a word of caution. There are two errors spell check will not find. One of them is a spacing error.

did enjoy pumpkin, however; but it was boiled. In addition the following were also on the table wild plums, dried berries, watercress, and leeks. Wild cranberries were collected, boiled, and mashed into a sauce for meat.

Challenge

You are probably becoming pretty good at counting at your computer. This time you will count for one minute following the steps below:

1. Count by ones—example: (1) [space] (2) [space], etc.

2. Count by ones—example: $1 [space] $2 [space], etc.

3. Count by ones—example: 1% [space] 2% [space], etc.

4. Count by ones—example: -1 [space] -2 [space], etc.

Copying Text

Objectives:
- To learn how to copy text
- To practice composing at the computer
- To practice proofreading
- To improve speed
- To improve accuracy

PART A

Warmup

Retrieve your Journal file. Add to your journal what you learned in the previous lesson about this topic:
- how to move text from one place to another
- the advantages of moving text

PART B

Composing at the Computer

Determine the birthday—month and day—of each student sitting in your row. Compose a short "make-believe" horoscope for each one. Print each horoscope out on a separate sheet of paper and give it to the person to whom it applies. Here are the astrological signs and dates:

Aries (March 21 to April 20)
Taurus (April 21 to May 20)
Gemini (May 21 to June 21)
Cancer (June 22 to July 22)
Leo (July 23 to August 22)
Virgo (August 23 to September 22)
Libra (September 23 to October 22)
Scorpio (October 23 to November 21)
Sagittarius (November 22 to December 21)
Capricorn (December 22 to January 19)
Aquarius (January 20 to February 18)
Pisces (February 19 to March 20)

PART C

The Copy Function

Copy is an editing function that allows you to duplicate a piece of text. First, you identify the part you want to copy. Second, you place that text in the temporary memory of the computer. Then you position your cursor where you want the copied text to go and retrieve the text. Your teacher will show you the commands your software uses to accomplish this.

SECTION 5

More Word Processing Functions

Application 10: Fragrance

Directions:
- 1-inch bottom and side margins
- Double space
- 2-inch top margin
- Wordwrap
- Center the title; Return/Enter twice after title
- File name: Scent

FRAGRANCE

Did you know that the way we relate to others is influenced by how we smell? Primitive tribes have gone to war because they did not like the way the other tribe smelled. Scientific research also shows that our physical well-being is influenced by what we smell.

Each of us has our own "scent fingerprint," which is different from anybody else's. Fragrance applied to skin differs from person to person. It depends on our skin type, weather, where the fragrance was applied, and how it was cared for.

Fragrance is available in different strengths. A good perfume is a blend of as many as 300 different elements. Perfume is the most concentrated and lasting. Toilet water is next in strength to perfume. Cologne is the lightest form of a fragrance for women but is the most concentrated form of men's fragrances. Shaving lotions, talcum powder, and men's bath oils have scents that last a shorter time than women's. Alcohol is blended in to determine the strength. Hot weather expands the smell, making it stronger. Always apply the scent from the feet up because scent rises. Once a bottle is opened, it begins to evaporate. Keep bottles tightly closed, away from heat and cold.

Print a copy before proceeding further. Then make these changes, using the move commands for your software, and print a second copy.

1. Move the sentence, *Alcohol is blended in to determine the strength.* to the beginning of the third paragraph.

2. Move the last four sentences to the end of the second paragraph.

Moving Text

Objectives:

- To learn how to move text
- To practice composing at the computer
- To practice proofreading
- To improve speed
- To improve accuracy

Warmup

Key the lines below **twice** each. As you key, try to avoid looking at your hands.

```
1 Angela will reduce her stock by 5% by November 19.
2 * Note:  Chart 1 on page 125 has been reduced 50%.
3 Your bill of May 18 for $784.24 has not been paid.
4 Do the following:  (1) exercise (2) eat good food.
  ....1....2....3....4....5....6....7....8....9....10
```

Composing at the Computer

As a student you have taken lots of quizzes. Here is your chance to make up a quiz about keyboarding. The quiz should have at least ten true/false questions and may cover anything contained in the lessons you have covered thus far. When you are finished, switch places with another person and see if you can answer each other's questions correctly. Then go back to your computer and grade the quiz.

The Move Function

An editing feature called "cut and paste" allows you to move text from one part of the document to another. First, you identify the part you want to move. Second, you place that text in the temporary memory of the computer. Then you position your cursor where you want the moved text to go and retrieve the text. Your teacher will show you the commands your software uses to accomplish this.

these early times tumblers, acrobats, and jugglers
existed.

The first modern circus was held in England.
Philip Astley started it by giving performances of
his trick horseback riding. Later he added more
stunts and an assortment of caged and leashed
animals. When he took his show to Paris, he started
the tradition of a traveling circus.

In this country the first circus was probably
run by a lone trapper who came to town with a tame
bear. For a few coins or a hot meal, the trapper
would put the bear through its paces. Gradually
other animals were added as well as clowns and
fearless horseback riders. Eventually small groups
of wagons traveled from town to town touring cross-
country.

As time went on, the circus became bigger and
bigger. Bands were added, and the wagons became more
colorful. Accomplished and fearless performers did
astonishing feats to entertain the audience. Some
did magic tricks. Some showed what the trained
animals could do. Others performed daredevil
breathtaking tricks in the air.

Print a copy before proceeding further. Then make the following
changes, using the move command, and print a second copy.

1. In the first paragraph, move *acrobats,* in front of *tumblers.*

2. In the second paragraph, switch *leashed* with *caged.*

3. In the third paragraph, switch *a few coins* with *a hot meal.*

4. In the last paragraph, move *breathtaking* before *daredevil.*

Practicing Moving Text

Key the paragraph below using wordwrap. Then use the appropriate commands to move the text as indicated.

```
        Efficient readers move their eyes quickly over
the material.  They comprehend thoroughly what they
read and retain the information for a long period of
time.  They know how to rapidly pass their eyes over
groups of words, rather than single words.  They find
the theme and constantly keep this in mind as they
read.
```

1. Move *quickly* in front of the word *move*.

2. Move *thoroughly* in front of *comprehend*.

3. Move *rapidly* after *eyes*.

4. Move *constantly* after *this*.

Speed Practice

Below are lines that contain alternate-hand words. Practice them for a few minutes. Your teacher will then time you for one minute on each line. Try to increase your speed by at least one word on the second timing on the same line. Then, on the third timing on that same line, try to increase your rate by even one more word.

```
1 flake worms burnt whale vogue tight theme ornament
2 ivory handy profit world title spend signal enamel
3 digit quake panels angle elbow gland formals shame
4 island theory visitor jangle gospel ambush workbox
  . . . .1. . . . 2. . . . 3. . . . 4. . . . 5. . . . 6. . . . 7. . . . 8. . . . 9. . . .10
```

Accuracy Practice

The lines on the next page contain one-hand words that may slow you down. When you have one line keyed with perfect accuracy, raise your left hand. When you have two lines done with perfect accuracy, raise your right hand. When you have three lines done accurately, raise both hands, and when you finish the fourth line, stand up. When there are ten people standing, your teacher will stop the exercise. You will have to flip to the next page and then turn your book around to see these words.

1 rests pink hill waters braved look pull jump beets
2 minimum car ill freezes taste average lollipop few
3 abstract draft gazette poppy savage cascade bazaar
4 John Art Polly Warsaw Honolulu Joplin Molly Teresa

Proofreading Practice

The paragraph below contains six errors. Use wordwrap as you key it. Your job is to find and correct all errors. If it is available, you might wish to use a spell check program. However, a word of caution. There is one word spell check will not find.

Pancakes were a major food in the anceint world, but they did not look like the pancakes do today. Early panckaes were flat sheets of greul cooked on top of the stove. The first people in American to eat pancakes were the Pilgrims. They called theirs "soft cakes." A century later "hoe cakes" were devloped. These were pancakes cooked low in the flames of a campfire. Because they colected ash, they were also called "ashcakes."

Production

Application 9: Circus History

Directions:
- 2-inch top margin
- 1-inch side and bottom margins
- Center the title; Return/Enter twice after title
- Double space
- Wordwrap
- File name: Circus

HISTORY OF THE CIRCUS

If you enjoy going to the circus, you have the ancient Greeks to thank for the idea. They invented it. The Romans continued the idea by featuring horse and chariot races. There is evidence that even in

(continued on next page)

Typewriter Operations

Different Kinds of Electric Typewriters

Electric typewriters can be classified into two general categories: electronic and electro-mechanical. Most electro-mechanical machines do their printing with either typebars or an element, which looks like a ball. Electronic machines use a "daisy wheel" for printing. The printing mechanism looks like a daisy with many petals, with the characters that print at the end of each "petal." Find the diagram that is similar to the typewriter you are using. If you are unsure, ask your teacher.

Parts of the Typewriter

As you read about the basic parts described below, see if you can locate them on the diagram and then on your own typewriter.

1. **Platen Knob (left and right):** used to turn the platen manually on some models

2. **Platen (cylinder):** provides a surface against which the letters strike

3. **Paper Guide:** used to position the paper for inserting into the machine

4. **Paper Bail:** used to hold the paper against the platen

5. **Paper Release Lever:** used to remove the paper

6. **Print Carrier:** includes the printing mechanism (ribbon cassette, daisy wheel, or element)

7. **Impact Selector:** used to set the degree of printer impact to light, medium, or heavy

8. **Line Space Regulator:** used to set the distance the paper will advance at the end of each line, either single space or double space

9. **Pitch Select Key:** used to determine the number of characters per inch of type

10. **Paper Support:** used to support the paper as it is fed into the machine

11. **Margin Scale:** shows the printing point and margin positions

12. **Alignment Scale:** used to line up words on paper that is reinserted into the typewriter

13. **Variable line spacer:** used to change the point where the line of typing is placed on the page

14. **Ribbon position indicator:** used to select the portion of a rewindable ribbon—top, middle, or bottom—that will be used

IBM Wheelwriter 3

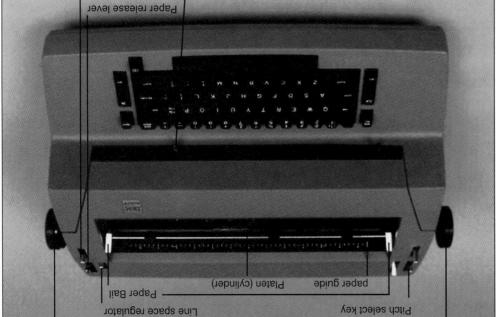

Margin scale

Paper bail

Platen (cylinder)

IBM Selectric

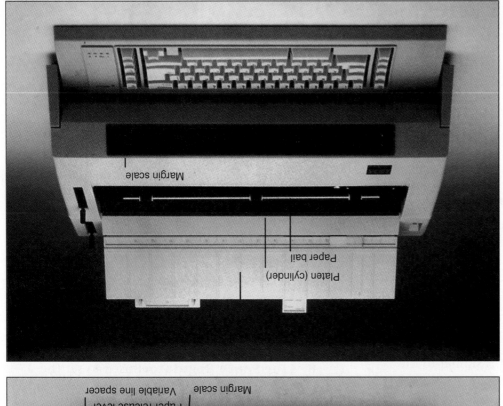

Paper release lever

Variable line spacer

Margin scale

Paper Ball

Platen (cylinder)

paper guide

Platen knob

Line space regulator

Pitch select key

Getting Ready to Keyboard on a Typewriter

Here are a few things you should do to get your typewriter ready for keyboarding:

1. Turn on the machine using the on/off switch. If nothing happens after you turn it on, check the floor plug to be sure it is plugged in.

2. Adjust the paper guide so the left edge of the paper lines up with zero or the beginning on the margin scale.

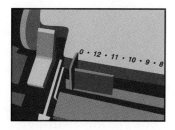

3. Pull the paper bail forward so it is out of the way.

4. Hold the paper in your left hand. Place the left edge of the paper against the paper guide behind the platen.

5. Roll the paper into the machine using the right platen knob or by pressing the Index key.

6. Stop when there is about 1½ inches of paper in the machine.

7. If the paper is not straight, pull the paper release forward, straighten the paper, and put the paper release back in position.

8. Push the paper bail back so it holds the paper against the platen.

9. Slide the paper bail rollers so they evenly divide the paper.

10. Set the line space regulator for the type of spacing desired: single spacing (SS or - or 1) or double spacing (DS or = or 2).

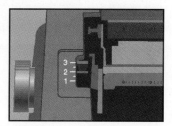

11. Set the margins for the space line desired.

PART D

Setting the Margins

Margin settings depend on the pitch, or how many characters per horizontal inch your typewriter can print. Most typewriters have print that is either 10 characters per inch (10 cpi), 12 characters per inch (12 cpi), or 15 characters per inch (15 cpi). Some typewriters have the ability to print in more than one pitch. Ten pitch is also called *pica*. Twelve pitch is also called *elite*. Below are common margin settings for both pica and elite.

Pica or **10 Pitch** (10 characters per horizontal inch), using 42 as center:

40-space line: 22 and 67

50-space line: 17 and 72

60-space line: 12 and 77

Elite or **12 Pitch** (12 characters per horizontal inch), using 50 as center:

40-space line: 30 and 75

50-space line: 25 and 80

60-space line: 20 and 85

Note: Actual center for elite is 51 but some people round the number down.

There are different ways to set the margins. Below are some of the most common ones. If you are not sure which is appropriate for you, ask your teacher. These procedures are intended to be general guidelines. If your typewriter user's manual is available, follow the procedures listed for your particular model.

Push Button/Lever Set

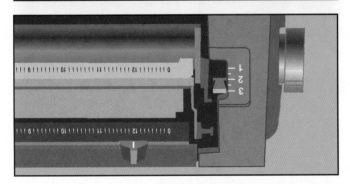

1. Press down on the left Margin Set button.
2. Slide it to the desired position on the scale.
3. Release the Margin Set button.
4. Follow the same procedure with the right button.

Key Set

1. Press the Return key to move the carriage to the left margin stop.

2. Depress and hold down the Margin Set key as you move the carriage to the new left margin setting.

3. Release the Margin Set key.

4. Follow the same procedure for the right margin.

Electronic Set

1. Space to the desired left margin position and strike the left Margin key.

2. Space to the desired right margin position and strike the right Margin key.

Now you are ready to learn the keyboard. Turn to Lesson 2 at the front of the book, or to the lesson assigned by your teacher. You will return to this section as your teacher refers you to special tasks.

Correcting Errors While the Paper is Still in the Machine

There are different ways to correct errors. Some of the most common methods are described below. Find the section that is appropriate for you. If you are unsure, ask your teacher.

Electronic Correction

Most machines have a correction key that removes errors from the paper or window/screen. Follow the steps in your user's manual to correct errors electronically.

LIFT-OFF Tape Contained in the Typewriter

1. Strike the special Lift-Off key to move the print carrier to the point where the error occurred.

2. Rekey the error exactly as you made it the first time. The lift-off tape will lift the error off the page.

3. Key the correction.

PART F

Correcting Errors After the Paper Has Been Removed from the Machine

You will want to proofread carefully before you remove your paper from the typewriter. Correcting errors after a paper has been removed requires a bit more skill. If you do find an error after the paper is out, follow these steps:

1. Remove the error using correction fluid or a typewriter eraser, or by rubbing chalk with your fingernail from a piece of correction tape.

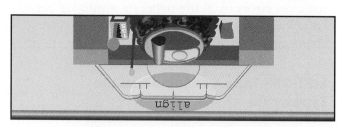

Typewriter Eraser

1. Roll the paper forward to make the error easy to reach.
2. Pull the paper bail forward so it is out of the way.
3. Erase the error; brush or blow the eraser crumbs off the paper but not inside the machine.
4. Position the paper where the correction begins and key the correction.

Correction Fluid

1. Roll the paper forward to make the error easy to reach.
2. Shake the bottle, remove the applicator, and dab excess fluid on the inside of the bottle.
3. Brush the fluid lightly over the error.
4. Wait for the white paint to dry. Replace the applicator inside the bottle and tighten the cap. Fluid dries out quickly if not capped tightly.
5. Backspace to the point where the correction begins and key the correction.

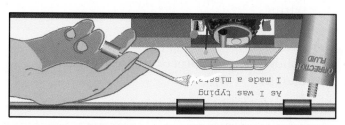

Correction Tape

1. Backspace to the beginning of the error.
2. Insert the correction tape or strip behind the ribbon and in front of the error, placing the coated side toward the copy.
3. Rekey the error exactly as you made it the first time. The powder from the correction paper is pressed over the error and covers it.
4. Remove the correction paper. Backspace to the point where the correction begins and key the correction.

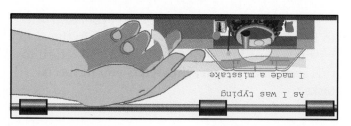

2. Reinsert the paper. Set the line so all letters are aligned with the alignment scale. This takes some practice until you learn to recognize the relationship between the printed line and the scale on your machine. Every typewriter is slightly different. You may have to adjust the variable line spacer to move the paper up or down. If you need to move the paper left or right, use the paper release.

3. If you want to check your alignment before typing in the correction, disengage the ribbon. Key the correction to check its placement. If necessary, adjust the paper again.

4. Adjust the ribbon position for normal typing and key the correction.

PART G

Listening for the Bell

Typewriters that do not automatically decide where to end a line have a bell that warns you the end of the line is coming up. The right margin is usually set at a point that will make the bell ring about five spaces before the desired ending of the line. This allows you to key about five more characters before the margin locks. If you ignore the bell and keep typing, the margin will lock and you will have to use the margin release to continue.

When the bell rings, you have two choices:

1. If the word is short, finish typing the word you are on and return to the next line.

2. If the word is long, divide it between syllables using the hyphen.

Example: Suppose the bell rang when you were typing the letter *x* in the word *excavation.* You could put *ex-* at the end of the

line and the rest of the word on the next line. Or you could continue typing and put *exca-* at the end of the line and the rest of the word on the next line. (If you are unsure where to break the syllables, you can always check the dictionary.)

It takes a little practice to get used to listening for the bell, especially if you are sitting in a room filled with typewriters. Do not get discouraged. Soon you will develop a special sense of hearing for your own bell. Also, most beginners often end up with ragged right margins when first starting to listen for the bell. You want your lines to end fairly evenly, but they do not have to be *exactly* even. If you start out with ragged margins, don't get discouraged. With a little practice, your line endings will soon even out.

PART H

Horizontal Centering

Sometimes you may want to key a line, such as the title for a report, so it is centered horizontally on the page. Centering horizontally means there is equal white space on both sides of the line. Follow these steps to center one line:

1. Move the margin stops to the edge of the paper.

2. Space Bar to the center of the paper: 42 if you are using pica or 10 pitch; 50 if you are using elite or 12 pitch.

3. Backspace once for every two characters, spaces, or punctuation marks in the line.

4. Do not backspace for an odd stroke left over at the end of a line.

5. Start typing the line where the backspacing ended.

PART I

Vertical Centering

Sometimes you may wish to center all the lines on a page so they are arranged with equal white space above and below them. This is called vertical centering. To do this, follow these steps:

1. Count the lines of typing and the blank lines between them. Remember, when using single spacing there are zero blank lines; when using double spacing there is one blank line; and when using triple spacing there are two blank lines between the lines of type.

2. Subtract the number of typed and blank lines from 66—the total number of lines that fit on a page.

3. Divide by two to get the top and bottom margins.

4. If the fraction ½ is part of the answer, disregard it. Your answer is the number of blank lines you should leave from the top edge of the paper before typing the first line. The first line you type on will actually be the answer you got in Step 3, plus 1.

PART J

Working with Tab Stops

The Tab key moves the carrier to a selected point on the margin scale. To set a tab stop, follow these steps:

1. Eliminate any stops that may already be set in the machine by one of these two methods:

   a. Move the carrier to the right margin; hold down the Tab Clear key as you return the carrier.

   b. Press the All-Clear key, if your machine has one.

2. Set the tab stop by moving the carrier to the point on the margin scale where you want it and press the Tab Set key.

3. Test the setting by bringing the carrier back to the left margin and pressing the Tab key to see if it stops where you set it. If not, repeat the process for setting the tab stop.

PART K

Centering Tables Horizontally

A table contains data arranged in columns. If the directions do not state how many spaces to leave between the columns, it is left to your judgment. Generally, the space between columns should not be so great that the reader has trouble following the line of type across the page. Nor should the space be so small that the reader has difficulty distinguishing where one column ends and another begins. Tables are usually centered horizontally on the page. To do this, follow these steps:

1. Move the margin stops to the edge of the paper.

2. Clear all the tab stops.

3. Space Bar over to the center of the paper (42 for pica; 50 for elite).

4. Backspace once for every two characters, spaces, or punctuation marks in the *longest* line in the first column. If an odd or leftover space occurs at the end of the longest item in the column, carry it forward to the next column.

5. Now backspace once for every two spaces to be left between the first and second columns.

6. Repeat this procedure until you have accounted for the longest line in all the columns and the spaces *between* the columns. Do not backspace for an odd character at the

end of the last column. *Do not backspace for spaces in front of the first column or after the last column.*

7. Set the left margin where the backspacing ended.

8. From the left margin, space forward once for every character, space, or punctuation mark in the *longest* line of the first column, *plus once for every space to be left between columns.*

9. Set the first tab stop where the forward spacing ended.

10. Repeat this procedure for additional columns.

PART L

Typing on a Printed Line

If you decide to fill out a form on a typewriter, you will need to learn how to type on a printed line. This takes a certain amount of skill because you want only a slight space separating the typed letters and the printed line. Downstem letters such as *p, y, q,* and *g* may touch the line.

To see just how much space your particular typewriter leaves between a printed line and a word typed on the line, follow these steps:

1. Using your underscore (underline) key, type a line that is 30 strokes long beginning at the left margin.

2. Backspace and type your name on the line.

3. Note how much space there is between the typed letters and the underline.

4. Now space down four lines and type another underline that is 30 strokes long beginning at the left margin.

5. Remove your paper.

6. Reinsert your paper. Align the paper using the variable line spacer and type your name on the blank line. Does the second name look like the first attempt when you did not take the paper out of the machine? If not, keep practicing. Repeat the exercise until you can type on a printed line with only a slight amount of space between the typing and the line.

Typewriter Keyboard

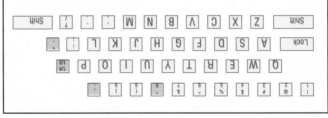

Most computer and typewriter keyboards are essentially the same except for a few keys. Exercises for these keys appear below.

PART A

' Key

On some keyboards the apostrophe is the shift of the number 8 key and is operated with the K finger. Key each line below **twice.**

k'k 'k' 'k' 'kk k'k 'k' 'kk k'k 'k' 'kk k'k 'k' 'kk
kkk ''' kkk ''' kkk ''' kkk ''' kkk '''

For practice on this key, use the apostrophe key drills on page 102 of the text.

PART B

" Key

On some keyboards the quotation marks key is the shift of the number 2 key and is operated with the S finger. Key each line below **twice.**

s"s "s"s "ss "s"s "ss "s"s "ss "s"s "ss "s"s
sss """ sss """ sss """ sss """ sss """

For practice on this key, use the question mark drills on page 115 of the text.

PART C

_ Key

On some keyboards the underline key is the shift of the number 6 key and is operated with the J finger. Key each line below **twice.**

jjj ___ jjj ___ jjj ___ jjj ___ jjj ___
jj _jj _jj _jj _jj _jj _jj _jj _jj _jj ___

For practice on this key, use the underlining key drill on page 136 of the text.

PART D

* Key

On some keyboards the asterisk (star) key is the shift of the hyphen key and is operated with the ; finger. Key each line below **twice.**

i*i *i! i*i *i! i*i *i! i*i *i! i*i *i!
!!! *** !!! *** !!! *** !!! *** !!! ***

For practice on this key, use the asterisk key drills on page 170 of the text.

Key

Some typewriter keyboards have a special ½ fraction key. It is located next to the P key and the ; finger operates it. Key each line below **twice.**

```
;½;  ½;;  ;½;  ½; ;  ;½ ;  ½; ; ;½ ;  ½;; ;½; ;  ½;;
;;; ½½½  ;;; ½½½  ;;; ½½½  ;;; ½½½  ;;;  ½½½
```

1 Buy ½ pint of cream and ½ gallon of
   milk for Tues.
2 She wants ½ of the team to go by bus
   and ½ by car.
3 If you do ½ the assignment, I will do
   the other ½.

Key

Some typewriter keyboards have a special ¼ fraction key. It is the shift of the ½ fraction key. Use your ; finger for the reach to this key. Key each line below **twice.**

```
;¼;  ¼;;  ;¼;  ¼;;  ;¼;  ¼;; ;¼;  ¼;; ;¼; ¼;;
;;; ¼¼¼  ;;; ¼¼¼  ;;; ¼¼¼  ;;; ¼¼¼  ;;; ¼¼¼
```

1 Marty ate ¼ of the pie and Jerry also
   ate ¼ of it.
2 That group has only completed about ¼
   of the work.
3 About ¼ of the group is made up of
   volunteer boys.

APPENDIX C

Word Division Guidelines

To avoid confusion by the reader, the following guidelines are recommended when you have to divide words at the end of a line:

1. Divide words between syllables; words of only one syllable should not be divided. If in doubt about syllables, consult a dictionary.

   Example: con-cern *not* conc-ern

   sleigh *not* sle-igh

2. Words of fewer than five letters should not be divided even if they have more than one syllable.

   Example: human *not* hu-man

   basic *not* ba-sic

3. Do not separate a one-letter syllable from the beginning of a word.

   Example: about *not* a-bout

   eclair *not* e-clair

4. Do not separate a one- or two-letter syllable from the end of a word.

   Example: frosty *not* frost-y

   likely *not* like-ly

5. When the final consonant is doubled before adding a suffix, divide between the double letters.

   Example: control-ling *not* controll-ing

   skip-ping *not* skipp-ing

6. Divide after a one-letter syllable within a word.

   Example: sepa-rate *not* sep-arate

   busi-ness *not* bus-iness

7. Divide between two one-letter syllables when they occur together.

   Example: gradu-ation *not* grad-uation

   idio-syncrasy *not* idi-osyncrasy

8. When the single-letter syllable *a*, *i*, or *u* is followed by the ending *ly*, *ble*, *bly*, *cle*, or *cal*, divide before the single-letter syllable.

   Example: read-ily *not* readi-ly

   miser-able *not* misera-ble

9. Divide hyphenated words at the hyphen.

   Example: self-defense *not* self-de-fense

   hand-launder *not* hand-laun-der

10. Do not divide a contraction or group of figures.

    Example: shouldn't *not* should-n't

    $3,788.23 *not* $3,-788.23

11. Avoid dividing proper names and dates.

    Example: Ms. Sue Jones *not* Ms. Sue Jones

    April 18, 1992 *not* April 18, 1992

Post Office Authorized Two-Letter Abbreviations for U.S. States and Territories

Alabama	AL	Nebraska	NE
Alaska	AK	Nevada	NV
Arizona	AZ	New Hampshire	NH
Arkansas	AR	New Jersey	NJ
California	CA	New Mexico	NM
Colorado	CO	New York	NY
Connecticut	CT	North Carolina	NC
Delaware	DE	North Dakota	ND
Dist. of Columbia	DC	Ohio	OH
Florida	FL	Oklahoma	OK
Georgia	GA	Oregon	OR
Guam	GU	Pennsylvania	PA
Hawaii	HI	Puerto Rico	PR
Idaho	ID	Rhode Island	RI
Illinois	IL	South Carolina	SC
Indiana	IN	South Dakota	SD
Iowa	IA	Tennessee	TN
Kansas	KS	Texas	TX
Kentucky	KY	Utah	UT
Louisiana	LA	Vermont	VT
Maine	ME	Virginia	VA
Maryland	MD	Virgin Islands	VI
Massachusetts	MA	Washington	WA
Michigan	MI	West Virginia	WV
Minnesota	MN	Wisconsin	WI
Mississippi	MS	Wyoming	WY
Missouri	MO		
Montana	MT		

Proofreader's Marks

Symbol	Meaning	Example	Symbol	Meaning	Example
≡	Capitalize	in the united states in the United States	/	lower case	try not to Worry try not to worry
◡	close up	mix the eggs and milk mix the eggs and milk	◯	spell out	ask (Dr.) Shay ask Doctor Shay
∽	switch around	run to catch up run to catch up	¶	paragraph	Buy it now. If you wait Buy it now. If you wait
∧	insert	ask the big question ask the big question	.....	let it stand	Do not stop on the way. Do not stop on the way.
℘	delete (take out)	a large gawdy box a large box			
#	space	now is the time now is the time			

400 Commonly Misspelled Words

abundant	attorney	carriage	confidential	discipline	experienced
accommodate	auditorium	cassette	congratulations	disconnected	experiment
accompanied	authorities	cataloging	conquer	discussion	exquisite
accomplished	automation	category	conscience	disposition	extraordinary
acknowledge	available	cautiously	conspicuous	disputable	extravagance
acquaintance	aviation	celebrate	constitution	dissatisfied	fascinating
acquired	balanced	cemetery	continuous	donor	fatigue
activities	ballot	census	controversial	economical	fiend
adjourned	bananas	certificate	convenient	editor	fierce
administration	banister	challenge	conversation	effective	fiery
affectionate	bankruptcy	chocolate	convey	elegance	finale
affordable	banquet	cinema	correspond	eligible	flourish
agricultural	baritone	circuit	coupon	embarrassment	foliage
aisle	belief	circumstances	courageous	emergency	forcible
allowance	benefit	civilization	courteous	emphasize	forfeit
ambassador	bestow	clammy	credentials	employees	fugitive
ambitious	biscuit	classify	crimson	endurance	furious
ambulance	blizzard	cocoon	crisis	engineer	gallery
ammunition	bluffed	coincidence	criticism	enormous	genius
analysis	bookkeeping	colonel	crystal	enthusiasm	geography
analyze	bough	colossal	curiosity	envy	gimmick
anchor	boulevard	column	cyclone	equipped	glimpse
animate	boundary	combustible	deceive	escapade	glorious
anniversary	brilliant	commercial	decision	especially	gopher
anticipate	bulletin	commissioner	definition	essay	gorgeous
anxiety	bureau	committee	delicate	essence	gracious
apologize	businesses	communities	delicious	estimate	grammar
apparent	cafeteria	comparatively	descend	evidence	gratitude
appearance	calamity	competition	destination	examination	grieve
appetite	campaign	complement	develop	exceed	guarantee
artificial	cancellation	conceit	dilapidated	excessive	gymnasium
assistance	candidate	condemn	dinosaur	executive	harried
assortment	capacity	conductor	disappointed	exhibition	helicopter
athletics	carnival	conference	disappointment	existence	historical

horrible
humiliate
hybrid
hygiene
hypnosis
icicle
illustrious
imagination
immediately
immense
incident
incite
individual
ineligible
inflammation
inhabitant
initial
initiated
innocent
instinct
intellect
intelligence
intentions
interrupt
intimate
invisible
irrigate
irritate
jarring
jubilant
judgment
juiciest
knight

laboratory
legion
leisure
levee
libel
library
license
lieutenant
likable
limitation
literacy
livable
loiter
luxury
magnificent
maintenance
malfunction
mammal
maneuver
manipulate
marriage
marvelous
maturity
mechanical
mechanism
memorable
memorandum
metropolitan
minimum
mischief
misinterpret
misspell
monopolize

mosquito
multiplication
museum
mutilate
narrator
necessity
negligence
notable
notorious
nuisance
obliging
obstacle
occasionally
occurrence
offend
omission
omitted
opposed
orchestra
ordinarily
oyster
pageant
pamphlet
parallel
participant
patience
pennant
performance
perishable
permanence
persevere
persistence
persuasive

pessimistic
petition
physician
physical
piece
pollutant
possession
practically
prairie
premium
preparation
primitive
privilege
prominent
prosperous
psychology
pursue
pursuit
quarrel
radiate
reasonable
receipt
receive
recognition
recommend
register
regretting
reign
relief
relieved
remnant
renewal
repetitious

responsibility
restaurant
ridicule
sacrifice
sanitary
sarcasm
scent
schedule
scheme
scholarship
sensible
sentiment
separately
shield
significant
similar
sincerely
skiing
sociable
solemn
solitary
somersault
spacious
specimen
stirring
strategy
strenuous
substantial
sufficient
suggestions
surrender
surround
suspicion

syllable
sympathy
tariff
temperature
therapy
thermometer
thief
thorough
tragedy
treasury
triumph
truly
unanimous
underrate
unimaginable
unnecessary
unoccupied
unusual
usage
variety
vengeance
vicinity
viewpoint
visible
warranty
weird
whimper
wholly
witness
wrestle
yield